# THE COUNTY COMMUNITY
# UNDER HENRY VIII

The Military Survey, 1522, and Lay Subsidy, 1524-5, for Rutland

Edited for the Rutland Record Society

by

JULIAN CORNWALL

Rutland Record Series
Volume 1

Published by the Rutland Record Society
Rutland County Museum, Oakham
1980

ISBN No. 0 907464 00 9

The publication of this book has been assisted
by a grant from the Twenty-Seven Foundation.

Printed in Great Britain by Dalkeith Press Ltd.
21-26 Dalkeith Place, Kettering, Northants NN16 0BS

# Contents

# Acknowledgements

An invitation to produce the first volume for a newly formed society is a rare distinction, and it is with pleasure that I record my thanks to Prince Yuri Galitzine and the Executive Committee. The labour of preparation has been greatly lightened by the unstinting support of Mr. Bryan Waites, the Hon. Editor. As on former occasions my wife has taken over the indexing as well as encouraging me to complete the project. I am indebted to Drs. J. J. Goring, R. S. Schofield and J. Sheaill for permission to consult their unpublished theses. Any shortcomings in the present edition are mine alone.

Crown copyright material from the Public Record Office appears by permission of the Controller of H.M. Stationery Office. © *Crown Copyright 1980. Document Nos. PRO E179/165/110. E179/166/112 (Part). E179/165/113 (Part). E36/54. E36/55 ff 1-44.*

The map of the Hundreds of Rutland is reproduced by permission of the General Editor from the *Victoria County History: Rutland,* vol. ii, London, 1935.

# COUNTY OF RUTLAND

MAP OF THE HUNDREDS OF RUTLAND

# Introduction

This volume comprises the muster book for Rutland in 1522 and the lay subsidy rolls of 1524-5 which are closely related to it. Each is acknowledged to be an indispensible source for the economic and social History of England in the sixteenth century. Forming a unique, intimate survey of a county and its inhabitants, the Rutland muster possesses many of the attributes appropriate to the inaugural volume of a new venture in record publication. The subsidy not only marks a significant stage in the evolution of direct taxation under the Tudors, it is also much the most comprehensive and realistic one levied in a period when truly effective taxation was seldom achieved. Independently projected and executed, each on its own forms an outstanding record of conditions at the time it was made—the eve of the Reformation and the price revolution. Nevertheless, the value of each is immeasurably enhanced by the light shed on it by the other which offers an alternative view of the selfsame community. Examples of each type of document have previously appeared in print, but so far only the returns for the city of Exeter have been presented together in a single volume, and unfortunately the muster book there is far from complete. No other county is as comprehensively documented as Rutland, which for this reason, as much as any other, stands out as by far the most complete example of a provincial society at this time.

Until very recently the musters of 1522 were unaccountably neglected by scholars, the standard modern histories of the period according them nothing better than a passing mention, while even specialised studies of government added little of substance. They were first seriously examined by Dr. J. J. Goring in an unpublished thesis, subsequently expanded into a study in depth of their genesis.[1] Simultaneously, Professor W. G. Hoskins and the present writer pioneered the quantitative analysis not only of the musters but also the related forced loans of 1522-3 and the lay subsidy.[2] Increasing interest has led to the recent publication of the Buckinghamshire and Exeter books, although the return for North Greenhoe hundred, Norfolk, had been printed as early as 1931.[3] This neglect is all the more surprising in face of the profound impression that the unprecedented character of the survey and the manner in which it was executed made on the contemporary chroniclers Edward Hall and Polydore Vergil.[4] Subsequently, however, it attracted the attention only of the eighteenth century Huguenot historian Rapin de Thoyras, although in fact his knowledge of it extended no further than a set of instructions circulated in Essex and reproduced in the 1631 edition of John Stow's *Annals*.[5] For all practical purposes the returns had dropped out of sight. Not only had few survived, those that were preserved in the Public Record Office were listed simply as musters—

1.   J. J. Goring, 'The Military Obligations of the English People, 1511-1558', unpublished Ph.D. thesis (London, 1955), and 'The general proscription of 1522', *English Historical Review*, lxxxvi (1971), 681-705.
2.   W. G. Hoskins, *The Age of Plunder* (1976); J. Cornwall, 'The People of Rutland in 1522', *Transactions of Leicestershire Archaeological Society*, xxxvii (1963), 7-28.
3.   *The Certificate of Musters for Buckinghamshire in 1522*, ed. A. C. Chibnall, Royal Commission on Historical MSS, JP 18 (1973); *Tudor Exeter: Tax Assessments, 1489-1595*, ed. M. M. Rowe, Devon and Cornwall Record Society, n.s. 22 (Exeter, 1977) 7-33: 'Musters for the hundred of North Grenowe, co. Norfolk, temp. Henry VIII', ed. [M. Dale], *Norfolk Record Society*, i (1931), 42-68.
4.   E. Hall, *Chronicle: Henry VIII*, ed. C .Whibley (1904), vol. i, *passim; The Anglica Historia of Polydore Vergil, 1485-1537*, ed. D. Hay, Camden 3rd series, lxxiv (1950), 301-3.
5.   J. Stow, *Annals* (1631), p. 515; Rapin de Thoyras, *History of England*, trans. N. Tindal (1732), i. 750.

correctly but at the same time inadequately. General musters, or views of the military resources of the king-
dom, were a regular feature of Tudor administration, but those held on the outbreak of the war with France
in 1522 were conceived and executed on a scale never previously attempted and never to be repeated. Ex-
ceptionally detailed and searching, they incorporated a comprehensive valuation of wealth, both real and
personal, resulting in a record that is so wide-ranging that the technical term 'musters' fails to do them
justice. Stow termed the project 'a general proscription'; Rapin compared it to Domesday Book, a happy
inspiration, although in many respects it outclasses the eleventh century survey. At the present time 'Military
Survey' is increasingly favoured as giving a more precise definition of the structure and content of the
documents.

The subsidy rolls have fared somewhat better. The Suffolk ones were published in full as early as 1910,
with those relating to Buckinghamshire and Sussex following in the 1950s; short excerpts had appeared
from time to time in the transactions of local societies.[1] It is of some interest to note that the first of the
muster returns to be printed—for Penwith hundred, Cornwall[2]—was discovered among the subsidy rolls,
and would seem to have attracted attention as a curiosity.

### i.  The Background

Although overtly cast in the form of a survey of military resources, the true significance of these
musters lies in the fact that they mark a new departure in the evolution of taxation under the first two Tudors.
Direct taxes took two forms. On the one hand there were the legal ones granted by Parliament, the long
established Tenths and Fifteenths and the new-fangled subsidy; on the other, the extra-legal benevolences—
nominally free gifts—and forced loans which the King periodically levied on his wealthier subjects, and
which, consequently, were popular with the community at large. In theory repayable, in practice loans were
increasingly written off—and *ipso facto* legalised—by a subsequent parliament.[3] The muster of 1522 is
related to both types.

By the beginning of the sixteenth century the need for a general reassessment of wealth for fiscal
purposes had long been apparent. The cost of government—of war in particular—was escalating, while
the resources available to the Crown through direct taxation had failed to keep pace. The traditional Tenth
and Fifteenth levied on personal property had been standardised in perpetuity in 1334 as a fixed grant of
approximately £37,430.[4] During the fifteenth century this had been whittled down to just under £30,000
as a result of reductions in the quotas of impoverished townships, while those which had prospered could
not be called on to make good the loss of revenue. With major shifts in the geographical distribution of
population and wealth the assessments had long ceased to bear much relationship to economic realities.
Experiments with alternative types of taxation had been tried and abandoned, culminating in 1513-15 in
an ambitious subsidy which combined the assessment of incomes from land and wages with that of the
capital value of goods and chattels. The yield, however, had fallen well short of the expected £160,000,

1.  *Suffolk in 1524*, ed. S. H. A. H[ervey], Suffolk Green Books x (Woodbridge, 1910); *Subsidy Roll for the County of Buckingham, anno 1524*, ed. A. C. Chibnall and A. V. Woodman, Buckinghamshire Record Society, 8 (1950); *The Lay Subsidy Rolls
for the County of Sussex, 1524-25*, ed. J. Cornwall, Sussex Record Society, 56 (Lewes, 1957); *Tudor Exeter*, ed. cit. pp. 35-44.
See also, e.g. J. Tait, *The Taxation of Salford Hundred*, Chetham Society, n.s. 83 (1924), *passim*.

2.  H. M. Whitley, 'A Valuation of the Lands and Goods of the Inhabitants of Penwith, temp. Henry VIII', *Journal of the
Royal Institution of Cornwall*, ix (1887), 222-70.

3.  G. R. Elton, *The Tudor Constitution* (Cambridge, 1965), pp. 43-4.

4.  *The Lay Subsidy of 1334*, ed. R. E. Glasscock, Records of Social and Economic History, new series, ii (1975), p. xvi.

thanks to the government's inability to obtain realistic assessments in the absence of permanent administrative machinery.[1] To complicate matters further, attempts to impose novel taxes were always liable to encounter resistance, and on two occasions in the reign of Henry VII had resulted in serious rebellions.[2]

With the termination of the war that had necessitated this grant the problem was shelved, but on the renewal of hostilities in 1522 it assumed a fresh urgency. During the intervening years of peace Cardinal Wolsey, the Lord Chancellor, had no doubt reflected on the problem of increasing the yield of taxes. The solution finally devised was to obtain new assessments by subterfuge, under the pretext of holding musters. But although the unprecedented scope of the survey created something of a sensation, no official record has been kept of the process by which the policy was formulated or how the project came to be initiated—whether planned in advance or improvised on the spur of the moment.[3] What is certain is that it achieved a remarkable and indeed alarming degree of success, enabling Polydore Vergil to observe that 'When the assessments had been made the king could readily see that his people were by no means poor.'[4] Hall, author of the only other contemporary account, represents it as bursting on an unprepared public like a bolt from the blue: 'Also this time [early March] commission was geven throughoute the realme for general musters to be had, to know what power might be made with in the same, and also men sworne of what substaunce and landes thei wer of. And the Cardinal advertised of the same: not wythout grudging of the people, and marveiling why thei shuld be sworne for their own goodes.'[5] Commissions, none of which has been preserved, were addressed to leading men in every county, hand-picked for their reliability. These in turn relayed instructions to local officials within their jurisdiction detailing the information to be gathered and the procedure to be followed; those issued by the commissioners for Essex to the bailiff and chief constable of Waltham half hundred were printed by Stow, and thus have come to be the only set preserved. They ordered ' . . . all Constables of euery towne, hamlet, Parish and village within the said hundred, personally to appeare before vs the said commissioners on Monday next comming, the last day of the month of March at Waltham holy crosse, and there to bring with them a certificate in writing of the names of all manner of men aboue the age of 16 yeeres, dwelling within . . . the said hundred . . . [And] also give . . . commandment to all manner of temporall men dwelling . . . within the same halfe hundred personally to appeare before vs . . . the said Munday next comming, furnished and apparelled in their best array for the war . . . Also also . . . certifie vs in writing . . . of all their names and whom they belong vnto. Also who is Lord of euery towne or hamlet . . . and who bee Stewards. Item who be parsons of the same townes, and what the benefices be worth by yeere. Also who be owners of euery parcell of land within any towne . . . with the yeerely value of euery mans land within the same townes . . . And of euery stocke and stocks of Cattell, or other things that be occupied vpon any ferme . . . and who be owners of them. Also what aliants or strangers dwell in any towne . . . and where they were borne, and vnder whose dominion. Item what occupation, mystery, or substaunce they be of. Item, the value and substance of euery person being of 16 yeeres and aboue . . . as well spirituall as temporall. Also what pensions goeth out of any lands there to and religious or spirituall men.'

As the sole surviving example this has necessarily been accepted as a pro forma, though without any actual warrant, and the internal evidence of the extant muster books suggests that the wording was anything but uniform. In the absence of reprographic facilities the dissemination of central government precepts must have posed serious problems, indeed it has been argued that they can only have been circulated

1. S. Dowell, *A History of Taxation in England from the Earliest Times to the Present Day*, vol. i (1884), *passim:* for the Tudor period see R. S. Schofield, 'Parliamentary Lay Taxation, 1485-1547', unpub. Ph. D. thesis (Cambridge, 1963).

2. J. D. Mackie, *The Earlier Tudors* (Oxford, 1951), pp. 91, 141.

3. See Goring, *loc. cit.* for a full discussion of the survey, on which the following account is largely based.

4. *Polydore Vergil*, p. 301.

5. Hall, i, 237.

in summary form.[1] On this occasion it is clear that misapprehensions were widespread in the first instance, for the preliminary returns failed to satisfy the government.

A daunting task for untrained administrators, the making of the survey occupied much of the year 1522. The fundamental problem was that the inquest sought to combine two disparate elements in a single all-purpose return. Separately each was relatively routine: the listing of able-bodied men liable for service in the militia, with their arms and acoutrements, and the sort of assessment such as might be made for tax purposes. Difficulty arose because at first the emphasis appeared to be placed on musters, although what the government was really interested in was the valuation of property: '... the king had a census taken partly to find out the condition of his people, but partly so that he could be able to find out from the census what tax each should pay for the general advantage of the state.'[2] Wolsey himself explained that the object was to enable the king '... to put hymself with the [aid] of hys loving subiectes in such state of substance and treasour that he may behable [to] contynew the warrys.'[3] Thus the first returns, completed before the end of April, failed to satisfy the Chancellor's stringent requirements, and in July—after a delay due to the visit of the Emperor Charles V—orders were issued for the survey, or rather the assessments, to be undertaken all over again. To combat widespread evasion the Council now directed the commissioners to require every man to make a sworn declaration of the whole of his assets, inclusive of debts, specialities, loans, merchandise, household effects and so forth: where necessary they were to investigate claims for allowances in respect of liabilities, and in cases of suspected concealment to approach men's neighbours for estimates of their wealth. Above all the commissioners were cautioned to maintain strict secrecy about the real object of the inquiry, giving out that it was undertaken solely in order to ascertain the rate at which each man should be assessed for the furnishing of harness. Once the survey had been completed they were to call together the leading inhabitants of the county, explain the king's great necessity due to the war, and ask for a loan of ten percent on all incomes and personal estate of from £20 to £300, and 13⅓ percent on assessments on £300-£1000.[4] This second phase took longer to complete. The Rutland commissioners were still working on it as late as 21 September when they witnessed the abjuration of the realm by John Robinson the Scotch shepherd of Thistleton, while the Buckinghamshire return was not ready for submission until the end of November. By the end of the year the books from 29 counties had been received in the Star Chamber, and partial returns from two more; six counties, all in the north of England, had still to make theirs.[5] Whether the yield of the loan proved disappointing or Wolsey felt encouraged by its success it is not possible to say, but early in 1523 a second one was levied, this time on persons worth £5 and under £20, bringing the total raised to an unprecedented £260,000 and causing burning resentment, for '... the people were sworne and some avaunced themselfes more than they were worth of pride, not remembryng what was comyng, and the commissioners did what they could to set the people to the uttermoste, which afterwardes turned the people to muche heavines, and by reason of this, great summes of money were levied, but the moste parte were not content, because the laone was so sodainly paied'.[6] Written promises of repayment had indeed been given, following the precedent of Henry VII who had always honoured his commitments. Wolsey, however, had other ideas: the object of the assessments was to enable a heavy burden of taxation to be imposed on the country, and so he 'put obstacles in the way' of repayment, treating the loans as a free gift.[7] They were never repaid, and the Parliament of 1529 duly cancelled them.[8]

1. L. F. Salzman, 'Early Taxation in Sussex', *Sussex Archaeological Collections*, xcix (Lewes, 1961), 6.
2. Polydore Vergil, *loc. cit.*
3. B. L. Cotton, Galba B vii, f. 280: q. by Goring, *op. cit.* p. 684.
4. *Letters and Papers, Henry VIII*, iii, 2484: instructions to the commissioners for Warwickshire.
5. *Ibid.* iii, 3683.
6. Hall, i, 274; Hoskins, *The Age of Plunder*, pp. 22-3.
7. Polydore Vergil, pp. 302-3.
8. K. Pickthorn, *Early Tudor Government: Henry VIII* (1934), pp. 137-8.

The loans had scarcely been gathered in when, on 15 April 1523, Parliament met at Blackfriars, London, the first to be called for eight years since its predecessor had been summarily dissolved to forestall an embarassing debate on the now burning issue of Church reform. Not surprisingly the mood of the assembly was hostile. Wolsey demanded a subsidy of £800,000 to be levied on the new assessments at the rate of four shillings in the pound. This met with stubborn resistance, and after prolonged and acrimonious debate, in the course of which the Cardinal tried unsuccessfully to browbeat the Commons, a compromise was effected. The subsidy finally voted[1] took the form of a graduated tax spread over two years, and it was tacitly understood that the now contentious assessments would be abandoned in favour of new and presumably less rigorous ones. To compensate for this the threshold was extended downwards to £1. For each instalment the rate was fixed at 1s in £ on all incomes from land—copyhold as well as freehold—and on goods worth £20 and upwards; 6d in £ on goods worth £2 but less than £20, and a poll tax of 4d on owners of goods worth less than £2, as well as on persons aged sixteen and over who had no goods but were earning at least 20s a year in wages. Aliens were to pay double these rates, or a poll tax of 8d if they had neither goods nor wages. A surtax element was also added: in the third year an additional shilling in the pound was payable on lands of £50 a year and upwards, and on goods of the same value in the fourth. Peers made a separate grant, while the clergy taxed themselves in their convocations.[2] The latter were however, assessed for lands held by secular tenure, i.e. property they owned as private individuals and not forming part of their benefices. Peers, and the heads of convents were also made responsible for the payment of their servants' taxes, and might deduct what was due from their wages; this is unlikely to have had any effect on the Rutland returns.

Unpaid commissioners, who had to be resident there, were appointed by the House of Commons for each shire. These were required to appoint high collectors who could not themselves be commissioners or act for more than one year; and sub-collectors were appointed for each township. Members of Parliament were ineligible for this duty. From the moneys collected the high collectors were authorised to deduct 6d in £, allowing the sub-collectors 2d, and the commissioners 2d to defray clerical and other expenses; the balance they might keep for themselves. The work of assessment was entrusted to teams of from two to eight persons empanelled by the commissioners in every hundred, parish or township. Persons suspected of owning greater wealth than they were prepared to admit might be summoned before the commission and, if they refused to appear or to be sworn, were to be taxed double. Anyone believing himself overrated could appeal to the commissioners. No one was to be taxed on more than one source of wealth, namely whichever would produce the largest sum. Reference to the muster shows us that this made little difference to the assessments of the majority of taxpayers in Rutland whose assets consisted chiefly of personal property with little or no income from land. In contrast, many of the gentry owned considerable wealth in both land and goods, and hence their assessments give only a partial account of their possessions: Simon Swaffeld, for instance, was taxed on lands of £17 a year, in addition to which he also owned goods to the value of £20. A man who owned more than one residence was to be taxed only in the place where he usually dwelt. When the collection had been completed the commissioners executed an indented certificate, one part of which, with the schedules of assessments annexed, had to be remitted to the Exchequer, the other, together with the money, to the Treasurer of the King's Chamber. Commissioners who failed to agree could make separate indentures, but no problem of this kind arose in Rutland.

Payment of the first instalment was due in the spring of 1524, but by October 1523 Wolsey found himself so pressed for money that he deputed special commissioners to demand immediate payment from

1.   Hall, i, 284-7; 14 & 15 Henry VIII, c. 16, *Statutes of the Realm*, iii, 230-9.

2.   *A Subsidy Collected in the Diocese of Lincoln in 1526*, ed. H. Salter, Oxford Historical Society, lxiii (Oxford, 1913), 145-8 gives the archdeaconry of Rutland.

everyone assessed at £40 and over. The assessments of 1522 provided the basis for this 'anticipation', as it was called, although in the event many people succeeded in getting reductions[1], and it is clear from the records of other counties which (unlike those of Rutland) have survived that the sums finally levied were identical with those entered on the main return.

The last had not been heard of the military survey. Nationally the lay subsidy netted a disappointing £151,215.[2] Once the second main instalment had been collected in January 1525 it was obvious that, despite the lowering of the threshold, the yield was bound to fall far short of what the loans had produced: in the event the 'surtax' was to add less than £15,000. On 21 March, therefore, commissions were issued for the levying of a fresh loan at the rate of one-sixth on the original assessments; the clergy would be asked to pay a fourth.[3] If Wolsey's calculations were the same as they had been previously, he must have reckoned on getting upwards of £650,000 and thus reaching his original target of £800,000. At the same time he may not in reality have set his sights so high, for at one point he was talking in terms of a graduated scale according to which the sixth would have been payable on assessments of £50 only. The question,[4] however, is academic. The Amicable Grant, as it was called, encountered determined resistance notwithstanding the fact that the collection was placed in the hands of the magnates, with the Chancellor personally taking charge of the City of London. It was claimed that the recent unprecedented taxation had drained the country of coin, bringing the economy to the verge of collapse. Serious disorders threatened in Kent and East Anglia, especially in the manufacturing district of Suffolk where the clothiers had laid off their workmen, and only tactful handling by the Duke of Norfolk averted a rebellion in May. Deterred perhaps by tidings of the peasant war in Germany, the government backed down and abandoned the project.[5] Whether and to what extent Rutland was affected is not known. The fact that the recorded disturbances were confined to the south-east rather suggests that the commissions commenced their work there and were suspended before reaching the Midlands.

With the vast sums already raised either spent or committed and political considerations inhibiting any further attempt at taxation, England ceased to play an active role in a war which dragged on until 1529— except to change sides. Parliament was not summoned again until after Wolsey's fall in 1529, and significantly it was not asked for a grant until 1532, when the amount offered was so small the King refused it. When at length another subsidy was granted in 1534 it was far from generous, but nonetheless created an important precedent, namely taxation in peacetime.[6] The subsidies of the 1540s succeeded in raising taxation to new levels, exceeding even those of the 'twenties. but since few of the rolls (which were paper instead of the more usual parchment) have survived in usable condition their value is inevitably limited. After the death of the autocratic Henry VIII the subsidy quickly degenerated into a more or less fixed sum which, like the fifteenths and tenths, not only declined in value but was progressively rendered unrealistic by inflation.[7]

1.  Hall, i, 316-7; *Subsidy Roll for the County of Buckinghamshire*, pp. xii, 90-5.

2.  Schofield, thesis, p. 416.

3.  *Letters & Papers*, iv, 1199, 1200.

4.  Hall, ii, 35.

5.  *Letters & Papers*, iv, 1272; Hall, ii, 32-46.

6.  G. R. Elton, *Reform and Reformation: England, 1509-1558* (1977), pp. 148, 190.

7.  Schofield, thesis, *passim;* F. C. Dietz, *English Government Finance, 1485-1558* (Urbanna, Ill. 1920), *passim*, and *English Public Finance, 1558-1641* (New York 1932), *passim*.

## ii.  *The Military Survey*

Few of the county muster books have been preserved, and it can only be concluded that, having been delivered to the Star Chamber, they shared the fate of many of the records of that court in the seventeenth century. A handful that escaped destruction probably owed their survival to having been previously transferred to the Treasury. Others now preserved among the records of the Court of Augmentations may have originated as copies retained locally in the shires and lodged for safe keeping in religious houses, falling into the hands of the Crown at the dissolution of the monasteries a few years later. Other returns remain in private ownership: the Gloucestershire one, which suffers from numerous omissions, could possibly have been one of the early versions that was rejected. The Buckinghamshire survey now exists only in the form of a Jacobean transcript, the purpose of which is not known. Altogether complete, or nearly complete returns for three counties and two cities have been preserved, with partial ones for five more counties.[1]

The Rutland muster book is one of the miscellaneous volumes of the Treasury of Receipt in the Public Record Office (class mark E. 36/55). It consists of 44 paper folios measuring 40mm x 28mm, mounted and rebound. The first ten folios are decayed at the edges; folio 44 is almost wholly illegible. The survey covers virtually the whole county, concluding with the entries for the deserted settlements of Gunthorpe and Martinsthorpe. Horn and Pickworth, the two other major depopulated medieval villages, would appear to have been ignored, as was Leighfield Forest. The volume is undated, but on folio 6 it is stated that the commissioners visited Thistleton on 21 September in the 14th year of the reign of Henry VIII, that is 1522. There is also a transcript (E. 36/54) which is also undated but was probably made in the middle or late eighteenth century.[2] The purpose is unknown and it was discontinued in the middle of the Uppingham section. It confirms that most of the deterioration in the original had already occurred, and hence one is tempted to speculate that it had been rescued at some stage by someone who recognised its value, and that the copy was undertaken as a precaution against further decay. An exact line for line copy, the transcript can be confidently substituted where the original is now inadequate. The list of payers of the second loan, on assessments of £5-20, is also extant;[3] with minor differences it virtually repeats the relevant entries from the muster book, and so has not been reproduced here.

Of the returns now surviving the Rutland survey is the most thorough. The material is arranged clearly in tabular form, thus avoiding the ambiguities found in certain other volumes and which at times make interpretation difficult. The entry for each township follows a fairly regular plan. It commences with the name of the chief lord, followed by the steward of the manor, the clergy and other owners of land, many of whom are defined as non-residents by the phrase 'nil quia manet extra' in the column devoted to the value of goods. Next are listed the inhabitants along with their occupations, the names of their landlords, and the values of their lands (if any) and goods, more or less in order of wealth and importance. The land in question can be assumed to have been freehold; most peasants, however, would have been copyholders, and as such their holdings would have remained outside the scope of the survey. The rear is brought up by poor men who owned neither land nor goods worth valuing. Information of a military nature is placed in the two outside columns, almost in the form of marginal annotations; on the left hand is given a man's rating, on the right his arms and harness in the rare cases that there were any. Occasionally it looks as though a landowner has been missed at first and his particulars inserted at the point at which the muster-takers are reminded of him—no doubt by his tenant. Finally come items concerning the community as a whole—

1.  See for details my 'A Tudor Domesday', *Journal of the Society of Archivists*, iii (1965), 19-24; some further returns relating to Norfolk have been identified in addition to those listed.
2.  I am indebted to the Public Record Office for the information that the watermark in the paper points to French manufacture, from the 1730s to the 1760s; the earliest date for the binding is indicated by the date 1826 on the end-papers.
3.  PRO, E. 179/165/266A.

any harness owned by it, and the value of the stock (funds) of the parish church which, although strictly moveable property, is here erroneously entered in the land value column. At the foot of each page the lands and goods columns are totalled in a different, though contemporary hand. The inference is that this was done in the course of planning the subsidy, for the initial demand for £800,000 at a rate of 4s in £ clearly postulated aggregate national wealth of £4,000,000.[1] Three features in particular distinguish the Rutland book from all others: it states the name of the lord of every person of substance, together with the status and occupations of most of the inhabitants, and it classifies persons lacking assessable property as 'poor'.

The descriptions of status and occupation can be regarded as something of a bonus, since in Essex such information was required for aliens only. Nevertheless, the wording is not entirely free of ambiguity, and there is no doubt that misunderstandings occurred in the preparation of both the musters and the subsidy.[2] Strictly it was unnecessary to give occupations. Except in isolated instances most other returns identify only the gentry and clergy, clearly lumping everyone else together under the broad classification characterised by Sir Thomas Smith as 'the fourth sort of men which do not rule', consisting of day labourers, poor husbandmen, merchants and retailers, copyholders and artificers; indeed even his third class, composed of citizens, burgesses and yeomen was ignored.[3] The clear inference is that in an overwhelmingly agrarian society it would have been understood as a matter of course that most men were peasant farmers and smallholders; in fact the commonest description in Rutland is 'husbandman'. It is further significant that some returns compromise by distinguishing servants and labourers, in addition to gentry and clergy,[4] that is to say persons whose status was one of dependence, and landless peasants who did not conform to the ideal of a society composed of small independent producers or husbandmen. Labourers and servants formed the second largest group in Rutland. The insignificant number of men designated as tradesmen or craftsmen were almost all represented as farmers or labourers in the subsidy roll (and vice versa) implying that their trades were by-employments.

The use of the epithet 'poor' seems to carry something of a sociological connotation. That all persons so designated owned no property of any description other than, say the clothes on their backs, seems on the face of it improbable. In fact the assessment *nil* should clearly be interpreted as meaning less than one pound, and some returns regularly record sums of a few shillings; in Rutland such entries are extremely rare, no more than a couple in North Luffenham. What probably happened was that, in the absence of any guidance, the commissioners adopted the tax threshold from the subsidy of 1513-15 as their standard.[5] What is especially interesting is the fact that many (though by no means all) of these people were not described as anybody's tenants, the implication being that they were poor in as much as they did not occupy holdings on which to support themselves. That most were also described as young suggests that they were unmarried and indeed unsettled.

This rare glimpse of the poorest members of the community is one of the most informative features of the survey; at the same time it has limitations. Although in theory every man aged sixteen and over should have been listed, in practice many were not, and a large number showed up in the subsidy who had not previously been mustered, and vice versa. Detailed comparison of the returns indicates that on average any given list is liable to omit approximately one third of the names it was supposed to contain. Some may have failed to qualify for inclusion, men who were too old for service and had no assessable wealth: while

---

1.   This figure was cited by Thomas Cromwell in a draft of a speech planned for the parliament of 1523 in which he estimated the value of lands at one million and moveables at three millions: *Letters and Papers, Henry VIII*, iii, 2959.

2.   *Letters & Papers*, iv, 122.

3.   Sir Thomas Smith, *De Republica Anglorum*, ed. L. Alston, (Cambridge, 1906), pp. 40-6.

4.   For example in Berkshire, PRO, E. 315/464.

5.   4 Henry VIII, c. 19, *Statutes of the Realm*, iii, 74-89.

a few townships returned 'old men and pore', it is noticeable that the majority did not. Even when full allowance has been made for changes due to natural causes and migration, turn over on this scale seems excessive for a period of two and a half years, more especially in view of the fact that, although a high degree of mobility was a characteristic of pre-industrial society[1], the number of actual cases that can be proved to have actually removed from one place to another is negligible. All that is certain is that in general the discrepancies between the various lists cannot have been entirely fortuitous. It is particularly noticeable that the great majority of people missing from one return or another had assessments of less than £2 and were predominantly labourers or servants. Conversely, most men worth upwards of £2 reappeared in each successive return. In Empingham, to take but one case, 20 out of 31 whose assessments never reached £2 occurred in one list only; in contrast, 23 out of 34 assessed at £2 or more appeared in all three lists. This is a moderate example; at Ketton no less than 84 percent of the sub-£2 men were listed only once.[2] The precise reasons for this turnover—carelessness apart—are a matter of speculation. There are grounds for inferring that local officials recognised varying degrees of poverty and treated people accordingly: there would, for example, appear to be a material difference in the circumstances of a man whose sole appearance was in 1522 with a nil assessment and one who was taxed twice on wages. Equally, and perhaps more realistically, the reason could have been that the labouring poor were migratory by nature, and that here we have a rare, fleeting glimpse of those elusive figures on the fringes of sixteenth century society, vagabonds and sturdy beggars.[3] Whichever it was, the enumeration of the poor proved either unproductive or too difficult, for it was never again attempted on this scale.

In all other respects the muster is remarkably free of serious omissions. A small number of assessments were left blank, presumably to be completed following further enquiries. These, unfortunately, include all the 19 lordships owned by the King. The defect can be tentatively remedied by applying the average value of £32 per thousand acres calculated from the figures relating to Surrey and part of Suffolk[4], although the result is not entirely satisfactory, as some assessments are misleading. Land was valued in separate parcels as and where it was situated. Most of the time this presents no problem: either it belonged to an absentee whose other property—if any—was not relevant, or if it belonged to a resident it was the only piece he owned. But the Essex instructions specified 'the yeerely value of euery mans land', and although they add 'within the same town', the possibility of misreading remains. The result was that some, though not all, of the greater landowners were assessed at their places of residence on all their property both there and in other parishes. In some of the other returns the occasional explanatory gloss makes it clear that an assessment is a global one[5], but the Rutland book does not, with the result that the practice can only be detected with the evidence of other sources. Richard Flower, for example, was assessed at £80 for land at Whitwell, but the feodary survey made after his death in 1528-9 valued his property there at no more than £3. 13s 9d, and it is obvious that the £80 was obtained by rounding down his actual income of £103.[6]

1.  P. Laslett and J. Harrison, 'Clayworth and Cogenhoe', in H. E. Bell and R. L. Ollard, eds., *Historical Essays, 1600-1750, presented to David Ogg* (1963), pp. 157-84.

2.  See my article in *Trans. Leics. Arch. Soc.* xxxvii, 24, and my 'English Population in the Early Sixteenth Century', *Economic History Review*, 2nd. Ser. xxii (1970), 33-6; where only two lists are available the combined total should be increased by an average ten percent to take account of the missing one.

3.  This problem will be examined in a forthcoming monograph to be published by Routledge & Kegan Paul, London.

4.  See *Trans. Leics. Arch. Soc.* xxxvii, 8, n.9.

5.  *Certificate of Musters for Buckinghamshire*, p. 118, &c.

6.  PRO, Wards 9/129, f. 78v. David Cecil, assessed at £46 at Tinwell, owned little property there, and lived in the manor house as the abbot of Peterborough's bailiff: *Victoria County History of Rutland*, ii 282.

The accuracy of individual assessments is not easy to test. Valuations of church property compare well with those stated in the *Valor Ecclesiasticus* of 1535 which frequently goes into much finer detail. For the lands of laymen we have to rely largely on a handful of feodary surveys which were made on behalf of the Crown when an estate was taken into wardship: the more familiar inquisitions post mortem are less reliable. The results, nonetheless, are by no means discouraging. In any case the tenant of a property could vouch for the rent paid for it, while if necessary a landowner's rentals and accounts could be, and on occasion were, inspected.[1]

The wage assessments in the subsidy present the fewest problems. The minimum of twenty shillings must be regarded as the disposable surplus of income net of essential expenditure on food and lodging. At the current statutory rate of 4d a day the annual earnings of a farm worker in full employment must have been of the order of £5; however, the wage of a "common servant of husbandry" boarded in his master's household was 16s 8d a year plus 4s for clothing, making a total of 20s 8d. Higher assessments, such as 26s 8d or 33s 4d, correspond to the rates laid down for superior servants like bailiffs and shepherds, while the fact that total remuneration for a woman was limited to 14s a year is sufficient to explain why female taxpayers were restricted to a handful of widows of landowners and farmers.[2]

There is no prima facie reason for supposing that the standard of assessment of goods and chattels was less rigorous. This is an important consideration since in the absence of probate inventories there can be no question of verifying individual valuations, but in general they do not conflict with the known facts regarding personal estates at this time.[3]

Perhaps the most significant aspect of this Rutland material is the light it sheds on Hall's intriguing, not to say incredible claim that certain people 'avaunsed themselfes more than they were worth of pride. . .' Although we have Polydore Vergil's assurance that the survey demonstrated that the nation was far from poor, the suggestion of shrewd peasants bragging of their affluence to the King's agents is not easy to swallow. Yet a comparison of the level of wealth in Rutland with that in other counties reveals a most significant feature. According to the loans of 1522-3 it ranked fourteenth, on a par with the rich county of Gloucester-shire, whereas in the subsidy of 1515 they had ranked 22nd and sixth, respectively. In 1524, moreover, on the basis of tax paid, the best that Rutland could achieve was 24th place, implying that this was more or less its 'normal' position for tax purposes.[4] More precisely, personal wealth in Rutland averaged £97 per thousand in 1522, or half as much again as in both 1515 and 1524 when it stood at approximately £62-64. In Buckinghamshire the difference was far smaller—£79 in 1522 compared with roughly £70 in the two subsidies, and in western Berkshire the level was only marginally higher than the £88 averaged by the whole county in 1515. Again, while many Rutland people secured substantial reductions in their assessments when the subsidy was levied such revisions were much rarer in Buckinghamshire, and were mostly concen-trated in the Chiltern hundreds in the south. In the northern district, the part most comparable to Rutland, most assessments were carried forward unchanged, while not a few were actually increased.

Improbable though it would appear, many Rutland men may actually have fallen for the commission-ers' blandishments, really believing that all they were being asked to do was to declare their ability to con-tribute to the defence of the realm. Possibly the commissioners there were more persuasive than in other counties, but in any event the very fullness of the return betrays an anxiety to play safe. It is feasible that Raddlemen found themselves committed to subscribing to the loan on the basis of the true value of their

1. Coventry City Record Office, Acc. 24; A96, f. 91.
2. 6 Henry VIII, c. 3, 1514-15: *Statutes*, iii, 124.
3. See, for example, W. G. Hoskins, *Essays In Leicestershire History* (Liverpool, 1950), *passim*. The problem will also be dis-cussed fully in my forthcoming monograph.
4. Hoskins, *Age of Plunder*, P. 24; R. S. Schofield, 'The Geographical Distribution of Wealth in England, 1334-1649'. *Economic History Review*, 2nd. ser. xviii (1965), 504; PRO, E. 314/41.

possessions; certainly the assumption must be that in 1524 the subsidy commissioners were prevailed on to restore assessments to approximately the levels of 1515. The fact that assessments in north Buckinghamshire were retained substantially unaltered speaks for itself: most people deemed it prudent to keep quiet and pay up, while those who were uprated presumably brought on themselves a further and more searching investigation of their assets as a penalty for claiming unwarranted abatements. Whether many men actually did overstate their assets may be doubted; at the same time it is entirely possible that an access of unwonted candour had given us a more or less accurate statement of the wealth of a rural community in the Midlands at the close of the middle ages.

The military aspects present no difficulty. Able-bodied men between the ages of 16 and 60 were classified as either archers or billmen. The scanty entries relating to arms and harness show that very few fulfilled their obligations under the Statute of Winchester, 1285, to furnish themselves according to their means. Most equipment was held by gentlemen and yeomen, complete harnesses especially; lesser men tended to have only odd pieces. The name of the lord of each town together with the record of tenurial relationships provided essential information about military potential since the raising of troops was almost always entrusted to leading landowners who in the first instance would call upon their servants and tenants. Several men are designated as servants or retainers of magnates; for the most part yeomen and the owners of full equipment, they may very well have semi-professional soldiers who acted as recruiting or training officers. Christopher Webster of Ridlington was listed as a household servant of Lord Hastings the Leicestershire magnate; despite appearances there is no anomaly in this, for some noblemen made a practice of working their households in relays.[1]

### iii. The Subsidy

The indenture and schedule for the first year, dated 3 May 1524 (PRO, E.179/165/110) is almost complete and generally in good condition. There is a separate membrane for each of the five hundreds made up of two or more smaller pieces of parchment stitched together. Part of the membrane which contains Martinsley has evidently been lost, for the sum total for the hundred follows the entry relating to Manton, while Ayston, Lyndon and Uppingham are missing. For the second instalment, levied in January 1525, roll 165/112 contains East hundred with fragments of Wrandike, and 165/113 fragments of Alstoe and Martinsley including the three parishes missing from 165/110. Both these rolls consist of loose, un-numbered membranes. Overall there is one complete list for every parish and hamlet in the county, and two for a third of them, including the whole of East hundred.

The indenture gives the names of the five commissioners, who executed it, as well as the five high collectors. The omission of the sub-collectors, of whom there would have been one or two for every township, is not unusual. The composition of the commission for musters is not known, except that it was headed by John Haryngton the elder of Exton, who died in 1523. As his son John the younger, who is named the first of the subsidy commissioners, evidently succeeded to his place in the local hierarchy, it seems likely that some or all of his colleagues had also served on the muster commission.

Unlike the military survey, the subsidy was never intended to apply to every man aged sixteen and over, only those who owned taxable assets. Thus the lists can be expected to be both shorter and less comprehensive. In practice, however, they are nearly always very similar in structure, the chief difference being the high turnover of persons assessed at less than £2. Not only were many assessments scaled down, the lists show a tendency to get shorter year by year. However, in a few cases where the number of low assessments was disproportionately small in 1522, the balance is restored in the subsidy return. Thus at Clipsham

1.  C. Rawcliffe, *The Staffords, Earls of Stafford and Dukes of Buckingham* (Cambridge, 1978), p. 88.

only 13 men were listed in the survey, including four worth less than £2, but in 1524 the total was increased to 27 of whom 19 were assessed at £1—an attempt, clearly to rectify a glaring oversight in the earlier return.

As regards the assessments, those made on land are intended to represent a man's total income in each case. Very few persons were in fact taxed on this basis, and the survey shows that in most villages there was only a tiny handful of resident landowners, most of whom had no more than a few shillings' worth. Most men were assessed on their goods, the definition of which was comprehensive embracing coin plate, and moneys owing—allowance being made for debts owed—and excluding only standing corn and personal attire. Values were subject to wide variations, not merely as between the muster and the subsidy, but also between the two instalments of the latter. Inevitably there must have been cases of avoidance and evasion; certainly misunderstandings occurred.[1] But there are no compelling reasons for suspecting widespread fraud, rather the opposite, and indeed glosses on returns from some counties specify grounds on which assessments were reduced: certain districts were clearly afflicted by livestock epidemics and heavy rains which levelled crops.[2]

Due perhaps to its experimental nature the taxation of wages gives rise to problems of interpretation. First attempted in 1513, it was abandoned after 1525, possibly because of difficulties over implementation, but certainly as one result of the steep decline in real wages. In line with the wording of the act assessments include not only wages as such but also 'profits for wages'. The distinction is not explained; profits could arguably have been used to describe the earnings of cottagers, especially those gained from piecework rather than day wages, and as opposed to the stipends of servants hired by the year, an occupational description that is not found in the subsidy rolls. The majority of assessments below £2 were made on wages. At this level, however, the amount of tax paid was the same, that is 4d, as for assessments on goods, and since a good many wage earners must have owned some personal estate, confusion arose from time to time. At Market Overton in 1524, for instance, the collectors clearly endeavoured to distinguish men who qualified to be taxed on goods from those who had to be assessed on wages: whether they did so successfully or not we have no way of telling, at any rate in 1525 everyone was taxed on goods regardless of status. Although the act did not envisage it, a number of men were assessed on wages of two or three pounds, and even more in a very few cases, tax being paid at the same rate as for goods. In the absence of any explanation it can only be supposed that they were either servants exercising exceptional responsibilities or the possessors of special skills.

In three of the hundreds occupations were recorded in 1524, though not in 1525. While it is to be presumed that this followed the precedent set by the muster book, there was no mere mechanical reproduction of earlier details. As previously noted, almost every tradesman listed in the one return was represented as a farmer or labourer in the other. Furthermore, while the survey distinguished servants from labourers, who were mostly described as tenants and as often as not owned some goods, the subsidy recognised only the latter category, thereby suggesting that in practice the distinction between the two kinds of wage-earner was not entirely clear cut.

### iv.  *The Transcripts*

For the military survey the text used is that of the original return, supplemented by the later copy. The aim has been to produce a complete transcript except insofar as it has been judged advisable to prune certain repetitious matter in the interests of clarity. Omissions are as follows:

1. *Letters & Papers*, iv, Part 1, no. 122.
2. PRO, E. 179/155/131; *Buckinghamshire Subsidy*, pp. 1-10. Cf also Schofield, thesis, pp. 334-40.

1. the words 'in lond' in the land value column wherever the words 'hath lond their' appear in the name column;
2. 'Nil' in the arms column where it serves no useful purpose; the very small number of substantive entries is thereby highlighted.

In the lands and goods columns, however, 'nil'is retained as constituting, despite its negative form, a positive statement that the person in question is a resident who does not own assessable property under either heading.

Subject to these exceptions the return is transcribed verbatim; the few items in Latin, mainly headings, are rendered into English and in the interests of clarity Arabic numerals are substituted for Roman. Non-resident landowners are identified by the gloss 'quia manet extra' or 'quia extra', frequently shortened to 'q.e.' which form has been adopted as standard. Suspensions and abbreviations have been extended except where the meaning is not apparent, but a few standardised abbreviations have been retained. Punctuation has been added sparingly and only where it seems essential to the sense. The suspension point is added to the shortened forms 'husb.' for husbandman, and 'laber.' for labourer. The latter, used only in the subsidy roll, occasionally has the symbol indicating a terminal 'er', that is laberer, but it has not been extended in the transcript. In the original the columns were totalled in a different hand. These totals are printed in bold type; errors have not been rectified.

Editorial emendations and insertions are enclosed in square brackets; glosses are italicised. The modern foliation of the original is followed, with the pagination of the eighteenth century copy given in parenthesis.

For purposes of comparison the entry relating to Ketton is reproduced *verbatim et literatim*.

The text of the subsidy presented here is a composite one. Basically it consists of the schedule for the first instalment (roll 165/110), supplemented by the second (165/112-3) in respect of three missing townships and four others for which the earlier list is imperfect. Where there are two complete returns new and revised assessments are appended. Names peculiar to the primary return are distinguished by an asterisk (*); assessments which are revised in the second return are distinguished by a dagger (†). For obvious reasons the asterisk can be employed only where there are two perfect lists. There is no return for the Soke of Oakham in 1525.

The numbering of the membranes of roll 165/110 is modern and incorrect. The text is transcribed in what is clearly its original order. The other rolls consist only of loose, un-numbered fragments.

Each individual entry consists of name, assessment and amount paid. In the interests of economy it has been considered superfluous to print the amounts paid. If desired they can be readily computed according to the following scale:

assessments on land, 1s in £;
assessments on goods of £20 and upwards, 1s in £;
assessments on goods of £2 but under £20, 6d in £;
assessments on goods and wages of £1 but less than £2, a flat 4d.

Some assessments intermediate between £1 and £2 were incorrectly taxed at 6d; these are noted as they occur.

# Glossary of Military Terms

**BILL**  a combined axe blade and spear point with a short rearward pointing spike, mounted on a pole; one of the two standard infantry weapons.

**BRIGANDINE**  body protection consisting of iron rings or plates sewn onto, and covered with canvas or leather; sometimes worn in two halves, hence 'a pair of brigandines'.

**GORGET**  piece of armour protecting the throat.

**HARNESS FOR A MAN**  sallet, jack, gorget and splints.

**JACK**  a coat of canvas or leather with small plates sewn in.

**JESTORN**  corrupt form of jesserant; a coat of splints or small plates, rivetted together.

**SALLET**  a helmet.

**SPLINTS, PAIR OF**  Pieces of armour protecting the elbows.

**STEEL BONNET**  similar to a sallet.

# The Military Survey, 1522

PRO E. 36/55   E.36/54

*f. 1 (1v)*

The names of the five Hundreds of County Rotlond, viz. Alstow Hundred, Mertley Hundred, Wrandyke Hundred Okam Sokon and the Esthundred.

*f. 1v (1A, 1Av) blank)*

*f. 2 (1B)*

**WYSSENDEN**                          **ALSTOW HUNDRED IN COUNTY ROTLOND**

| Persons' ability | Persons' names and qualities & of whom holding | Value of lands | | Value of goods | | Equipment and horses |
|---|---|---|---|---|---|---|
| | The Kyng ower souereign lord is cheyef lord of the seid Town .. | — | — | — | — | — |
| | [Willi]am Overton Gent. is steward of the seid town .. .. | in Feez | 6s 8d | in goods nil q.e. | | — |
| | The Prior of Sempryngham is parson of the seid town .. .. | parsonage | 20 marks | in goods nil q.e. | | — |
| | William Hyde is vicar their .. | vicarige | 10 marks | in goods | 40s | — |
| | Robert Brudenell Esquier hath an annuite goyng out of certain londs & tenements within the seid Town .. | — | £8 | in goods nil q.e. | | — |
| Bill man | Laurence Barkeley Gent. hath londs to the yerely value within the seid Town | — | £14 | in goods | £4 | — |
| | Moris Barkeley Esquier hath lond ther to the yerely value .. .. | — | £8 | in goods nil q.e. | | — |
| | William Villers hath lond their to the yerely value .. .. .. .. | — | 5 marks | in goods nil q.e. | | — |
| | Thomas Pochyn hath lond their to the yerely value .. .. .. | — | £3 | in goods nil q.e. | | — |
| | John Pudsey hath lond their to the yerely value .. .. .. | — | 10s | in goods nil q.e. | | — |
| Bill man | Jamys Obyns hath londs their to the yerly value is Thomas Sherrards tenant & his bailly their .. .. | — | 13s 4d | in goods £40 | | & hath a Bill |
| | William Wartley tenant to Laurence Barkeley .. .. | in londs | nil | in goods | £8 | & hath 2 Bills |
| Archer | Hugh Sharpe tenant to the seid Laurence .. .. .. .. | in londs | nil | in goods £36 | | & hath a Bow with a Sheff of arrows & .... Bills |
| | Thomas Sherrard Esquier hath londs their to the yerly value .. .. | — | £16 | in goods nil q.e. | | — |

| | | | | |
|---|---|---|---|---|
| Bill man | Thomas Wortley tenant to Laurence Barkeley hath londs their the yerly value .. .. .. | — | 12[s] | ............... |
| | Thomas Watkyn tenant to the Kyngs grace .. .. | .. in londs | [nil]1 | ............... |
| | Richard Wortley tenant Laurence Barkeley .. .. | .. in londs | [nil] | ............... — |
| Bill man | William Masson tenant to Thomas Pochyn .. | .. in londs | [nil] | ............... — |
| Bill man | John Greneham tenant to William Villers .. .. .. | .. in lond | [nil] | ............... — |
| | William Lovet tenant to Thomas Sherrard .. .. | ............... | | ............... — |
| Bill man | Robert Malton tenant to Moris [Barkeley] aforenamed .. | ............... | | ............... — |
| Bill man | William Ber .... [tenant to] Moris Barkeley .. .. | ............... | | ............... — |
| Bill man | William Glover [tenant to Thomas] Sherrard .. .. | ............... | | ............... — |

*f. 2v (2)*

| | | | | | | |
|---|---|---|---|---|---|---|
| | ..... tenant to Thomas ...... | .. in londs | nil | in goods | £8 | — |
| | ...... tenant to the [Prior of Sempryngham?] .. .. | .. in londs | nil | in goods | £3 | — |
| | Thomas Baker tenant to Laurence Barkeley .. .. | .. in londs | nil | in goods | £3 | — |
| | Robert Machyn tenant to Laurence Barkeley .. .. | .. in londs | nil | in goods | 40s | — |
| | Richard Spencer tenant to Laurence Barkeley .. .. | .. in londs | nil | in goods | 40s | — |
| | Edward Wortley tenant to Laurence Barkeley .. .. | .. in londs | nil | in goods | 20s | — |
| | Agnes Baker widow tenant to the seid Laurence .. .. | .. in londs | nil | in goods | 20s | — |
| ...... | John Wayt tenant to William Villers | in londs | nil | in goods | 40s | — |
| Bill man | William Hertford tenant to Laurence Barkeley .. .. | .. in londs | nil | in goods | 20s | |
| | William Jenkynson tenant to Moris Barkeley .. .. | .. in londs | nil | in goods | 20s | |
| Bill man | John Kyrkeale tenant to Laurence Barkeley .. .. | .. in londs | nil | in goods | 20s | |
| Archer | Thomas Goodrode tenant to Laurence Barkeley .. .. | .. in londs | nil | in goods | 20s | — |
| Archer | Roger Rylay tenant to Thomas Sherrard .. .. | .. in londs | nil | in goods | 40s | & Hath Bowe & Arrows & a Bill |
| Bill man | William Stanylond tenant to William Villers .. .. .. | .. in londs | nil | in goods | 40s | & Hath a Bonytt |
| | William Page tenant to the seid Laurence .. .. | .. in londs | nil | in goods | 40s | — |

---

1. *In this section only 'in londs' is regularly followed by 'nil' but omitted if a positive value is given.*

| | | | | | | |
|---|---|---|---|---|---|---|
| Bill man | Cristofer Batson tenant [to Thomas] Sherrard .. .. .. | in londs | nil | in goods | 40s | |
| | . . . . . . . . . . . . . . . . . . . . . . . . . . . . | | | in goods | 20s | |
| | . . . . . . . . . . . . . . . . . . . . . . . . . . . . | | | in goods | 30s | — |
| | . . . . . . . . . . . . . . . . . . . . . . . . . . . . | | | in goods | 40s | — |
| | . . . . . . . . . . . . . . . . . . . . . . . . . . . . | | | in goods | £3 | & hath a jestorn |
| | . . . . . . . . . . . . . . . . . . . . . . . . . . . . | | | in goods | £6 | — |
| | . . . . . . . . . . . . . . . . . . . . . . . . . . . . | | | in goods | 20s | — |
| | . . . . . . . . . . . . . . . . . . . . . . . . . . . . | | | . . . . . . . . . . . . . . . . | | — |
| | . . . . . . . . . . . . . . . . . . . . . . . . . . . . | | | . . . . . . . . . . . . . . . . | | — |
| | . . . . . . . . . . . . . . . . . . . . . . . . . . . . | | | . . . . . . . . . . . . . . . . | | — |

*f. 3 (3)*

| | | | | | | |
|---|---|---|---|---|---|---|
| | Henry Magdaunce tenant to the seid Laurence .. .. .. | in londs | nil | in goods | 40s | — |
| | Thomas Man tenant to Thomas Sherrard .. .. .. | in londs | nil | in goods | 40s | — |
| Bill man | William Man tenant to William Villers .. .. .. | in londs | nil | in goods | £3 | — |
| Bill man | Robert Robyns tenant to Thomas Sherrard .. .. .. | in londs | nil | in goods | £3 | — |
| Bill man | William Lovet the yonger tenant to Thomas Sherrard .. .. .. | in londs | nil | in goods | 40s | — |
| | Richard Wayte tenant to Laurence Barkeley .. .. .. | in londs | nil | in goods | 26s 8d | — |
| Bill man | Edward Lovet tenant to Laurence Barkeley .. .. .. | in londs | nil | in goods | 20s | — |
| Bill man | Hugh Pudsey tenant to Laurence Barkeley .. .. .. | in londs | nil | in goods | 30s | — |

| | | |
|---|---|---|
| Bill man | Thomas Hastyngs tenant to John Pudsey a yong man & pore .. | |
| Bill man | William Fareday tenant to the Kyng a yong man & pore .. | |
| | William Wortley tenant to William Villers pore man & old | |
| Bill man | William Poole tenant to Laurence Barkeley yong man & pore .. | |
| Archer | Robert Bellamy tenant to Thomas Sherrard yong man & pore .. | |
| Bill man | Thomas Lednam tenant to Laurence Barkeley yong man & pore .. | |
| Bill man | Thomas Grove seruant to Hugh Sharpe, yong man & pore .. | in londs nil     in goods nil |
| Archer | William Baker seruant to Thomas Wortley a yong man & pore .. | |
| Archer | Thomas Brown seruant to Thomas Wortley a yong man & pore .. | |
| Archer | Richard Perkyn seruant to Richard Lover a yong man & pore .. | |
| Archer | Bartill' Standyll seruant to Richard Bylkley, a yong man & pore .. | |
| Bill man | John Gourton seruant to Jamys Reve, a yong man & pore .. | |
| Archer | Hugh a Greneham seruant to John Greneham a yong man & pore | |

| | | | | | |
|---|---|---|---|---|---|
| Bill man | William Sparke seruant to Richard Watkyn a yong man & pore .. | in londs   nil | | in goods nil | |
| Bill man | John Collyn seruant to Thomas Wortley, a yong man & pore .. | | | | |
| | The Township hath half a harnesse for a man | | | | |
| | The Church Stoke is worth nil | | | | |
| | | £36   16s   8d | | | nil |

*f, 3v (4)*

## COTISMORE

| | | | | | |
|---|---|---|---|---|---|
| | The Kyng owr souereign lord is chief lord of the seid Town ..   .. | — | — | —   — | — |
| | Edward . . . . . y Esquier is steward of the seid town   ..   .. | in londs   nil | | in goods nil q.e. | — |
| | William Urmeston is parson of the seid Town   ..   ..   ..   .. | parsonage   £22 | | in goods   £40 | — |
| | John Haryngton thelder Esquier hath londs ther to the yerly value ..   .. | — | £4 | in goods nil q.e. | — |
| | Jerram Markham hath londs ther to the yerly value ..   ..   .. | — | £8 | in goods nil q.e. | — |
| | Thomas Duraunt hath londs ther to the yerly value   ..   ..   .. | — | 40s | in goods   £20 | & hath harnesse for on man & a bill |
| | William Adam hath londs ther to the yerly value ..   ..   ..   .. | — | 40s | in goods nil q.e. | — |
| | John Bate hath londs ther to the yerly value & tenant to Jerram Markham   ..   ..   .. | — | 13s   4d | in goods   £20 | & hath a jestorn a Sallet with an appryn of mayle |
| | Richard Markham hath an annuite goyng owte of certen londs their   .. | — | £8 | in goods nil q.e. | — |
| | Robert Chamberlyn tenant to the kyng | in lond   nil | | in goods   £22 | — |
| | Thomas Collyn tenant to Jerram Markham   ..   .. | in lond   nil | | in goods   £18 | & hath a sallet & a Bill |
| | Edmond Cooper tenant to the Kyng | in lond   nil | | in goods   £16 | & hath a sallet |
| Archer | John Hichecok tenant to Jerram Markham   ..   .. | in lond   nil | | in goods   £8 | — |
| | John Sharpe tenant to the Kyng   .. | in lond   nil | | in goods   £4 | — |
| | Henry Starke tenant to Jerram Markham   ..   .. | in lond   nil | | in goods   £3 | — |
| Bill man | Robert Snetht tenant to the Kyng   .. | in lond   nil | | in goods   £4 | — |
| Bill man | Stephyn Gibson tenant to the parson | in lond   nil | | in goods nil | a pore yong man |
| . . . . . . | William Man tenant to John Haryngton thelder   ..   .. | in lond   nil | | in goods   £4 | — |
| | Edmond Dawson tenant to the Kyng | in lond   nil | | in goods   £10 | — |
| Bill man | William Cark tenant to John Haryngton   ..   .. | in lond nil | | in goods    40s | & hath a Sallet & a Bill |
| | John Allen tenant to the seid John Haryngton   ..   .. | in londs   nil | | in goods   £4 | — |
| Bill man | William Turpyn tenant to Jerram Markham   ..   .. | in londs   nil | | in goods   £5 | — |
| | John Russhell tenant to Jerram Markham   ..   .. | in londs   nil | | in goods   £6 | — |
| Bill man | Robert Stubbe tenant to the Kyng   .. | in londs   nil | | in goods    40s | — |
| Bill man | John Dove tenant to the seid John Haryngton   .. | in londs   nil | | in goods    20s | — |
| | | £46   13s   4d | | £189 | — |

*f. 4 (5)*

| | | | | | | |
|---|---|---|---|---|---|---|
| Bill man | John Bett tenant to the Kyng | .. in londs | nil | | in goods 20s | — |
| | John Plomer tenant to John Bate | .. in londs | nil | | in goods 20s | — |
| Archer | Niccolis Oldham tenant to the seid Jerram Markham .. | .. in londs | nil | | in goods 20s | — |
| Archer | Niccolis Ashlyn tenant to the seid Jerram Markham .. | .. in londs | nil | | in goods 20s | — |
| Archer | Robert Parker tenant to Jerram Markham .. .. | .. in londs | nil | | in goods £3 | — |
| | John Walker tenant to the Priorisse of Stamford .. .. | .. in londs | nil | | in goods 20s | — |
| | The Priorisse of Seynt Michell by Syd Stamford hath lond their to the yerly value .. .. .. | — | | 6s 8d | in goods nil q.e. | — |
| | An Fyssher widow tenant to William Adams .. .. | .. in londs | nil | | in goods 20s | — |
| Archer | John Coper seruant to Edmond Coper | in londs | nil | | in goods 20s | — |
| | Robert Coper seruant to the same .. | in londs | nil | | in goods 20s | — |

| | | | | | |
|---|---|---|---|---|---|
| Bill man | Thomas Heryng seruant to the seid John Haryngton .. .. | | | | |
| Bill man | Hugh Morley tenant to the Kyng | | | | |
| Bill man | William Buchibek tenant to the Kyng .. .. .. | | | | |
| Bill man | William Wells tenant to the parson their .. .. | in londs nil | in goods nil | yong men & pore | |
| Archer | William Pery tenant to the seid parson their .. .. | | | | |
| Bill man | William Wood weuer tenant to the Kyng .. .. .. | | | | |
| Bill man | John Bretten tenant to the Kyng | | | | |
| Bill man | Thomas Leyland tenant & seruant to the seid parson .. .. | | | | |

| | | | | | |
|---|---|---|---|---|---|
| | Thomas Hunt tenant to the Kyng | in londs nil | in goods nil | old men & pore | |
| | John Alee tenant to the parson | | | | |
| Bill man | Robert Hill seruant to John Bate | | | | |
| | Hugh Hichecok seruant to Thomas Duraunt .. .. | in londs nil | in goods nil | yong men & pore | |
| Bill man | Richard Turpyn laborer .. | | | | |
| Archer | Thomas Egaley seruant to John Bate | | | | |

The Church Stoke is worth their of the seid Town £5

|   |   |
|---|---|
| 6s 8d | £16 |

*f. 4v (6)*

## MERKITOUERTON

| | | | | | |
|---|---|---|---|---|---|
| | William [Sey Knyght] is chef lord of the seid Town .. .. | .. in londs | £18 | in goods nil q.e. | — |
| | John Haryngton thelder is steward their .. .. .. | .. in Feez | [blank] | in goods nil q.e. | — |
| | Thomas Byrch is parson of the seid town .. .. | .. parsonage | 24 marks | in goods nil q.e. | — |
| | Raff [blank] is chapeleyn their of the seid Town .. .. | .. stipend | £5 | in goods 20s | — |
| Archer | Robert Rysse bailly of the seid Town & seruant to the Lord Mountjoy & tenant to the seid William Sey | .. in londs | nil | in goods £10 | & hath a Bill |

| | | | | | | |
|---|---|---|---|---|---|---|
| | Thomas Sherrard Esquier hath londs their .. .. .. | — | 10s | in goods | nil q.e. | — |
| | Jamys Waren hath londs their to the yerly value .. .. .. | — | 13s 4d | in goods | nil q.e. | — |
| Bill man | John Suckstob hath londs their & reteyned to the Lord Scrop .. .. .. | | 33s 4d | in goods | £10 | & hath a Jak, Sallet gorgit & pair of Splynts & a Bill |
| Archer | Thomas Suckstob tenant to the seid William Sey .. .. .. in londs | nil | | in goods | £5 | — |
| Archer | Henry Baxster seruant to Lord Mountjoy .. .. .. in londs | | 33s 4d | in goods | £6 | & hath a Bowe & a Sheff of Arrows |
| Bill man | Thomas Blomfeld tenant to Sir William Sey .. .. .. in londs | | 6s 8d | in goods | £4 | — |
| | John Bretfield tenant to Sir William Sey .. .. .. in londs | | 3s 4d | in goods | 5 marks | — |
| | John Cowes tenant to the seid William Sey .. .. .. in londs | nil | | in goods | 20s | — |
| | John Nyke tenant to the seid Sir William Sey .. .. in londs | nil | | in goods | £10 | — |
| Bill man | Richard Hall tenant to the seid Sir William Sey .. .. in londs | nil | | in goods | £6 | — |
| ........ | Richard Smarte tenant to the seid Sir William Sey .. .. in londs | nil | | in goods | 20s | — |
| ........ | Henry Porter tenant to the seid Sir William Sey .. .. in londs | nil | | in goods | £10 | — |
| ........ | Jamys Holt tenant to the seid Sir William Sey .. .. in londs | nil | | in goods | £8 | & hath a Bill |
| Bill [man] | Richard Nyk tenant to the seid Sir William Sey .. .. in londs | nil | | in goods | £10 | — |
| Bill man | William Stallok tenant to the seid Sir William Sey .. .. in londs | nil | | in goods | £8 | — |
| Bill man | William Grey tenant to the seid Sir William Sey .. .. on londs | nil | | in goods | 5 marks | — |
| Bill man | Thomas Rushall tenant to the seid Sir William Sey .. .. in londs | nil | | in goods | 20s | — |
| | William Porter tenant to the seid Sir William Sey .. .. in londs | nil | | in goods | £3 | — |
| Bill man | William Ward reteyned to Thomas Sherrard Esquier & his tenant .. in londs | nil | | in goods | 20s | — |
| | | **£44 17s** | | | **£101 13s 4d** | — |

f.5 (7)

| | | | | | |
|---|---|---|---|---|---|
| | Robert Faconer Husbond tenant the seid Sir William Sey .. .. in londs | nil | in goods | 40s | — |
| Archer | Andrew Hogyn laborer tenant to the seid Sir William Sey .. .. in londs | nil | in goods | 20s | — |
| | Thomas Wylson laborer tenant to the seid Sir William Sey .. .. in londs | nil | in goods | 20s | — |
| | John Multon laborer tenant to the seid Sir William Sey .. .. in londs | nil | in goods | 20s | — |
| | John Player Weuer tenant to the seid Sir William Sey .. .. in londs | nil | in goods | 20s | — |
| | John Spendyng laborer tenant to the seid Sir William Sey .. .. in londs | nil | in goods | 20s | — |
| Bill man | Robert Porter Husbond tenant to the seid Sir William Sey .. .. in londs | nil | in goods | £4 | — |

| | | | | | | |
|---|---|---|---|---|---|---|
| | Thomas Jakson laborer | .. | | | | |
| Archer | John Suckstob laborer | .. | in londs nil | in goods nil | | yong men & pore |
| Archer | Richard Sawnson laborer | .. | | | | |
| Archer | John Sawnson laborer | .. | | | | |

The Church of the seid Town 10*s*

The seid Town hath the third part of a Harnesse for a man.

## BARROW

| | | | | | |
|---|---|---|---|---|---|
| | Thomas Sherrard is chyeff lord of the seid Town .. .. .. | in londs | £10 | in goods nil q.e. | — |
| | William Urmeston is parson their of the parish of Cotismore town & their valued .. .. .. .. | parsonage parcel of Cotismore | | in goods nil q.e. | — |
| | The Abbot of Valle Dei hath londs their .. .. .. | — | 8 marks | in goods nil q.e. | — |
| | The Priorisse of Seint Michell besyde Stamford hath londs their .. .. | — | £4 | in goods nil q.e. | — |
| | The Prior of Seint John of Jerusalem in Englond hath londs their .. .. | — | 10*s* | in goods nil q.e. | — |
| | William Niccolls Husbond tenant to the seid Abbot .. .. .. | in londs | nil | . . . . . . . . . . . . . . . | — |
| | William Cristian Husbond tenant to the seid Thomas Sherrard .. .. | in londs | 10*s* | . . . . . . . . . . . . . . . | — |
| | Richard Whithed tenant to the seid Thomas Sherrard & Husbond .. | in londs | nil | . . . . . . . . . . . . . . . | — |
| Bill man | Thomas Clerk Husbond tenant to the seid Prior .. .. .. .. | in londs | nil | . . . . . . . . . . . . . . . | — |
| | | | £20 6s 8d | . . . . . . . . . . . . . . . | — |

*f. 5v (8)*

| | | | | | |
|---|---|---|---|---|---|
| | John A . . . gham Husbondman & tenant to Thomas Sherrard .. .. | in londs | nil | in goods £5 | — |
| | John Rosse Husbond & tenant to the seid Thomas Sherrard .. .. | in londs | nil | in goods £5 | — |
| Bill man | John Depyng laborer & tenant to the seid Thomas Sherrard .. .. | in londs | nil | in goods 26*s* | — |
| | Robert Dunmore Husbond & tenant to the seid Thomas Sherrard .. .. | in londs | 12*s* | in goods £4 | — |
| Bill man | Thomas Robberd laborer & tenant to the seid Thomas Sherrard .. .. | in londs | 4*s* | in goods 20*s* | — |
| | Thomas Ways laborer & tenant to the seid Thomas Sherrard .. .. | in londs | nil | in goods 26*s* | — |
| | John Cristian seruant to William Cristian .. .. .. | in londs | nil | in goods £3 | — |
| | Robert Cristian laborer & seruant to William Cristian .. .. .. | in londs | nil | in goods £3 | — |
| | William Whithed seruant to Richard Whithed .. .. .. | in londs | nil | in goods £4 | — |
| | Robert Clerk seruant to Thomas Clerk | in londs | nil | in goods £4 | — |
| | He[nry] Frekyngham seruant to John Fre[kyngham] .. .. .. | in londs | nil | in goods 30*s* | — |
| | . . . . . . . . . . / . . . . . . . . . . { pore men & old / . . . . . . . . . . | in londs | nil | in goods nil | |

| | | | | |
|---|---|---|---|---|
| · · · · · · · · · · }<br>· · · · · · · · · ·<br>· · · · · · · · · ·<br>· · · · · · · · · · } yong men & pore | in londs nil | in goods nil | — |
| | · · · · · · · · · · | | 33s 2d |

## *f. 6 (9)*
### THISTILTON

| | | | | |
|---|---|---|---|---|
| | Miles Bushey Knyght is Chieff lord of the seid Town .. .. .. | in londs £5 | in goods nil q.e. | — |
| | Cristoforus Hudson is parson of the seid town .. .. .. .. | parsonage £4 | in goods £5 | — |
| | John Jakson Husbondman & tenant to the seid Miles .. .. .. | in londs nil | in goods £16 | & hath a jak a Sallet & a gorgit |
| | Thomas Coope Husbondman & tenant to the seid Miles .. .. | in londs nil | in goods £10 | — |
| | John Lamore Husbondman & tenant to the seid Miles .. .. | in londs nil | in goods £5 | — |
| Bill man | William Midbroke Husbondman & tenant to the seid Miles .. .. | in londs nil | in goods £3 | — |
| | Richard Short Husbond & tenant to the seid Miles .. .. | in londs nil | in goods £3 | — |
| | William Ray Husbond & tenant to the seid Miles .. .. | in londs nil | in goods £5 | — |
| | John Browghton Husbondman & tenant to the seid Miles .. .. | in londs nil | in goods £4 | — |
| Bill man | John Rasse Husbond & tenant to the seid Miles .. .. | in londs nil | in goods £4 | — |
| | William Grene laborer .. | in londs nil | in goods nil | a pore man and old |
| Bill man | Robert Fysshlak tenant to the seid Miles laborer .. .. | in londs nil | in goods 30s | — |
| Archer | Jamys Ottes seruant to John Jakson } | | | |
| | William Drewe seruant to the person .. .. .. } in londs nil | | in goods nil | Yong men & pore |
| Archer | William Richemond seruant to Thomas Coope .. .. } | | | |

The Church Stoke is nil

John Robynson sheperd of the seid Town Born in Scotlond the xxj*te* day of September in the xiiij yere of the reigne of owr Souereign lord the Kyng that now is before John Haryngton thelder & other the Kyngs Comissioners of the Countie of Rotlond for the takyng of views & musters within the seid Countie was abjured the seyd Realme of Englond & his passage & days to him assigned by the seid Comissioners accordyng to the Kyngs instruccions annexid to the Kyngs Comision.

| | | |
|---|---|---|
| Abjured | | An old man & pore |
| | £9 | £56 10s |

## *f. 6v (10)*
### WHITWELL

| | | | | |
|---|---|---|---|---|
| | The Prior of Seint John of Jerusalem in Englond is Chieff lord of the seid Town .. .. .. .. | in londs 22s | in goods nil q.e. | — |
| | Steward of the seid town is Henry Wykley .. .. | feez 6s 8d | in goods nil q.e. | — |

| | | | | | |
|---|---|---|---|---|---|
| | Richard Flower Esquier hath londs their to the yerely value of .. .. | — | £80 | in goods £60 | & hath horse & harnesse for vj men |
| | Henry Hasley is parson of the seid Town & is worth by yere | parsonage | 5 marks | in goods £4 | — |
| | John Reynold chauntre prest their & his .. .. .. .. .. | stipend | 6 marks | in goods £5 | — |
| | Thomas Sherrard Esquier hath londs their worth by the yere .. | — | £4 13s 4d | in goods nil q.e. | — |
| | John Haryngton thelder Esquier hath londs their by yere .. .. | — | 6s | in goods nil q.e. | — |
| | William Haryngton Gentilman hath londs their worth by yere .. .. | — | 20s | in goods nil q.e. | — |
| | Richard Fylynley Husbond & tenant to the seid Richard Flowre .. | — | 25s | in goods £3 | — |
| | William Belamy Husbond & tenant to the seid Thomas Sherrard .. .. | in londs nil | | in goods £10 | — |
| | Richard Wryght Husbond & tenant to the seid Richard Flowre .. .. | in londs nil | | in goods £8 | — |
| Archer | Thomas Nettils Husbond & tenant to the seid Thomas Sherrard .. .. | in londs nil | | in goods £10 | — |
| | John Siston laborer & tenant to the the seid Richard Flowre .. .. | in londs nil | | in goods 40s | — |
| Bill man | Thomas Broge laborer .. | | | | |
| | Robert Smyth laborer .. | yong men & pore | | in londs nil | in goods nil |
| Archer | William Ward laborer .. | | | | |
| | William Monee laborer .. | | | | |

The Church Stoke of the seid Town [blank]


**STRETTON**

| | | | | | |
|---|---|---|---|---|---|
| | William Hussey Knyght is Chief lord of the seid Town .. .. .. | in londs | [blank] | in goods nil q.e. | — |
| | .... Clark Gentilman is Steward of the seid Town .. .. | in Feez | 6s 8d | in goods nil q.e. | — |
| | The Prior of Seint John of Jerusalem in Englond hath londs their .. .. | — | 20s | in goods nil q.e. | — |
| | | | **£190 6s 8d** | **£102** | |


*f. 7 (11)*

| | | | | | |
|---|---|---|---|---|---|
| | The seid Prior of Seint John of Jerusalem in Englond is parson their | parsonage | 26s | in goods nil q.e. | — |
| | William Tedryngton is Vicar of the seid Town & is worth by yere .. | Vicarige | £4 6s 8d | in goods 5 marks | — |
| | The Warden of the Halmeshowse of Stamford hath an annuite goyng owte of certen londs .. .. .. | annuite | 36s 8d | in goods nil q.e. | — |
| | John Barker hath londs & tenements their by yere .. .. | — | 8s | in goods nil q.e. | — |
| Archer | William Wezelhed Husbond & tenant to the seid William Hussey .. .. | in londs nil | | in goods £15 | — |
| Bill man | John Queneborow Husbond & tenant to the seid William Hussey .. .. | in londs nil | | in goods £11 | — |
| | Robert Wells Husbond & tenant to the seid William Hussey .. .. | in londs nil | | in goods £18 | & hath a gestorn & a Bill |

| | | | | | |
|---|---|---|---|---|---|
| | Robert Skillyngton tenant to the seid William Hussey & Husbondman | in londs | nil | in goods £18 | & hath a jestorn a Sallet & a Bill |
| | John Skillyngton Husbond & tenant to the seid William Hussey .. .. | in londs | nil | in goods £15 | — |
| Bill man | Roger Stephen Husbond & tenant to the vicar their .. .. .. | in londs | nil | in goods £10 | — |
| Bill man | Thomas Kensall tenant to the seid William Hussey & Husbondman .. | in londs | nil | in goods £7 | — |
| | Richard Fyshlak tenant to the seid William Hussey & Husbondman .. | in londs | nil | in goods 20s | — |
| Bill man | John Quenebroow thelder Husbond & tenant to the seid William Hussey | in londs | nil | in goods £4 | — |
| | William Coke Husbond & tenant to the seid William Hussey .. .. | in londs | nil | in goods £4 | — |
| Bill man | John Dalymer Husbond & tenant to the seid William Hussey .. .. | in londs | nil | in goods £12 | — |
| Archer | William Washyngborow Husbond & tenant to the seid William Hussey .. | in londs | nil | in goods £3 | — |
| | Thomas Lame laborer & tenant to the seid William Hussey .. .. | in londs | nil | in goods 20s | — |
| Archer | Thomas Wesilhed Husbond & tenant to the seid William Hussey .. | in londs | nil | in goods 40s | — |
| Bill man | George Rogerson seruant to William Wezelhed .. .. .. | in londs | nil | in goods £4 | — |
| | John Skellit laborer & tenant to the seid Warden of the Almeshowses .. | in londs | nil | in goods 20s | — |
| | Thomas Kensall laborer .. .. | in londs | nil | in goods nil | pore man & yong |

The Church Stoke nil

            £7 16s 4d           £130 6s 8d

*f. 7v (12)*

**ASHWELL**

| | | | | | |
|---|---|---|---|---|---|
| | Brian Palmes Esquier is Chieff lord of the seid Town .. .. | in londs | £25 | in goods nil q.e. | — |
| | John Haryngton thelder is Steward their .. .. .. | in Feez | 10s | in goods nil q.e. | — |
| | Miles Hago chapelyn to the Bishop of Wynchester is parson their .. | parsonage | £14 | in goods nil q.e. | — |
| | Thomas Norton Knyght Master of Burton Lazars hath londs their .. | in londs | £3 | in goods nil q.e. | — |
| Bill man | Robert Wilcokes Husbond & tenant to the seid Brian .. .. | in londs | 10s | in goods £18 | — |
| | Agnes Castelyn Wydow tenant to the seid Brian .. .. .. | in londs | 26s 8d | in goods 40s | — |
| | Henry Thorp Husbond & tenant to seid Brian .. .. .. | in londs | nil | in goods £5 | — |
| | Thomas Stencall Husbond & tenant to the lord aforesaid .. .. | in londs | nil | in goods 40s | — |
| Archer | John Castelyn Husbondman & tenant to the seid Brian .. .. | in londs | nil | in goods £3 | — |
| Bill man | William Chapman Husbond & tenant to the seid Brian .. .. | in londs | nil | in goods £5 | — |
| | Thomas Redmile Husbondman & tenant to the seid Brian .. | in londs | nil | in goods £15 | — |

| | | | | | | |
|---|---|---|---|---|---|---|
| | Robert Heryng Husbond & tenant to the seid Brian | in londs | nil | in goods | £3 | — |
| | Thomas Cartlech Husbond & tenant to the seid Brian | in londs | nil | in goods | £3 | — |
| | Thomas Ierman laborer & tenant to the seid Brian | in londs | nil | in goods | 30s | — |
| Bill man | Raff Bothome laborer & tenant to the seid Brian | in londs | nil | in goods | 20s | — |
| Bill man | John Wynnowe Husbond & tenant to the seid Brian | in londs | nil | in goods | 40s | — |
| Bill man | John Day laborer & tenant to the seid Brian | in londs | nil | in goods | 30s | — |
| | William Irenes Husbond & tenant to the seid Brian | in londs | nil | in goods | 40s | — |
| | Thomas Greneham laborer | in londs | nil | in goods | 20s | — |
| Bill man | John Castelyn the yonger Husbond & tenant to the seid Brian | in londs | nil | in goods | £8 | — |
| Bill man | Thomas Andrew Husbond & tenant to the seid Brian | in londs | nil | in goods | £16 | — |
| Bill man | John Wells Husbond & tenant to the seid Brian | in londs | nil | in goods | £10 | — |
| | John Redmyle Husbond & tenant to the seid Brian | in londs | nil | in goods | £3 | — |
| Bill man | Thomas Bredsale Husbond & tenant to the seid Brian | in londs | nil | in goods | £8 | — |
| | | | **£44  6s  8d** | | **£110** | |

*f. 8 (13)*

| | | | | | | |
|---|---|---|---|---|---|---|
| Bill man | John Mason Husbond & tenant to the seid Brian Palmes | in londs | nil | in goods | £8 | — |
| | John Rutlond laborer | in londs | 20s | in goods nil | | a pore old man |
| Archer | Thomas Spenyng Taillor & tenant to the seid Brian Palmes | in londs | nil | in goods | 30s | — |
| | Emmot Spennyng Widow & tenant to the seid Brian Palmes | in londs | nil | in goods | £10 | — |
| | William Castelyn Husbond & tenant to the seid Brian Palmes | in londs | nil | in goods | £5 | — |
| Archer | Nicholis Castelyn Husbondman & tenant to the seid Brian Palmes | in londs | nil | in goods | £10 | — |
| Bill man | Richard Heryng Husbond & tenant | | | | | — |
| | to the seid Brian Palmes | in londs | nil | in goods | £3 | — |
| | William Spennyng laborer | in londs | nil | in goods | 20s | — |
| Archer | John Wilkokes laborer | | | | | |
| Bill man | John Watson laborer | in londs | nil | in goods nil | | pore men & yong |
| Bill man | John Stowe laborer | | | | | |
| Archer | Iosie Spennyng laborer | | | | | |

The Church Stoke 26s  8d

The Town Schipp of Asshwell hath Harnesse for a man         Hernes for a man

## GRETHAM

| | | | | | | |
|---|---|---|---|---|---|---|
| | The Kyng ower souereign lord is Chieff lord their | | | | | |
| | Edward Digby Esquier is Steward of the seid Town | in Feez | 20s | in goods nil q.e. | | — |

|  |  |  |  |  |  |
|---|---|---|---|---|---|
|  | The Prior of Warwyke is parson of the seid Town .. .. .. | parsonage | £3 | in goods nil q.e. | — |
|  | John Boare Clerk is Vicar of the seid Town .. .. .. .. | vicarige | 8 marks | in goods nil q.e. | — |
|  | The Heirez of Plompton hath londs their to the yerly value .. .. | — | 20s | in goods nil q.e. | — |
| Archer | John Brown Bailly of the seid Town & seruant to owr seid lord the Kyng | in londs | 20s | in goods £10 | — |
| Bill man | Robert Laxston Husbond & tenant to the seid Plompton .. .. .. | in londs | nil | in goods £20 | & hath harnesse hole for a man with a Bill |
|  | William Allee Husbond & tenant to the Kyng .. .. .. .. | in londs | nil | in goods £7 | — |
| Bill man | Robert Nyk husbond & tenant to the Kyng .. .. .. .. | in londs | nil | in goods £8 | — |
|  | Thomas Wells Husbond & tenant to the Kyng .. .. .. .. | in londs | nil | in goods £10 | — |
|  | John Fairechild Husbond & tenant to the Kyng .. .. .. .. | in londs | nil | in goods £12 | & hath a Bill |
|  |  |  | £12 16s 8d | £105 10s |  |

*f. 8v (14)*

|  |  |  |  |  |  |
|---|---|---|---|---|---|
| Bill man | John Somerby Husbondman & tenant to the Kyng .. .. | in londs | nil | in goods £8 | — |
| Bill man | Thomas Torry Husbondman & tenant to the Kyng .. .. | in londs | nil | in goods £5 | — |
|  | John Chamberlyn Husbondman & tenant to the Kyng .. .. | in londs | nil | in goods 5 marks | — |
| Bill man | Thomas Hopkyn Husbond & tenant to the Kyng .. .. .. | in londs | nil | in goods £3 | — |
|  | Thomas Swyfte Husbond & tenant to the Kyng .. .. .. | in londs | nil | in goods 40s | — |
| Bill man | John Stark Husbond & tenant to the Kyng .. .. .. | in londs | nil | in goods 40s | — |
|  | Thomas Gooll Husbond & tenant to the Kyng .. .. .. | in londs | nil | in goods 40s | — |
| Bill man | Robert Wich laborer & tenant to the Kyng .. .. .. | in londs | nil | in goods 40s | — |
| Bill man | John Brown laborer & tenant to the Kyng .. .. .. | in londs | nil | in goods 40s | — |
| Bill man | William Hawley laborer & tenant to the Kyng .. .. .. | in londs | nil | in goods 20s | — |
|  | Thomas Johnson laborer & tenant to the Kyng .. .. .. | in londs | nil | in goods 20s | — |
| Bill man | Richard Crosse laborer & tenant to the Kyng .. .. .. |  |  |  |  |
|  | John Maw laborer & tenant to the Kyng .. .. .. |  |  |  |  |
| Bill man | Henry Freman laborer & tenant to the Kyng .. .. .. | Yong men & pore | | in londs nil | in goods nil |
| Bill man | Stephen Bett laborer & tenant to the Kyng .. .. .. |  |  |  |  |
| Bill man | Robert Sawer laborer & tenant to the Kyng .. .. .. |  |  |  |  |

|  | William Daley laborer | .. |  |  |  |  |
|---|---|---|---|---|---|---|
| Bill man | Robert Stubbs laborer | .. | } Yong men & pore | in londs nil | in goods nil |  |
| Bill man | John a Wood laborer .. | .. |  |  |  |  |

The Church Stoke nil

## BURLEE

|  | Name | land | lands | in goods | goods | harness |
|---|---|---|---|---|---|---|
|  | Edward Sapcote Esquier is Chieff lord of the seid Town .. .. .. | in londs | £60 | in goods | £20 | & hath harness for hymself & iij men, & iij horses, ij bills, ij Bowies ij Sheff of Arrowies |
|  | William Ouerton Gentil. is Steward their .. .. .. .. | in Feez | 40s | in goods nil q.e. |  | — |
|  | Gilbert Urmeston Vicar their of the seid Town & chapelyn to the lord Cobham in howshold .. .. .. | Vicarige | £12 | in goods nil q.e. |  | — |
|  | The Priorisse of Nounetton is parson their .. .. .. | parsonage | 10 marks | in goods nil q.e. |  | — |
|  | Thomas Crispe is parish prest of the seid town .. .. .. | stipend | £5 | in goods | 26s 8d | — |
|  |  |  | £83 16s 8d |  | £4 13s 4d |  |

f. 9 (15)

| Role | Name | land | lands | in goods | goods | | harness |
|---|---|---|---|---|---|---|---|
| Archer | William Wilkynson yoman, bayly to the seid Edward Sapcote .. .. | in londs | nil | in goods | £30 | | & hath a Bill a Bow & a Sheff of arrowies |
| Bill man | John Tyller Husbond & tenant to the seid Edward .. .. .. | in londs | nil | in goods | £20 | | & hath a Bill |
|  | John Thorp Husbond & tenant to the seid Edward .. .. .. | in londs | nil | in goods | £15 | | — |
| Bill man | John Hunton Husbond & tenant to the seid Edward .. .. .. | in londs | nil | in goods | £6 | | |
| Archer | John Stubbs Husbond & tenant to the seid Edward .. .. .. | in londs | nil | in goods | £4 | | & hath a Jestorn |
| Bill man | John Wymark Husbond & tenant to the seid Edward .. .. .. | in londs | nil | in goods | £5 | | & hath a Bill |
| Archer | John Bakhowse Husbond & tenant to the seid Edward .. .. .. | in londs | nil | in goods | £3 | | — |
|  | William Thornton Husbond & tenant to the seid Edward .. .. .. | in londs | nil | in goods | £4 | | — |
| Bill man | William Curlew Husbond & tenant to the seid Edward .. .. .. | in londs | nil | in goods | £4 | | — |
|  | Robert Vellam Husbond & tenant to the seid Edward .. .. .. | in londs | nil | in goods | 40s | | — |
| Bill man | Thomas Cotton Miller & tenant to the seid Edward .. .. .. | in londs | nil | in goods | £3 | | — |
| Bill man | William Kyrkman Husbond & tenant to the seid Edward .. .. | in londs | nil | in goods | £4 | | — |
| Bill man | Richard Rose Weuer & tenant to the seid Edward .. .. .. | in londs | nil | in goods | 13s | 4d | — |
|  | Richard Briggs laborer & tenant to the seid Edward .. .. .. | in londs | nil | in goods | 26s | 8d | — |
| Bill man | John Webster laborer & tenant to the seid Edward .. .. .. | in londs | nil | in goods | 30s | | — |
| Archer | Thomas Dicconson laborer & tenant to the seid Edward .. .. | in londs | nil | in goods | 30s | | — |

| | | | | | | |
|---|---|---|---|---|---|---|
| Bill man | John Hauer laborer & tenant to the seid Edward | in londs | nil | in goods | 30s | — |
| Bill man | Robert Brown Husbond & tenant the seid Edward | in londs | nil | in goods | 30s | — |
| Bill man | Thomas Day laborer & tenant to the seid Edward | in londs | nil | in goods | 20s | — |
| Archer | Henry Clerk laborer & tenant to the seid Edward | | | | | |
| Bill man | William Hardy laborer & tenant to the seid Edward | | | | | |
| Archer | John Cotton laborer | in londs | nil | in goods nil | | yong men & pore |
| Bill man | Richard Dalbe laborer | | | | | |
| Bill man | Richard Jobson laborer | | | | | |
| Bill man | Henry Teysdale laborer | | | | | |

The Church Stoke 30s

         30s          £109

## f. 9v (16)
## EXTON

| | | | | | | |
|---|---|---|---|---|---|---|
| | John Haryngton thelder Esquier is Chieff lord of the seid Town | in londs | 40 marks | in goods | [blank] | & hath harnesse sufficient for x men |
| | Richard Flower Esquier hath londs their | — | 13s | in goods nil q.e. | | — |
| | Richard Sapcot Esquier hath londs their | — | 26s 8d | in goods nil q.e. | | — |
| | William Ouerton Gent is Steward there of the seid Town | in feez | 40d | in goods nil q.e. | | — |
| | Thomas Pochyn Gent hath londs their | — | 11s | in goods nil q.e. | | — |
| | John Gylberd yoman hath londs their | — | 40s | in goods nil q.e. | | — |
| | The Prior of Seint Andrews of the town of Northampton is parson their | parsonage | £10 | in goods nil q.e. | | — |
| | Thomas Ives Vicar of the seid Town | Vicarige | £8 | in goods | £5 | — |
| | William Souter Husbond hath londs their | — | 13s 4d | in goods | 30s | — |
| | Phillip Colles Husbond hath londs their | — | 10s | in goods | 20s | — |
| Bill man | William Moysez Husbond & tenant to the seid John Haryngton | in londs | nil | in goods | £14 | — |
| Bill man | Thomas Tiller Husbond & tenant to the seid Richard Sapcot | in londs | nil | in goods | £7 | — |
| | Robert Clark Husbond & tenant to the seid John Haryngton | in londs | nil | in goods | £12 | — |
| Archer | John Freman Husbond & tenant to the seid John Haryngton | in londs | nil | in goods | £15 | — |
| Bill man | Robert Loke Husbond & tenant to the seid John Haryngton | in londs | nil | in goods | £12 | — |
| Bill man | Robert Wright Husbond & tenant to the seid John Haryngton | in londs | nil | in goods | £12 | — |
| Bill man | John Royse Husbond & tenant to the seid John Haryngton | in londs | nil | in goods | £14 | — |
| Bill man | Thomas Sowter Husbond & tenant the seid John Haryngton | in londs | nil | in goods | £10 | — |
| Bill man | John Byrd Husbond & tenant to the seid John Haryngton | in londs | nil | in goods | £10 | — |

| | | | | | | | |
|---|---|---|---|---|---|---|---|
| | Thomas Smyth Husbond & tenant to the seid John Haryngton .. .. in londs | nil | in goods | £10 | — |
| | Thomas Sisson Husbond & tenant to the seid John Haryngton .. .. in londs | nil | in goods | £8 | — |
| Bill man | John Smyth Husbond & tenant to the seid John Haryngton .. .. in lands | nil | in goods | £8 | — |
| Bill man | John Wright Husbond & tenant to the seid John Haryngton .. .. in londs | nil | in goods | £5 | — |
| | Richard Derby tenant to the seid Richard Flower .. .. .. in londs | nil | in goods | £5 | — |
| Bill man | William Parke Husbond & tenant to the seid John Haryngton .. .. in londs | nil | in goods | £3 | — |

**£50 10s 8d**      **£152 10s**

*f. 10 (17)*

| | | | | | | | | |
|---|---|---|---|---|---|---|---|---|
| Bill man | John Freyney Husbond & tenant to the seid Master John Haryngton .. in londs | nil | in goods | £3 | — |
| | John Persyvall laborer & tenant to the seid John Haryngton .. .. in londs | nil | in goods | 40s | — |
| Bill man | Jamys Armoror Husbond & tenant to the seid John Haryngton .. .. in londs | nil | in goods | £4 | — |
| | Thomas Horton Husbond tenant to the seid John Haryngton .. .. in londs | nil | in goods nil | | a pore old man |
| Bill man | Raff Brigge Husbond & tenant to the seid John Haryngton .. .. in londs | nil | in goods | 40s | — |
| | Robert Sharpe Husbond & tenant to the seid John Haryngton .. in londs | nil | in goods | 42s | — |
| | Robert Colles Husbond & tenant to the seid Haryngton .. .. .. in londs | nil | in goods | 40s | — |
| Bill man | John Turnor Husbond & tenant to the seid John Haryngton .. .. in londs | nil | in goods | £3 | — |
| Archer | Thomas Masson Smyth & tenant to the seid John Haryngton .. .. in londs | nil | in goods | 40s | — |
| Bill man | Edward Smyth Husbond & tenant to the seid John Haryngton .. .. in londs | nil | in goods | £3 | — |
| | John Colles Husbond & tenant to the seid John Haryngton .. .. in londs | nil | in goods | £3 6s 8d | — |
| Bill man | Hugh Clark Husbond & tenant to the seid John Haryngton .. .. in londs | nil | in goods | £6 | — |
| | John Clark Husbond & tenant to the seid John Haryngton .. .. in londs | nil | in goods | 40s | — |
| Archer | Thomas Whitley Husbond & tenant to the seid John Haryngton .. .. in londs | nil | in goods | 40s | — |
| Bill man | George Sowter Husbond & tenant to the seid John Haryntgon .. .. in londs | nil | in goods | £6 | — |
| | John Nyke Husbond & tenant to the seid John Haryngton .. .. in londs | nil | in goods | £4 | — |
| | Thomas Watson Husbond & tenant to the seid John Haryngton .. .. in londs | nil | in goods | £6 | — |
| | Robert Stevenson Husbond & tenant to the seid John Haryngton .. .. in londs | nil | in goods | 40s | — |
| Bill man | William Muse Miller & tenant to Elizabeth Haryngton Wydow .. in londs | nil | in goods | 40s | — |

| | | | | | | | |
|---|---|---|---|---|---|---|---|
| Bill man | Robert Gunthorp Taillor & tenant to John Harynton | .. | .. | .. in londs | nil | in goods | 40s | — |
| Archer | Richard Nottyngham Weuer & tenant to the seid John Haryngton .. | .. in londs | nil | in goods nil | a pore yong man |
| | William Stephyn Sheperd | .. | .. in londs | nil | in goods nil | a pore man |

The Church Stoke [blank]

nil      £58   8s   8d

*f. 10v (18)*

**TYGHT**

| | | | | |
|---|---|---|---|---|
| | Thomas Sherrard Esquier is Chieff lord of the seid Town ..   ..   .. in londs | £30 | in goods nil q.e. | — |
| | Thomas Masson is parson of the seid Town   ..   ..   .. parsonage | 20 marks | in goods   26s   8d | — |
| | William Forrist is parich prest their of the seid Town   ..   ..   .. stipend | £5 | in goods   20s | — |
| Bill man | Richard Grene Bailly of the seid Town & seruant to the seid Thomas Sherrard in londs | nil | in goods £20 | & hath a Jestorn a Sallet a Bill |
| | William Crane fermer of the seid parsonage Husbondman   ..   .. in londs | nil | in goods £16 | & hath a Jestorn a Sallet, a pair of splynts, a gorgit, a Bill |
| | Thomas Monee Husbond & tenant to the seid Thomas Sherrard   ..   .. in londs | nil | in goods £10 | — |
| Archer | Robert Chapman Husbond & tenant to the seid Thomas Sherrard ..   .. in londs | nil | in goods £8 | — |
| | William Chapman Husbond & tenant to the seid Thomas Sherrard ..   .. in londs | nil | in goods £5 | — |
| Archer | William Wilcok Husbond & tenant to the seid Thomas Sherrard ..   .. in londs | nil | in goods £5 | — |
| Bill man | Richard Grene the yonger Husbond & tenant to the seid Thomas Sherrard in londs | nil | in goods £5 | — |
| Bill man | William Queneborow Husbondman & tenant to the seid Thomas Sherrard .. in londs | nil | in goods £4 | — |
| | John Dyng Husbond & tenant to the seid Thomas Sherrard   ..   .. in londs | nil | in goods £5 | — |
| | William Wodde Husbond & tenant to the seid Thomas Sherrard ..   .. in londs | nil | in goods £4 | — |
| | Richard Waltham tenant to the seid Thomas Sherrard & Husbond   .. in londs | nil | in goods £4 | — |
| Archer | Thomas Plimgar Husbond & tenant to the seid Thomas Sherrard ..   .. in londs | nil | in goods £3 | & hath a Bill |
| Bill man | William Monee Husbond & tenant to the seid Thomas Sherrard ..   .. in londs | nil | in goods £3 | — |
| | John Waltham Husbond & tenant to the seid Thomas Sherrard   ..   .. in londs | nil | in goods £3 | — |
| Bill man | John Stanelond Husbond & tenant to the seid Thomas Sherrard ..   .. in londs | nil | in goods   20s | & hath a stele Bonytt with a Bill |
| Bill man | Laurence Waltham Husbond & tenant to the seid Thomas Sherrard ..   .. in londs | nil | in goods   20s | — |
| Bill man | Thomas Queneborow laborer | | | |
| Bill man | John Maye laborer   ..   .. | in londs   nil | in goods nil | pore men & yong |
| Bill man | Richard Bett laborer   .. | | | |
| | Thomas Clyfford laborer   .. | | | |

| Habilitas | | | | |

Bill man   Robert Dyng laborer .. ..  
Bill man   John Chapman laborer .. ..  
Bill man   John Truk laborer .. ..  
Archer   John Haminer laborer ..  
} in londs nil    in goods nil    pore men & yong

The Town hath the third part of harnesse for a man

The Church Stoke nil

£48  6s  8d      £99  6s  8d

End of this Hundred

*f. 11 (19)*
**KETTON**

### LE ESTHUNDRED IN COUNTY ROTLOND

| Habilitas personarum | Nomina personarum cum qualitatibus & cui tenens | Valor terrarum | Valor Bonorum | Armature er qui |
|---|---|---|---|---|
| | The Kyng ower Souereign lord is chieff lord of the seid town | | | |
| | John Calcott Esquier hath londs to the yerly value .. .. | in londs xxix*li* | in goods xxx*li* | & hath harnesse for man |
| | Edward Derby Clerk is parson of the seid town .. .. | parsonage xxxiij*li* iij*s* | in goods nil quia extra manet | nil |
| | Thomas Greneham Gent. hath londs ther .. .. | in lond xv*li* | in goods nil quia extra manet | nil |
| | Thomas Clerk Gent. is steward ther .. .. .. | in feez vj*s* viij*d* | in goods nil quia extra manet | nil |
| | William Oxon is vicar of the the seid Town .. .. .. | Vicarige viij*li* | in goods [blank] | nil |
| Archer | Richard Willoughby Gent. & fermer of the parsonage of the seid Town .. | in londs vij marce vj*s* | in goods l pounds | reteyned to Sir John Zouch & hath horse & harnesse for a man & hym selfe |
| | John Oxon yoman hath londs their within the seid Town .. .. | in lond xl*s* | in goods xx pounds | & hath harnesse for a man |
| Archer | William Kyng yoman & tenant to the Prior of Newsted hath londs .. | in londs iiij marce | in goods l pounds | & hath harnesse for a man |
| | The seid Prior of Newsted hath londs ther .. .. .. | in londs xl*s* | in goods nil quia extra | nil |
| | The Prior of Sempryngham hath lond their .. .. .. | in londs iiij*li* xiij*s* | in goods nil quia extra manet | nil |
| Bill man | Richard Niccolls Husbond & tenant to Thomas Greneham | in londs nil | in goods xlv*li* | & hath harnesse for a man |
| | Henry Betten Husbond & tenant to the seid Thomas .. .. | in londs xlvj*s* | in goods xij*li* | nil |
| Archer | Thomas Hogeson Yoman & tenant to Edward Sapcote .. .. | in londs v marce | in goods xij*li* | & hath harnesse for a man |
| | The Warden of the Hospitall of Tatersall hath londs their .. | in londs iij*li* xv*s* | in goods nil q.e. | nil |
| | Edward Sapcote Esquier hath lond their .. .. .. | in londs ix marce | in goods nil q.e. | nil |
| | Richard Sapcote Esquier hath lond their .. .. .. | in londs iiij*li* vj*s* | in goods nil q.e. | nil |
| Bill man | Richard Aburn Husbond & tenant to the Warden of Tatershall .. | in londs nil | in goods xxv pounds | & hath a sallet & a paire of splyntts |

| | | | | | |
|---|---|---|---|---|---|
| Archer | John Picher Husbond & tenant to the seid Warden | in londs | nil | in goods twenty pounds | nil |
| Archer | Nicholis Hogeson Husbond & tenant to the Prior of Sempryngham | in londs | nil | in goods v pounds | & hath a bill |
| Bill man | John Woode Husband & tenant to John Caldecote | in londs | xiij*s* iv*d* | in goods vij pounds | nil |
| Archer | Thomas Mathew laborer & tenant to the parson of the seid Town | in londs | nil | in goods xx*s* | nil |
| Bill man | William Kechyn Husbond & tenant to the seid parson | in londs | nil | in goods iiij*li* | nil |
| | John Collyn Husbond & tenant to Thomas Greneham | in londs | ij*s* | in goods vij pounds | nil |
| | | | **cxxij*li* iiij*s* iiij*d*** | **cclxxxiij*li*** | |

*f. 11v (20)*

| | | | | | |
|---|---|---|---|---|---|
| Bill man | William Johnson tenant to the parson and Husbond | in londs | nil | in goods xxvj*s* viij*d* | nil |
| | Richard Clark laborer & tenant to the seid Richard Sapcote | in londs | nil | in goods xl*s* | nil |
| | Richard Brawell laborer & tenant to the seid Henry Bretten | in londs | nil | in goods xxvj*s* viij*d* | nil |
| Bill man | Gilbert Yong[er] laborer & tenant to the seid John Caldecote | in londs | nil | in goods xxvj*s* viij*d* | nil |
| | William Brawell Husbond & tenant to the seid John Calcote | in londs | nil | in goods iij*li* | nil |
| Archer | Harry Adam Husbond & tenant to the seid Henry Bretten | in londs | nil | in goods ten pounds | nil |
| Bill man | Robert Walker laborer & tenant to the seid John Caldecote | in londs | nil | in goods xl*s* | nil |
| | William Lovet Husbond & tenant to the seid John Caldecote | in londs | x*s* | in goods iiij*li* | nil |
| | Thomas Porter laborer & tenant to the seid John Oxon | in londs | nil | in goods xx*s* | nil |
| | William Chatton Husbond & tenant to the seid Thomas Greneham | in londs | nil | in goods iiij*li* | nil |
| | Thomas Sisson Husbond & tenant to the seid Richard Sapcote | in londs | nil | in goods xij*li* | nil |
| Bill man | Thomas Cley Husbond & tenant to the seid Prior of Sempryngham | in londs | nil | in goods xl*s* | nil |
| Bill man | Thomas Grey Husbond & tenant to the seid Richard Sapcote | in lond | nil | in goods vj*li* | nil |
| | Richard Willner laborer & tenant to the seid parson | in londs | nil | in goods xx*s* | nil |
| Bill man | William Knyght Husbond & tenant to the seid parson | in londs | nil | in goods iij*li* | nil |
| Bill man | Robert Niccoll Husbond & tenant to the seid Thomas Greneham | in londs | nil | in goods xl*s* | nil |
| | William Mason laborer & tenant to the said Thomas Greneham<br>Peter Yonger laborer & tenant to the seid Prior of Sempryngham<br>John Caworth tenant to the seid John Calcote<br>Thomas Hargrave laborer<br>Brice Sherman laborer | in londs | nil | in goods nil | old men & pore |

|  | | | | | |
|---|---|---|---|---|---|
| | William Hyxson tenant to John Cley .. .. .. | | | | |
| | John Dalby laborer tenant to the parson .. | in londs nil | in goods nli | old men & pore |
| | William Gilbon seruant .. | | | | |
| | Thomas Wylnes seruant .. | | | | |
| Archer | Richard Burley seruant .. | | | | |
| Bill man | George Faux seruant .. .. | | | | |
| Archer | John Lane seruant .. .. | | | | |
| Archer | Thomas Roo seruant .. .. | in londs nil | in goods nil | yong men & pore nil |
| Bill man | John Malard seruant .. .. | | | | |
| Bill man | John Roo seruant .. .. | | | | |
| Bill man | John Flecher seruant .. .. | | | | |
| Archer | Richard Wright seruant .. | | | | |
| Archer | Richard Holme seruant .. | | | | |
| Bill man | John Aburn seruant .. .. | | | | |

The Trinite Gild in Stoke x*li* ij*s*
The Church Stoke nil
x*s*          lxvj*li* ij*s*

*f. 12 (21)*

## EMPYNGHAM

| | | | | | |
|---|---|---|---|---|---|
| | George Mackworth Esquier is chieff lord of the seid Town .. .. .. | in londs £40 | | in goods £36 | & hath horse & harnesse for iij men |
| | William Ouerton is steward of the seid Town .. .. .. | in feez 40*d* | | in goods nil q.e. | — |
| | Cristoforus Massingberd Clerk is parson of the seid Town .. | parsonage £24 | | in goods nil q.e. | — |
| | Richard Fowler prest is vicar of the seid Town .. .. .. | vicarige £5 6*s* 8*d* | | in goods 24 marks 6*s* 8*d* | — |
| | The Prior of Seint John of Jerusalem in Englond hath lond ther .. .. | — | 40*s* 8*d* | in goods nil q.e. | — |
| | The lord Souch hath lond their .. | — | 7*s* | in goods nil q.e. | — |
| | William Dall Gent hath lond their .. | — | 25*s* | in goods nil q.e. | — |
| | John Eldred yoman hath lond their .. | — | 40*s* | in goods nil q.e. | — |
| | John Parker yoman hath lond their .. | — | 6*s* 8*d* | in goods nil q.e. | — |
| | Elizabeth Edmonds widow hath lond their .. .. .. | in lond £3 | | in goods £50 | — |
| | John Collyn Husbond tenant to the seid George .. .. | in lond nil | | in goods £22 | & hath harnesse for a man |
| | William Barnys Husbond tenant to the seid George .. .. | in lond nil | | in goods £23 | & hath a sallet |
| Bill man | John Laxon Husbondman & tenant to the seid George .. .. | in lond nil | | in goods £21 | — |
| | Richard Collyn Husbond & tenant to the seid William Dale .. | in lond 12*s* | | in goods £10 | — |
| | John Spenethorn Husbond & hath lond their .. .. .. | in lond 10*s* | | in goods £10 | & hath a sallet & a Bill |
| | Thomas Exton Husbond & tenant to the seid George .. .. | in lond nil | | in goods £8 | — |
| | William Sisson Husbond & tenant to the seid George .. .. | in lond nil | | in goods £7 | — |
| Archer | Raff Caterns seruant to the seid George & tenant .. .. | in lond nil | | in goods £3 | — |

| | | | | | | |
|---|---|---|---|---|---|---|
| Bill man | John Faux tenant & seruant to the seid George .. .. .. | in lond | nil | in goods | 30s | — |
| Archer | Nicholis Fowler Husbond & tenant to the parson .. .. .. .. | in lond | nil | in goods £13 | | — |
| Bill | Robert Williamson Taillor & tenant to the lord .. .. .. .. | in lond | nil | in goods £8 | | — |
| Bill | Richard Brown Husbond & tenant to the lord .. .. .. .. | in lond | nil | in goods £4 | | — |
| | John Leyff Husbond & tenant to the Lord .. .. .. .. | in lond | nil | in goods £4 | | — |
| | Gye Spenethorn Husbond & tenant to the seid George .. .. .. | in lond | nil | in goods £5 | | — |
| Bill man | Robert Careby Husbond & tenant to the lord their .. .. .. .. | in lond | nil | in goods | 40s | — |
| | | **£79 11s** | | **£253 16s** | **8d** | |

*f. 12v* (22)

| | | | | | | |
|---|---|---|---|---|---|---|
| | Thomas Langton Husbond & tenant to the lord .. .. .. .. | in lond | nil | in goods £8 | | — |
| Bill man | Thomas A Bowre miller & tenant to the seid George .. .. .. | in lond | nil | in goods £3 | | — |
| Bill man | Thomas Turnor Husbond & tenant to the lord .. .. .. .. | in lond | nil | in goods £6 | | — |
| Bill man | William Gooll laborer & tenant to the lord .. .. .. .. | in lond | nil | in goods nil | | a pore yong man |
| | Thomas Prodfote Husbond & tenant to the seid George .. .. .. | in lond | nil | in goods | 40s | — |
| | Robert Wright Husbond & tenant to the seid George .. .. .. | in lond | nil | in goods £13 | 6s 8d | — |
| | Thomas Wright laborer & tenant to the lord .. .. .. .. | in lond | nil | in goods | 40s | — |
| Bill man | Richard Turnor Husbond & tenant to the seid lord .. .. .. | in lond | nil | in goods | 40s | — |
| Archer | Robert Whithed Husbond & tenant to the seid George .. .. .. | in lond | nil | in goods £3 | | — |
| Bill man | William Pepeer Husbond & tenant to the vicar .. .. .. .. | in lond | nil | in goods £12 | | — |
| | Margaret Wetherly widow & tenant to the lord .. .. .. .. | in lond | nil | in goods £3 | | — |
| | William Fox Husbond & tenant to the lord aforesaid .. .. .. | in lond | nil | in goods £3 | | — |
| Bill man | Richard Robinson seruant & tenant to the lord .. .. .. .. | in lond | nil | in goods £4 | | — |
| Archer | John Hill laborer & tenant to the lord | in lond | nil | in goods | 20s | — |
| | John Wezelhed laborer & tenant to the lord .. .. .. .. | in lond | nil | in goods | 20s | — |
| | Richard Wetherly Husbond & tenant to the lord .. .. .. | in lond | nil | in goods | 40s | — |
| | Thomas Collyn Husbond & tenant to the lord .. .. .. .. | in lond | nil | in goods £4 | | — |
| | Robert Burnes laborer & tenant to the lord .. .. .. .. | in lond | nil | in goods | 20s | — |
| Bill man | John Brown laborer & tenant to the Prior of Saint John of Jerusalem | in lond | nil | in goods | 20s | — |

|  | | in lond | | in goods | | |
|---|---|---|---|---|---|---|
|  | Thomas Symys laborer & tenant to the lord of the seid town | in lond | nil | in goods | 40s | — |
|  | Richard Pittes laborer & tenant to the Prior of Saint John of Jerusalem | in lond | nil | in goods | 20s | — |
| Bill man | John Brown Husbond & tenant to the lord their of the seid town | in lond | nil | in goods | 40s | — |
| Bill man | John Careby seruant to Elizabeth Edmonds | in lond | nil | in goods | £11 | — |
|  | Cristofer Barnys laborer & tenant to the lord | in lond | nil | in goods nil | | a pore man |
|  | | **nil** | | **£87 6s 8d** | | |

*f. 13 (23)*

|  | | in londs | | in goods | |
|---|---|---|---|---|---|
|  | Robert Umfry laborer & tenant to the lord of the seid Town | in lond | nil | in goods nil | — |
| Bill man | Robert Brown laborer & tenant to the lord | | | | |
|  | William Swan laborer & tenant to the lord | in londs | nil | in goods nil | pore men & yong |
| Archer | John Edmond son to Elizabeth Edmond | | | | |
| Bill man | William Toller seruant to the seid Vicar | | | | |

The Church Stoke £3

## TYKENCOTE

|  | | | in lond | | in goods | | |
|---|---|---|---|---|---|---|---|
|  | William Dale Gentilman is Chief lord of the seid Town | in lond | £15 | | in goods nil q.e. | | — |
|  | The Priorisse of Seint Michell by syde Stamford hath a pension going oute their | | — | 13s | 4d | in goods nil q.e. | — |
|  | Cristoforus Pykryng Clerk is parson | parsonage | £6 | 13s | 4d | in goods nil q.e. | — |
|  | The Abbot of Osolveston hath a pension their yerely | | — | 26s | 8d | in goods nil q.e. | — |
| Bill man | William Watson yoman & tenant to the seid William Dale | in lond | nil | | in goods | £15 | & hath a jestorn & a Sallet |
|  | William Baxster Husbond & tenant to the seid William | in lond | nil | | in goods | £30 | & hath a gorgit a pair of Splynts & a Sallet |
| Archer | Arthur Watson Husbond & tenant to the seid lord | in lond | nil | | in goods | £4 | — |
|  | Thomas Greneham Gent & farmer to the seid parson | in lond | £16 | | in goods | £12 | — |
|  | Thomas Okeley Husbond & tenant to the seid lord | in lond | nil | | in goods | £10 | — |
|  | John Okeley Husbond & tenant to the seid lord | in lond | nil | | in goods | £20 | — |
|  | Geffrey Baxster Husbond & tenant to the seid lord | in lond | nil | | in goods | £8 | — |
|  | Thomas Baxster Husbond & tenant to the seid lord | in lond | nil | | in goods | £6 | — |
| Bill man | Raff Payn Husbond & tenant to the seid lord | in lond | nil | | in goods | £5 | — |
|  | Thomas Turner Husbond & tenant to the seid lord | in lond | nil | | in goods | 40s | — |

| | | | | |
|---|---|---|---|---|
| | William Pope Husbond & tenant to the lord .. .. .. .. in lond | nil | in goods £3 | — |
| | John Grenesid Husbond & tenant to the seid lord .. .. .. in lond | nil | in goods 40s | — |
| | John Thomplyn Husbond & tenant to the lord .. .. .. in lond | nil | in goods 40s | — |
| Bill man | Robert Baxster Husbond & tenant to the lord .. .. .. in lond | nil | in goods £8 | — |
| | Thomas Belle Husbond & tenant to the lord .. .. .. .. in lond | nil | in goods 40s | — |
| | | **£42 13s 4d** | **£129** | |

*f. 13v (24)*

| | | | | |
|---|---|---|---|---|
| | Richard Gilbon laborer .. | | | |
| | Henry Baxster seruant .. | | | |
| Archer | Richard Barret laborer .. } in londs | nil | in goods nil | pore men & yong |
| | Thomas Watson laborer .. | | | |
| Archer | Richard Carter laborer & tenant to the lord .. .. .. .. in londs | nil | in goods 20s | — |
| | | The Church Stoke 33s 4d | | |

### YNGTHORP

| | | | | |
|---|---|---|---|---|
| | The Abbot of Peterborowgh is Chieff Lord of the seid Town .. .. in lond | £9 | in goods nil q.e. | — |
| Archer | John Page Husbond & tenant to the seid Abbot .. .. .. in lond | nil | in goods £6 | — |
| | Henry Fairchild Husbond & tenant to the seid Abbot .. .. in lond | nil | in goods £4 | — |
| Archer | Richard Martyndale Husbond & tenant to the seid lord .. .. in lond | nil | in goods £5 | — |
| Archer | Richard Thistilton Husbond & tenant to the lord .. .. .. in lond | nil | in goods £10 | — |
| | Roger Farechild Husbond & tenant to the lord .. .. .. in lond | nil | in goods £6 | — |
| Bill man | Mark Lee laborer & tenant to the seid lord .. .. .. in lond | nil | in goods 40s | — |
| | John Spenlong Husbond & tenant to the lord .. .. .. in lond | nil | in goods £4 | — |
| | | The Church Stoke nil | | |

### LITIL CASTERTON

| | | | | |
|---|---|---|---|---|
| | Fraunces Brown Esquier is Chieff lord of the seid town .. .. in londs | 100 marks | in goods £100 | & hath harnesse for vj men |
| | Robert Brown gent. & brother to the seid Fraunces in the custody of the same Fraunces .. .. .. in londs | nil | in goods £100 | — |
| Archer | Edmond Brown gent. & brother to the seid Fraunces in the custody of the same Fraunces .. .. .. in londs | nil | in goods £100 | — |
| | Anne Brown gentilwoman & sister to seid Fraunces in the custody of the same Fraunces .. .. .. in londs | nil | in goods £100 | — |
| | Katern Brown gentilwoman & sister to the seid Fraunces in the custody of the same Fraunces .. .. in londs | nil | in goods £100 | — |

| | | | | | |
|---|---|---|---|---|---|
| | The lord Scrop hath lond their .. | — | £4 | in goods nil q.e. | — |
| | The Prior of Newsted byside Stamford hath lond their .. .. .. .. | — | £5 | in goods nil q.e. | — |
| | Richard Beyerege prest is parson of the seid Town .. .. .. .. | parsonage | £8 | in goods £10 | — |
| | | | **£94 6s 8d** | **£547** | |

*f. 14 (24)*

| | | | | | |
|---|---|---|---|---|---|
| | The Abbot of Croston hath lond their | in londs | 8*s* | in goods nil q.e. | — |
| Bill man | Henry Bokyngham yoman & reteyned to John Hussey knyght & tenant to prior of Newsted .. .. .. | in londs | nil | in goods £60 | — |
| Bill man | Richard Cossyn Husbond & tenant to the seid Fraunces .. .. .. | in londs | nil | in goods £10 | nil vitium scriptoris[1] |
| Bill man | William Walker laborer & tenant to the seid Fraunces .. .. | | | | |
| Archer | Cristofer Bokyngham seruant to Henry Bokyngham .. .. | | | | |
| | Thomas Hudson laborer .. | | | | |
| Archer | Jarrard Dood seruant to the seid Fraunces .. .. .. | in londs | nil | in goods nil | yong men & pore |
| Bill man | Richard Miller seruant to the same Fraunces .. .. .. | | | | |
| Archer | John Palar seruant to the same | | | | |
| Archer | Thomas Plattes seruant to the same | | | | |

The Church Stoke nil

## ESSYNDEN

| | | | | | |
|---|---|---|---|---|---|
| | The Kyng ower souereign lord is Chieff lord of the seid Town | | | | |
| | Edward Digby Esquier is Steward of the seid Town .. .. .. .. | in fez | 6*s* 8*d* | in goods nil q.e. | — |
| | The Prior of Seint Andrews of Northampton is parson their .. | parsonage | 4 marks | in goods nil q.e. | — |
| | Henry Netlam prest is vicar of the seid Town .. .. .. | vicarige goyth with Riall | | in goods £5 | — |
| | Thomas Roo Husbond & tenant to the Kyng .. .. .. | in londs | nil | in goods £20 | — |
| | Thomas Dalby Husbond & tenant to the Kyng .. .. .. | in londs | nil | in goods £7 | — |
| Archer | John Revell Husbond & tenant to the Kyng .. .. .. | in londs | nil | in goods £6 | & hath a Jak & a Bill |
| | Thomas Smyth Husbond & tenant to the Kyng .. .. .. | in londs | nil | in goods £7 | — |
| Archer | John Biard Husbond & tenant to the Kyng .. .. .. | in londs | 9*s* | in goods £3 | & hath a Bill |
| | Roger Fyssher Husbond & tenant to the Kyng .. .. .. | in londs | nil | in goods £4 | — |
| | Robert Cosby Husbond & tenant to the Kyng .. .. .. | in londs | nil | in goods 40*s* | — |
| | Thomas Sharpe laborer & tenant to the Kyng .. .. .. .. | in londs | nil | in goods 20*s* | — |
| Bill man | William Wadforth laborer & tenant to the Kyng .. .. .. | in londs | nil | in goods 20*s* | — |

1. *Literally, 'nothing, clerical error'.*

| | | | | | |
|---|---|---|---|---|---|
| Bill man | William Allet laborer    .. | | | | |
| Bill man | Henry Bullok seruant to | | | | |
| | John Biard   ..   ..   .. | in londs   nil | | in goods nil | yong men & pore |
| | John Day laborer   ..   .. | | | | |
| | William Jakson laborer   .. | | | | |

The Church Stoke nil

           77s            £126

*f. 14v (26)*

## BRIGCASTERTON

| | | | | | |
|---|---|---|---|---|---|
| | John Hussey knyght is chieff lord of the seid Town   ..   .. | in lond | £12 | in goods nil q.e. | — |
| | Thomas Clerk gentilman is Steward of the seid Town   ..   .. | in feez | 6s 8d | in goods nil q.e. | — |
| | Olyuer Lokwood prest is parson of the seid Town ..   ..   .. | parsonage | £10 | in goods £10 | — |
| Bill man | Henry Laxston yoman reteyned to the seid John Hussey knyght & his tenant | in londs | 11s 8d | in goods £80 | & hath harnesse for 3 men |
| | Henry Thistilton Husbondman & tenant to the seid lord   ..   .. | in londs nil | | in goods £50 | & hath a Sallet |
| | Thomas Wilkynson Husbond & tenant to the seid lord   ..   .. | in londs nil | | in goods £3 | — |
| | Robert Bishope Husbond & tenant to the seid lord   ..   .. | in londs nil | | in goods 15s | — |
| | Thomas Bishope Husbond & tenant to the seid lord   ..   .. | in londs nil | | in goods £8 | — |
| Bill man | Henry Shorthose Husbond & tenant to the lord   ..   ..   .. | in londs nil | | in goods £6 | — |
| Bill man | Thomas Thompson Husbond & tenant to the lord   ..   .. | in londs nil | | in goods £7 | — |
| Bill man | John Collyn Husbond & tenant to Fraunces Brown Esquier   .. | in londs nil | | in goods 40s | — |
| Bill man | William Watte Husbond & tenant to John Hussey   ..   .. | in londs nil | | in goods 40s | — |
| Bill man | Robert Allen Husbond & tenant to the lord ..   ..   ..   .. | in londs nil | | in goods £3 | — |
| | John Wilhowse laborer & tenant to the lord ..   ..   ..   .. | in londs nil | | in goods 20s | — |
| | John Looff laborer & tenant to the lord | in londs nil | | in goods 20s | — |
| | John Strynger Husbond & tenant to the lord ..   ..   ..   .. | in lond nil | | in goods £5 | — |
| | Thomas Fairchild Husbond & tenant to the lord   ..   ..   .. | in lond nil | | in goods 40s | — |
| | Henry Pyxe laborer & tenant to the lord ..   ..   ..   .. | in lond nil | | in goods 20s | — |
| | William Rooke laborer & tenant to the seid John Huseey ..   .. | in londs nil | | in goods 20s | — |
| | John Gunby laborer & tenant to the seid John Hussey   ..   .. | in lond nil | | in goods 20s | — |
| | William Weuer laborer   .. | | | | |
| Bill man | Thomas Gillam laborer   .. | in londs nil | | in goods nil | yong men & pore |
| Bill man | Robert Nawyn laborer   .. | | | | |
| | Robert Horsely laborer   .. | | | | |

The Church Stoke nil

        £24   7s   8d         £198

*f. 15 (27)*

**TINWELL**

| | | | | | |
|---|---|---|---|---|---|
| | The Abbot of Peterborough is chieff lord of the seid Town .. .. .. | in londs | £21 10s | in goods nil q.e. | — |
| | Dauid Cecill Esquier & seruant to the Kyng .. .. .. .. | in londs | £46 | in goods £100 | & hath harnesse for 20 men Sufficient |
| | Thomas Grenehow Gent. is Steward of the seid Town .. .. .. | in feez | [blank] | in goods nil q.e. | — |
| | John Denham Clark is parson of the seid Town .. .. .. | parsonage | 20 marks | in goods nil q.e. | — |
| | Boniface Martyn Gent. & fermer to the seid parson .. .. .. | in londs | nil | in goods 20 marks | — |
| | Richard Antony is parish prest .. | stipend | £5 | in goods 20 marks | — |
| | Thomas Amyth Husbond & tenant the seid Abbott .. .. .. | in londs | nil | in goods £20 | — |
| | Thomas Thistilton Husbond & tenant to the seid Abbott .. .. .. | in londs | nil | in goods £15 | — |
| Bill man | Richard Knott Husbond & tenant to the seid Abbott .. .. .. | in londs | nil | in goods 40s | — |
| | John Wetherley Husbond & tenant to the seid Abbott .. .. .. | in londs | nil | in goods £5 | — |
| | Richard Andrew Husbond & tenant to the seid Abbott .. .. .. | in londs | nil | in goods 40s | — |
| | Roger Knott Husbond & tenant to the seid Abbott.. .. .. | in londs | nil | in goods £10 | — |
| Bill man | William Careby Husbond & tenant to the seid Abbott .. .. .. | in londs | nil | in goods £10 | & hath a Bill |
| | John Smyth Husbond & tenant to the seid Abbott .. .. .. | in londs | nil | in goods 40s | — |
| | Richard Iermyn laborer & tenant to the seid Abbott .. .. .. | in londs | nil | in goods 26s 8d | — |
| | Richard Faireday Husbond & tenant to the seid Abbott .. .. .. | in londs | nil | in goods £3 | — |
| | John Armystrong Husbond & tenant to the seid Abbott .. .. .. | in londs | nil | in goods 40s | & hath a Bill |
| | Elizabeth Hare Widow & tenant to the seid Abbott .. .. .. | in londs | nil | in goods 20s | — |
| Bill man | John Fairechild laborer & tenant to the seid Abbott .. .. .. | in londs | nil | in goods 30s | — |
| Bill man | John Wynch laborer & tenant to the seid Abbott .. .. .. | in londs | nil | in goods 30s | — |
| | Thomas Edmond Husbond & tenant to the seid Abbott .. .. .. | in londs | nil | in goods £3 | — |
| | Richard Stanyerd laborer & tenant to the seid Abbott .. .. .. | in londs | nil | in goods 20s | — |
| | Margery Cooper Widow & tenant to the seid Abbott .. .. .. | in londs | nil | in goods 30s | — |
| | Richard the Netherd laborer & tenant to the seid Abbott .. .. .. | in lond | nil | in goods 20s | — |

£80 16s 8d          £209 10s

*f. 15v (28)*

| | | | | | |
|---|---|---|---|---|---|
| Archer | William Bircheford laborer & tenant to the Abbott .. | | | | |
| Bill man | William Bradley laborer & tenant to the Abbott .. .. .. | | in londs nil | in goods nil | yong men & pore |
| Bill man | Richard Symmys laborer & tenant to the Abbott .. | | | | |
| | Richard Wynch laborer .. | | | | |
| Archer | William Fairechild laborer .. | | | | |
| | Henry Sage laborer .. .. | | | | |

The Township hath a Jak a Sallet a gorgit & a paire of Splynts

The Church Stoke nil

**RIALL**

| | | | | | |
|---|---|---|---|---|---|
| | Thomas Lovell knyght is chieff lord of the seid Town .. .. .. | in londs | £30 | in goods nil q.e. | — |
| | Henry Lacy Gent. is Steward their | in feez | 6s 8d | in goods nil q.e. | — |
| | The Prior of Saint Andrew of Northampton is parson their .. | parsonage | £12 | in goods nil q.e. | — |
| | The seid Prior hath londs their .. | — | 30s 4d | — — | — |
| | Henry Netlam Clerk is Vicar .. | vicarige | £10 | in goods £5 | — |
| Archer | Thomas Netlam yoman Bayly & tenant to the seid Mr. Lovell .. | in londs | 5 marks | in goods £80 | & hath harness sufficient for iij men with a bow a Sheff of Arrows & ij Bills |
| Archer | William Netlam yoman & A nother bayly of the seid Mr. Lovell & tenant | in londs | 24s | in goods £80 | & hath harnesse sufficient for iij men with iij bows & iij Sheff of Arrows |
| | Robert Sherman Husbond & tenant to the seid Mr. Lovell .. .. | in londs | nil | in goods £20 | & hath a Sallet & a Bill |
| | John Thistilton Husbond & tenant to the seid Mr. Lovell .. .. | in londs | nil | in goods £20 | & hath a Bill |
| Bill man | Robert Wallet Husbond & tenant to the seid Mr. Lovell .. .. | in londs | nil | in goods £8 | & hath a Jak with a Bill |
| | Thomas Watters Husbond & tenant to the seid lord .. .. | in lond | 4s | in goods £22 | & hath harnesse sufficient for a man |
| | John Watson Husbond & tenant to the seid lord .. .. .. | in londs | nil | in goods £12 | & hath a Bill |
| | Thomas Waterfall Husbond & tenant to the seid lord .. .. | in londs | 20s | in goods £12 | — |
| | Thomas Wadyngton Husbond & tenant to the seid lord .. | in londs | nil | in goods £6 | — |
| | Henry Clark Husbond & tenant to the seid lord .. .. .. | in londs | nil | in goods £6 | — |
| | Robert Tagell Husbond & tenant to the seid lord .. .. .. | in londs | nil | in goods £5 | & hath a Bill |
| | Henry Scot Husbond & tenant to the seid lord .. .. .. | in londs | nil | in goods £6 | & hath a Bill |
| | | | £59 11s 8d | £282 | |

*f. 16 (29)*

| | | | | | |
|---|---|---|---|---|---|
| | John Reve Husbond & tenant to the seid Mr. Lovell .. .. | in londs | nil | in goods £5 | — |
| | Johane Blood widow & tenant to the seid Chieff lord .. .. | in londs | nil | in goods £3 | — |

| | | | | | | |
|---|---|---|---|---|---|---|
| | Richard Smyth laborer & tenant to the seid lord .. .. .. .. | in londs | nil | in goods | 30s | — |
| | William Watson laborer & tenant to the seid lord .. .. .. | in londs | nil | in goods | 20s | — |
| | John Foster Husbond & tenant to the seid lord .. .. .. .. | in londs | nil | in goods | 40s | — |
| | Richard Everton Husbond & tenant to the seid lord .. .. | in londs | 13s 4d | in goods | 40s | — |
| | Richard Clerk Husbond & tenant to the lord .. .. .. .. | in londs | nil | in goods | 40s | — |
| Bill man | Thomas Burbage Husbond & tenant to the lord .. .. .. .. | in londs | nil | in goods | 40s | — |
| Bill man | John Gan Husbond & tenant to the lord .. .. .. .. | in londs | nil | in goods | £8 | — |
| Bill man | Richard Uffyngton Husbond & tenant to the lord .. .. | in londs | nil | in goods | 40s | — |
| | Thomas Uffyngton Husband & tenant to the lord .. .. | in londs | nil | in goods | 40s | — |
| | Jamys Paterson laborer & tenant to the lord .. .. .. | in londs | nil | in goods | 20s | — |
| Archer | Thomas Thistilton laborer & tenant to the lord .. .. .. | in londs | nil | in goods | 20s | — |
| Archer | William Sherman laborer & tenant to the lord .. .. .. | in londs | nil | in goods | 20s | — |
| Archer | Richard Saunderson laborer & tenant to the lord .. .. | in londs | nil | in goods | 20s | — |
| | Alis Wright Widow & tenant to the lord .. .. .. .. | in londs | nil | in goods | 20s | — |
| Archer | Edward Thistilton Husbond & tenant to the seid lord .. .. | in londs | nil | in goods | 20s | — |
| | Richard Dalby laborer & tenant to the seid lord .. .. .. | in londs | nil | in goods | 20s | — |
| | Robert Everton laborer & tenant to the seid lord .. .. .. | in londs | nil | in goods | 20s | — |

| | | | | |
|---|---|---|---|---|
| | Hugh Fuller laborer & tenant to the seid lord .. .. | | | |
| | Robert Turner laborer .. | | | |
| Archer | Thomas Watson laborer .. | | | |
| Archer | Raff Waterfall laborer .. | | | |
| Archer | Richard Laxston laborer .. | in londs nil | in goods nil | Yong men & pore |
| Archer | William Flecher laborer .. | | | |
| Bill man | Thomas Scott laborer .. .. | | | |
| | Nicholas Bocher laborer .. | | | |
| Bill man | William Bland laborer .. | | | |
| Archer | John Fether laborer .. .. | | | |
| Bill man | Thomas Flecher laborer .. | | | |

The Township hath horse & harnesse for a man with a bow & a Sheff of Arrowis

The Church Stoke nil

13s 4d          £38 10s

End of this Hundred.

**WRANDYK HUNDRED IN COUNTY ROTLOND**

*f. 16v (30)*
**SEYTON**

| | | | | | |
|---|---|---|---|---|---|
| | The Kyng ower Souereign lord is Chieff lord of the Town | | | | |
| | Edward Digby Esquier is Steward of the seid Town | in fez | 10s | in goods nil q.e. | — |
| Archer | Edward Catesby Gentilman hath lond their to the value | — | £24 | in goods 13s 4d | — |
| Archer | John Sheffeld Gent hath lond their | — | £11 | in goods £12 | — |
| | Thomas Bassit Gent & John Lynch hath lond their | — | £10 | in goods nil q.e. | — |
| | Jane Wymark widow hath lond their | — | £6 13s 4d | in goods nil q.e. | — |
| | Rowlond Sheffeld Gent hath lond their | — | 20s | in goods nil q.e. | — |
| | John Digby knyght hath lond their | — | 46s 8d | in goods nil q.e. | — |
| | Thomas Saunders Clerk is parson of the seid Town | parsonage | £20 | in goods £2 | — |
| | Thomas Berige Husbond & tenant to the seid Catesby | in londs | 26s 8d | in goods £40 | — |
| Archer | William Niccolls Husbond & tenant to the seid John Sheffeld | in londs nil | | in goods £40 | & hath a Sallet |
| | John Bishop Husbond & tenant to the seid John Sheffeld | in londs nil | | in goods £6 | — |
| | William Looff Husbond & tenant to the seid Catesby | in londs nil | | in goods £10 | — |
| | William Wylle Husbond & tenant to the seid Thomas Berige | in lond nil | | in goods £20 | — |
| | William Baxster Husbond & tenant to the seid Catesby | in lond nil | | in goods £12 | — |
| | Jane Toky widow & tenant to the seid John Sheffeld | in lond nil | | in goods 26s 8d | — |
| | Henry Beyvill Husbond & tenant to seid John Sheffeld | in lond nil | | in goods £4 | — |
| | William Ilson Husbond & tenant to the seid Catesby | in lond nil | | in goods 40s | — |
| | John Boley Husbond & tenant to the seid Edward Catesby | in lond nil | | in goods £40 | — |
| Archer | Richard Edwards Husbond & tenant to the seid John Sheffeld | in lond nil | | in goods £10 | — |
| | Henry Tog Husbond & tenant to the seid John Sheffeld | in lond nil | | in goods £9 | — |
| Archer | Henry Horn Husbond & tenant to the seid Catesby | in londs nil | | in goods £6 | — |
| Archer | Robert Bewhowe Husbond & tenant to the seid Catesby | in londs nil | | in goods £30 | — |
| Archer | Robert Thomplynson Husbond & tenant to the seid John Sheffeld | in londs nil | | in goods £3 | — |
| Archer | John Yett Husbond & tenant to the seid Edward Catesby | in londs nil | | in goods £6 | — |
| Archer | Raff Yett Husbond & tenant to the seid John Sheffeld | in londs nil | | in goods nil | |
| | Raff Whit seruant | in londs nil | | in goods 26s 8d | Yong men & pore |
| | Richard Sheperd seruant | in londs nil | | in goods 26s 8d | |

The Town hath Harnes for a man
The Church Stoke [blank]

                 **£76 16s 8d**               **£261 13s 4d**

*f. 17 (31)*
**PYLTON**

| | | | | | |
|---|---|---|---|---|---|
| | John Haryngton the yonger Esquier is Chieff lord of the seid Town .. .. in lond | 5 marks | in goods nil q.e. | — |
| | Edward Digby Esquier is Steward their of the seid Town .. .. in feez | 6s 8d | in goods nil q.e. | — |
| | John Digby Knyght hath lond their in the seid Town .. .. .. — | £6 | in goods nil q.e. | — |
| | Rauff Sacheuerell Gent hath lond their .. .. .. .. — | 22s | in goods nil q.e. | — |
| | Richard Alcok prest is parson of the seid Town .. .. .. .. parsonage | 13s 4d | in goods nil q.e. | — |
| Bill man | John Faconer Husbond & tenant to Sir John Digby .. .. .. in londs | 30s | in goods £8 | — |
| | Thomas Awyng thelder Husbond & tenant to the seid John Digby .. in lond | 13s 4d | in goods 10s | — |
| | Thomas Roberds Husbond hath lond their .. .. .. .. — | 12s | in goods nil q.e. | — |
| | Roberd Cooke Husbond & tenant to the seid John Haryngton .. .. in lond nil | | in goods £20 | — |
| Bill man | William Carter Husbond & tenant to the seid John Digby .. .. .. in lond nil | | in goods £20 | — |
| Bill man | John Awyng Husbond & tenant to the seid Rauff Sacheuerell .. .. in lond nil | | in goods £3 | — |
| Archer | Thomas Smyth Husbond & tenant to the said John Digby .. .. in lond nil | | in goods £8 | — |
| Bill man | William Avstyn laborer .. | | | |
| | Roger Prodfote laborer .. | | | |
| | Thomas Blackborn laborer .. } in londs nil | | in goods nil | pore men & yong |
| Bill man | John Akyrk laborer .. | | | |
| | Thomas Mynggo laborer .. | | | |
| | Thomas Awyng the yonger laborer .. in lond nil | | in goods 20s | — |
| | John Cook thelder laborer .. .. in lond nil | | in goods 20s | — |

The Church Stoke 20s

**SOUTH LUFFENHAM**

| | | | | | |
|---|---|---|---|---|---|
| | The Kyng ower Souereign lord is Chieff lord of the seid Town | | | |
| | Edward Digby Esquier is Steward their in feez | 6s 8d | in goods nil q.e. | |
| | John Digby Knyght hath lond their within the seid Town .. .. .. — | £20 | in goods nil q.e. | — |
| | Edward Sapcote Esquier hath lond their .. .. .. .. — | 26s 8d | in goods nil q.e. | — |
| | Nicolis Meysyng prest is parson of the seid Town .. .. .. .. — | £12 | in goods nil q.e. | — |
| | | **£48 17s 4d** | **£6 10s** | |

*f. 17v (32)*

| | | | | | |
|---|---|---|---|---|---|
| | Thomas Basset Gent hath lond their — | 4 marks | in goods nil q.e. | — |
| | Margaret Stombill widow hath lond their .. .. .. .. — | 13s 4d | in goods nil q.e. | — |
| | John Wytham Husbond hath lond their .. .. .. .. — | 10s | in goods nil q.e. | — |
| Bill man | John Toky yoman hath lond to the yerely value & retened to Sir John Digby — | £8 | in goods £20 | & hath a Jak a Sallet with a Bill |

| | | | | | | |
|---|---|---|---|---|---|---|
| | William Peck laborer & tenant to the seid Sir John Digby | — | — | in goods | 20s | — |
| Bill man | John Scarborowe Husbond & tenant to the seid John Toky | in lond | nil | in goods | 40s | — |
| | Peter Gybbon Husbond & tenant to the seid John Toky | in lond | nil | in goods | £9 | & hath a Sallet |
| | John Sheperd laborer & tenant to the seid John Digby | in lond | nil | in goods | 20s | — |
| | John Machyn laborer & tenant to the seid John Toky | in lond | nil | in goods | 20s | — |
| | John Bollond laborer & tenant to the seid John Toky | in lond | nil | in goods | 20s | — |
| | William Bentley Husbond & tenant the seid Sir John Digby | in lond | nil | in goods | £9 | — |
| Bill man | Thomas Cooke Husbond & hath lond their | in lond | 13s | in goods | £3 | — |
| | John Wright Husbond & tenant to the seid Sir John Digby | in lond | nil | in goods | £4 | — |
| Bill man | Thomas Dowghty laborer & tenant to the seid Margaret Stombill | in lond | nil | in goods | 20s | — |
| Bill man | Henry Bonyt Husbond & tenant to the seid Edward Sapcote | in lond | 10s | in goods | 40s | — |
| | Robert Irelond Husbond & tenant to the seid Sir John Digby | in lond | nil | in goods | £12 | — |
| Bill man | Thomas Johnson Husbond & tenant to the seid Sir John Digby | in lond | nil | in goods | £8 | — |
| | Thomas Wylles Husbond & tenant to the seid Sir John Digby | in lond | nil | in goods | £10 | — |
| Bill man | William Gudlok Husbond & tenant to the seid Henry Bonett | in lond | nil | in goods | 40s | — |
| Bill man | William Cooper Husbond & tenant to the seid Sir John Digby | in lond | nil | in goods | 40s | — |
| Bill man | William Irelond son to the seid Robert Irelond & his seruant | in lond | nil | in goods | 30s | — |
| Bill man | Robert Croft seruant to Thomas Johnson | in lond | nil | in goods | 20s | — |
| Archer | William Willes seruant to the seid Thomas Willes .. Raff Barker seruant to the seid John Toky .. Bartolmew Holme seruant to Maragret Gudlocke | in lond | nil | in goods nil | | yong men & pore |

The Church Stoke blank

£13   9s   8d      £90   10s

*f. 18 (33)*

**PYSBROKE**

| | | | | | | |
|---|---|---|---|---|---|---|
| | The Master of the House of Fotheryngay is Chieff lord of the seid Town | in lond | £5 16s 8d | in goods nil q.e. | | — |
| | John Digby knyght hath lond their to the value | — | 33s 4d | in goods nil q.e. | | — |
| | The Prior of Daventre is parson of the seid Town | parsonage | 28s | in goods nil q.e. | | — |
| | Thomas Brewster Chapelyn is Vicar of the seid Town | vicarige | 10 marks | in goods | £5 | — |

| | | | | |
|---|---|---|---|---|
| | The Chauntre of Stokerston hath an annuite goyng oute of yerely londs their | — £3 | in goods nil | — |
| | Robert Brudenell knyght hath lond their .. .. .. | — 32s | in goods nil q.e. | — |
| | William Elond yoman hath lond & tenantes their .. .. .. .. | — 5 marks 5s | in goods nil q.e. | — |
| | Richard Chisselden gent hath lond their .. .. .. .. | — 26s 8d | in goods nil q.e. | — |
| | John Ashbe yoman hath lond their .. | — 4s | in goods 40s | — |
| | William Wells Husbond hath lond their .. .. .. .. | — 8s | in goods nil q.e. | — |
| Bill man | Richard Fancourt Husbond & tenant to the seid William Elond .. .. in lond | nil | in goods £60 | & hath harnes for a man |
| Bill man | Robert Baxster Husbond & tenant to the seid Chieff lord .. .. in lond | nil | in goods £25 | — |
| Archer | Jamys Edmond Husbond & tenant to the seid Richard Chisselden .. in lond | nil | in goods £40 | — |
| | Henry Gambell Husbond & tenant to the seid Sir John Digby .. .. in lond | nil | in goods £10 | — |
| Bill man | Richard Byshope Husbond & tenant to the seid Vicar of the Town .. in lond | nil | in goods £12 | — |
| | Thomas Wellis Husbond & tenant to the seid Chieff Lord .. .. in lond | nil | in goods £20 | — |
| Bill man | William Cley Husbond & tenant to the seid Master of Fotheryngay .. in lond | nil | in goods £12 | — |
| Bill man | John Morris Husbond & tenant to the seid Robert Brudenell knyght .. in lond | nil | in goods £12 | — |
| | John Croley Husbond & tenant of the land that belongith to the seid Chauntre .. .. .. in lond | nil | in goods £4 | — |
| Bill man | Thomas Jakson Husbond & tenant to the seid William Wellis .. .. in lond | nil | in goods 40s | — |
| | William Grainger laborer & on the other tenant to to [sic] seid Chauntre in lond | nil | in goods 30s | — |
| | William Horsehall Husbond & tenant to the seid Chauntre .. .. .. in lond | nil | in goods £3 | — |
| | Robert Martyndall Husbond & tenant to the seid Chieff lord .. .. in lond | nil | in goods £8 | — |
| Archer | Robert Cranewell laborer & tenant to the seid Chauntre .. .. in lond | nil | in goods 20s | — |
| | John Skulthorp laborer & tenant to the seid Chieff lord .. .. .. in lond | nil | in goods 30s | — |

The Church Stoke 6s 8d

£25 11s 4d      £219

*f. 18v (34)*

## GLASTON

| | | | | |
|---|---|---|---|---|
| | The Kyng ower Souereign lord is chieff lord of the seid Town | | | |
| | Seth Atlclyff clerk is parson of the seid Town .. .. .. .. parsonage | £9 | in goods nil q.e. | — |
| | Issabell Conyers Gentilwoman Widow hath lond their for tyme of lyff .. | — 20 marks | in goods 200 marks | & hath a Jak & a paire of splynts |

| | | | | | |
|---|---|---|---|---|---|
| | William Collyn is parich prest of the seid Town .. .. .. .. stipend | 8 marks | in goods | 20s | — |
| | The Prior of Fynzed Abbey hath lond their .. .. .. .. — | 27s 8d | in goods nil q.e. | | — |
| | John Wymark Gent hath lond their — | 4 marks | in goods nil q.e. | | — |
| | Antony Ardes Gent hath lond their — | 30s | in goods nil q.e. | | — |
| | John Roks Husbond & tenant to the seid Issabell Conyers .. — | 9s | in goods | 24s | — |
| | Richard Acrosse Husbond & tenant to the seid Issabell Conyers .. .. — | 9s | in goods | 40s | — |
| | William Mason Husbond & tenant to the seid Issabell Conyers .. .. in lond | nil | in goods £10 | | — |
| Bill man | Richard Barker Husbond & tenant to the seid Issabell Conyers .. .. in lond | nil | in goods £20 | | — |
| Bill man | Nicholis Lacy Husbond & tenant to the seid Issabell Conyers .. .. in lond | nil | in goods £30 | | — |
| Bill man | William Blake Husbond & tenant to the seid Issabell Conyers .. .. in londs | nil | in goods £20 | | — |
| | John Lyghtfoote Husbond & tenant to the seid Mastres Conyers .. .. in londs | nil | in goods £15 | | — |
| | William Faconer Husbond & tenant to the seid Issabell Conyers .. .. in lond | nil | in goods £12 | | — |
| | Thomas Leycey Husbond & tenant to the seid John Wymark .. .. in londs | nil | in goods £6 | | — |
| | Richard Bretfeld Husbond & tenant to the seid Antony Ardes .. .. in londs | nil | in goods £8 | | — |
| | Robert Stevenson Husbond & tenant to the seid Issabell Conyers .. .. in lond | nil | in goods £12 | | — |
| | John Leycey Husbond & tenant to the seid Issabell Conyers .. .. in lond | nil | in goods £5 | | — |
| | Richard Payke Husbond & tenant to the seid Issabell .. .. .. in lond | nil | in goods | 40s | — |
| Archer | John Cranwell laborer & tenant to the seid John Wymark .. .. in lond | nil | in goods | 20s | — |
| | Thomas Lacy laborer & tenant to the seid Issabell .. .. .. in lond | nil | in goods | 20s | — |
| | George Johnson laborer & tenant to the seid Issabell Conyers .. .. in lond | nil | in goods | 30s | — |
| | Thomas Masson laborer & tenant to the seid Issabell .. .. .. in lond | nil | in goods | 20s | — |
| Archer | John Woodward seruant to Mastres Conyers .. .. | | | | |
| Bill man | William Jermyn seruant to the same .. .. .. | in londs nil | in goods nil | | yong men & pore |
| Bill man | Thomas Murdok seruant to John Lyghtfote .. .. | | | | |
| | John Lacy seruant to John Blake | | | | |

The Church Stoke 26s 8d

£35 10s                £282 0s 8d

*f. 19 (35)*

## THORP BY WATTER

| | | | | |
|---|---|---|---|---|
| Edward Catesby is Chieff lord of the seid Town .. .. .. .. in londs | 40s | in goods nil q.e. | | — |
| Edward Digby Esquier is Steward their in feez | 40d | in goods nil q.e. | | — |

| | | | | | | | | |
|---|---|---|---|---|---|---|---|---|
| Bill man | Cristofer Sheffeld Gent. hath londs their .. .. .. .. in londs | £5 13s 4d | in goods £7 | — |
| | William Harryson yoman hath lond their .. .. .. .. in lond | 40s | in goods £16 | — |
| | Elizabeth Scarborow Widow & tenant to the seid William Harryson .. in lond | nil | in goods £10 | — |
| Archer | William Uffyngton Husbond & tenant to the seid lord .. .. .. in lond | nil | in goods £16 | — |
| Bill man | Richard Irelond Husbond hath lond their .. .. .. .. in lond | 20s | in goods £5 | — |
| | John Harryson Husbond & tenant to the seid Chieff lord .. .. in lond | 6s 8d | in goods £5 | — |
| | John Colly Husbond & tenant to the lord .. .. .. .. in lond | 10s | in goods 40s | — |
| | Henry Angill Chappelyn hath lond their .. .. .. .. in lond | 50s | in goods nil q.e. | — |

The Church Stoke nil

## TIXOUER

| | | | | | | |
|---|---|---|---|---|---|---|
| | The Warden of Tatershall is Chieff lord of the Town .. .. .. in lond | £10 | in goods nil q.e. | — |
| | Robert Whalley gent. is steward their in feez | 6s 8d | in goods nil q.e. | — |
| | Edward Darby Clerk is parson of the seid Town .. .. .. .. parsonage goes with Ketton | | | |
| | John Smyth yoman hath lond their .. in lond | £3 | in goods £26 | — |
| Bill man | William Brettyn Husbond & tenant to the seid Warden .. .. .. in lond | 24s | in goods £20 | — |
| Bill man | John Plattis Husbond & tenant to the seid Warden .. .. .. in lond | nil | in goods £16 | — |
| Bill man | Richard Johnson Husbond & tenant to the seid Warden .. .. .. in lond | nil | in goods £15 | — |
| Bill man | John Euerton Husbond & tenant to the seid Warden .. .. .. in lond | nil | in goods £10 | — |
| Bill man | Robert Strawker Husbond & tenant to the seid Warden .. .. .. in lond | nil | in goods £4 | — |
| | Henry Fairman Husbond & tenant to the seid Warden .. .. .. in lond | nil | in goods 40s | — |
| | William Hochyn laborer & tenant to the seid Warden .. .. .. in londs | nil | in goods 20s | — |
| | Richard A Wood laborer .. | | | |
| | Richard Taillor laborer .. | in lond nil | in goods nil | old men & pore |
| | Thomas Smyth laborer .. | | | |

| £29 | £106 |
|---|---|

f. 19v (36)

| | | | | |
|---|---|---|---|---|
| Bill man | Thomas Rotherby seruant to John Euerton | | | |
| | William Kyng seruant to John Pattes | | | |
| Bill man | Henry Watson seruant to John Pattes .. .. .. | | | |
| Bill man | Richard Grene seruant to John Smyth .. .. .. | in lond nil | in goods nil | yong men & pore |
| Archer | John Hochyn seruant to the seid John Smyth .. .. | | | |
| Archer | Richard Crooker seruant to Richard Johnson .. .. | | | |

The Church Stoke £3

**MORCOTT**

| | | | | | |
|---|---|---|---|---|---|
| | The Kyng ower souereign lord is Chieff lord of the seid Town | | | | |
| | Edward Digby Esquier is Steward of the seid Town | in Feez | 6s | in goods nil q.e. | — |
| | John Digby Knyght hath londs their within the seid Town | — | 100s | in goods nil q.e. | — |
| | Edward Catesby Gent. hath lond their within the seid Town | — | 33s | in goods nil q.e. | — |
| | Thomas Duraunt Gent. hath lond their within the seid Town | — | 5 marks | in goods nil q.e. | — |
| | Rowlond Sheffeld Gent. hath lond their | — | 4 marks | in goods nil q.e. | — |
| | Issabell Pekryng Widow hath lond their | — | 23s 4d | in goods nil q.e. | — |
| | Issabell Conyers Gent. & Widow hath lond their for tym of lyffe | — | 40s | in goods nil q.e. | — |
| | Richard Wymark yoman hath an anuite their goyng oute yerely of lond | anuite | 8s | in goods nil q.e. | — |
| | Bartilmew Ouerton Gent. hath an anuite goyng oute of certen lond | anuite | 8s | in goods nil q.e. | — |
| | William Ouerton Gent. hath their lond within the seid Town | — | 40s | in goods £20 | — |
| Archer | Henry Tampon Husbond hath lond their within the said Town | — | 20s | in goods £20 | — |
| | Thomas West Husbond & tenant to the Kyng | in lond | nil | in goods £20 | — |
| Bill man | Richard . . . . . . the seruant of the seid Thomas West | in lond | nil | in goods 20s | — |
| Archer | Thomas Spicer Husbond & tenant to the seid Issabell Conyers | in lond | nil | in goods £20 | — |
| | William Brightmere Husbond & tenant to the Kyng | in lond | nil | in goods £14 | — |
| | Johan Messynger Widow & tenant to the seid Thomas Duraunt | in lond | 20s | in goods £10 | — |
| | Agnes Pertre Widow & tenant to the Kyng | in lond | 10s | in goods £8 | — |
| | Thomas Pegell laborer & tenant to the seid William Ouerton | in lond | nil | in goods 20s | — |
| | | | **£24 8s 4d** | **£114** | |

*f. 20 (37)*

| | | | | | |
|---|---|---|---|---|---|
| Bill man | John Spire Husbond & tenant to the Kyng | in lond | nil | in goods £15 | — |
| Bill man | John Frank Husbond & tenant to the Kyng | in lond | 10s | in goods £3 | — |
| Bill man | John Grevis Husbond & tenant to the Kyng | in lond | nil | in goods £5 | — |
| | Robert Shene laborer & tenant to the Kyng | in lond | nil | in goods 20s | — |
| Bill man | Raff Weuer laborer & tenant to the Kyng | in lond | nil | in goods £6 | — |
| | Richard Weuer Husbond & tenant to the Kyng | in lond | nil | in goods £5 | — |
| Archer | Robert Baker Husbond & tenant to the Kyng | in lond | nil | in goods £3 | — |

| | | | | | |
|---|---|---|---|---|---|
| Archer | William Jakson Husbond & tenant to the Kyng .. .. .. .. in lond | nil | | in goods 40s | — |
| | Thomas Presgrave Husbond & tenant to the Kyng .. .. .. .. in lond | nil | | in goods £6 | — |
| | John Bull Husbond & tenant to the Kyng .. .. .. .. in lond | 13s 4d | | in goods 40s | — |
| | John Spicer thelder tenant to the Kyng & Husbond .. .. .. in lond | 12s | | in goods £10 | — |
| Bill man | John Tampion Husbond & tenant to the Kyng .. .. .. .. in lond | nil | | in goods £12 | — |
| | John Kyrke Husbond & tenant to to the Kyng .. .. .. .. in lond | nil | | in goods £15 | — |
| Archer | Richard Cooke Husbond & tenant to the Kyng .. .. .. .. in lond | nil | | in goods £10 | — |
| | Thomas Smyth Husbond & tenant to the Kyng .. .. .. .. in lond | nil | | in goods £3 | — |
| Archer | John Smyth Husbond & tenant to the Kyng .. .. .. .. in lond | 6s | | in goods £5 | — |
| Bill man | John Ketilborowe Husbond & tenant to the Kyng .. .. .. in lond | nil | | in goods 40s | — |
| Bill man | Thomas Corbe Husbond & tenant to the Kyng .. .. .. .. in lond | nil | | in goods 40s | — |
| Bill man | John Forster laborer & tenant to the Kyng .. .. .. .. in lond | nil | | in goods 20s | — |
| Archer | Robert Turlyngton laborer & tenant to the Kyng .. .. .. .. in lond | nil | | in goods 20s | — |
| | Richard Sheffeld prest is parson of the seid Town .. .. .. .. parsonage | £10 | | in goods 14 marks | — |
| | Richard Sandall is parich prest their stipend | £5 6s 8d | | in goods 20s | — |
| | Raff Bull laborer .. .. .. in lond | nil | | in goods 20s | — |
| | Alice Bull Singlewoman .. .. in lond | nil | | in goods 20s | — |
| | Robert Laurence laborer .. | | | | |
| Bill man | John Hyngton laborer .. | } in lond | nil | in goods nil | yong men & pore |
| Bill man | William Brown laborer .. | | | | |
| | .. .. The Church Stoke | 13s 4d | | | |
| | | **£18 1s 4d** | | **£121 6s 8d** | |

*f. 20v (38)*

**NORTH LUFFENHAM**

| | | | | | |
|---|---|---|---|---|---|
| | Thomas Basset Gentilman is Chieff of the seid Town .. .. .. in lond | £6 6s 8d | | in goods £20 | & hath Harnes for a man |
| | John Digby Knyght hath lond their within the seid Town .. .. .. — | £4 | | in goods nil q.e. | — |
| | Richard Stokesley prest is parson of the seid Town .. .. .. .. parsonage | £16 | | in goods nil q.e. | — |
| | Jane Wimarke widow .. .. .. in lond | £4 | | in goods £20 | & hath a Jak a Sallet & a paire of Splynts |
| | John Wymark Gent & seruant to the seid Sir John Digby .. .. in lond | 4 marks | | in goods nil q.e. | — |
| Archer | Robert Goodman Yoman & hath lond their .. .. .. .. — | £4 | | in goods £30 | & hath a Jestorn a Sallet a pair of splynts with a Bill |
| | Thomas Hunt Yoman hath lond their — | 7 marks | | in goods £12 | — |
| | Margery Wilkynson widow & hath lond their & tenant to the seid lord Zouch .. .. .. .. in lond | 30s 4d | | in goods £20 | & hath harnes for a man |

|  | Name | | Land | Goods | | |
|---|---|---|---|---|---|---|
|  | The lord Zouch hath lond their .. | — | 13s 4d | in goods nil q.e. |  | — |
|  | The Prior of Broke hath lond their .. | — | 26s 8d | in goods nil q.e. |  | — |
|  | The Prior of Fynneshed hath lond their | — | 16s | in goods nil q.e. |  | — |
|  | Sir Henry Aunger prest hath lond their | — | 46s 8d | in goods nil q.e. |  | — |
|  | The Warden of the almes house of Stamford hath lond their .. .. | — | £3 | in goods nil q.e. |  |  |
|  | William Chamberleyn Husbond hath lond their .. .. .. | — | 26s 8d | in goods nil q.e. |  |  |
|  | Richard Sapcote Esquier hath lond their | — | 26s 8d | in goods nil q.e. |  |  |
|  | The Gilde of owr Lady the Virgin hath lond their .. .. .. .. | — | £3 6s 8d | in lond nil q.e. |  | — |
|  | Agnes Dudley widow hath lond their | in lond | 13s | in goods | 6s 8d | — |
|  | John Brown laborer hath lond their .. | in lond | 6s 8d | in goods | 10s | — |
|  | William Sculthorp Husbond hath lond their & tenant to Richard Sapcote .. | in lond | 3s 4d | in goods £24 |  | — |
|  | John Sculthorp laborer & tenant to Thomas Basset .. .. .. | in lond | 20s | in goods | 20s | — |
|  | William Scarborow Husbond & tenant to the Almeshowse of Stamford forseid | in lond | nil | in goods £15 |  | — |
|  | Thomas Royse Husbondman & tenant to the seid Henry Aunger .. | in lond | nil | in goods £20 |  | — |
|  | John Tilton Husbond & tenant to Thomas Basset .. .. .. | in lond | 40s | in goods | 40s | — |
|  | Robert Colle Husbond & tenant to Thomas Basset .. .. .. | in lond | 12s | in goods £30 |  | — |
| Bill man | Thomas Cotes Husbond & tenant to the Chauntre of Okham .. .. | in lond | nil | in goods | 40s | — |
|  | The seid Chauntre of Okham hath londs their .. .. .. .. | in lond | 6s | in goods nil q.e. |  | — |
|  | William Jerman Husbond & tenant to Thomas Basset .. .. .. | in lond | 6s 8d | in goods | 40s | — |
|  |  |  | **£62 14s** | **£198 16s 8d** |  |  |

*f. 21 (39)*

|  | Name | | Land | Goods | |  |
|---|---|---|---|---|---|---|
|  | Jamys Taillor Shomaker & tenant to the seid Thomas Basset .. .. | in lond | nil | in goods £6 |  | & hath a Sallet & a Bill |
| Archer | William [I]sslepp[1] Husbond & tenant to Thomas Marham .. .. | in lond | nil | in goods £6 |  | — |
|  | William Croft Husbond & tenant to William Chamberlyn .. .. | in lond | nil | in goods | 40s | — |
|  | Simon Wade Husbond & tenant to Thomas Hunt .. .. .. | in lond | nil | in goods £6 |  | — |
|  | Robert Lauley Husbond & tenant to the seid Thomas Basset .. .. | in lond | nil | in goods | 40s | — |
|  | Richard Spencer Husbond & tenant to the seid Thomas Basset .. .. | in lond | 13s | in goods | 40s | — |
|  | John Thorp Husbond & tenant to the seid John Wymark .. .. | in lond | nil | in goods £4 |  | — |
|  | John Parr Husbond & tenant to the seid Robert Godman .. .. | in lond | nil | in goods | 40s | — |
|  | John Jerman tenant to Edward Burton & Husbond .. .. | in lond | nil | in goods | 40s | — |

1. *Cf.* *William Islepe in the Subsidy Roll.*

|  | | | | | | |
|---|---|---|---|---|---|---|
| | John Johnson Husbond & tenant to | | | | | |
| | the seid Thomas Basset .. .. in lond | nil | in goods | 40s | — |
| | Henry Wylle laborer & tenant to | | | | | |
| | the seid Thomas Basset .. .. in lond | nil | in goods | 20s | — |
| | Cristofer Cooper laborer & seruant | | | | | |
| | to Sir John Digby .. .. in lond | nil | in goods nil | | — |
| Bill man | William Hopkyn laborer .. | | | | |
| Bill man | John Montor laborer .. .. | | | | |
| Bill man | John Tatham laborer .. .. | in lond | nil | in goods nil | yong men & pore |
| Bill man | Richard Royse laborer .. | | | | |
| Bill man | Roger Bamborow laborer .. | | | | |
| Bill man | Thomas Godman Husbond & tenant | | | | |
| | to the seid Thomas Basset .. .. in lond | nil | in goods | £4 | — |
| Bill man | Edward Taillor laborer & tenant to | | | | |
| | the seid Thomas Basset .. .. in lond | nil | in goods | 20s | — |
| | The Town hath harnesse sufficient for a man | | | | |

The Church Stoke   nil

       **13s**             **£4**

*f.21 v (40)*

**DRYE STOKE**

|  | | | | | |
|---|---|---|---|---|---|
| | The Bishop of Lincoln is Chieff lord | | | | |
| | of the seid Town .. .. .. in lond | [blank] | in goods [blank] | | — |
| | William Skevington Knyght is Steward | | | | |
| | of the seid Town .. .. .. in fez | 6s | in goods nil q.e. | | — |
| | Thomas Webster prest is parson of | | | | |
| | the seid Town .. .. .. .. parsonage | £10 | in goods | 20 marks | — |
| Bill man | John Faconer Husbond & tenant | | | | |
| | to Edward Digby Esquier .. .. in lond | nil | in goods £10 | | — |
| | John Peyke Husbond & tenant to | | | | |
| | the seid Edward Digby .. .. in lond | nil | in goods £8 | | — |
| Archer | Robert Islepp Husbond & tenant to | | | | |
| | the seid Edward .. .. .. in lond | nil | in goods £10 | | — |
| Bill man | John Peyke the yonger Husbond & | | | | |
| | tenant to the seid Edward .. .. in lond | nil | in goods £10 | | — |
| Bill man | Robert Imyng Husbond & tenant | | | | |
| | the seid Edward .. .. .. in londs | nil | in goods £7 | | — |
| Bill man | Thomas Billyng Husbond & tenant | | | | |
| | to the seid Edward .. .. .. in lond | nil | in goods | 40s | — |
| | John Cooper Husbond & tenant to | | | | |
| | the seid Edward .. .. .. in lond | nil | in goods £4 | | — |
| | William Dudley Husbond & tenant | | | | |
| | to the seid Edward .. .. .. in lond | nil | in goods | 40s | — |
| | William Barker seruant to the | | | | |
| | seid Edward .. .. .. .. in lond | nil | in goods nil | | |
| | Rowlond Humfrey seruant to the | | | | yong men & pore |
| | seid Edward .. .. .. .. in lond | nil | in goods nil | | |
| | Edward Digby Esquier .. .. in lond | [blank] | in goods [blank] | | & hath harness |

The Church Stoke   £3

**CALCOTT**

|  | | | | |
|---|---|---|---|---|
| | The Reuerent Father in good William | | | |
| | the Bishop of Lincoln is chieff lord of | | | |
| | the seid Town .. .. .. .. in lond | [blank] | in goods [blank] | — |

| | | | in lond | in goods | |
|---|---|---|---|---|---|
| | William Skevyngton Knyght is Steward their .. .. .. .. in Feez | | 6s | in goods nil q.e. | — |
| | John Tippyng is parich prest their .. stipend | | £6 | in goods 26s 8d | — |
| Bill man | Thomas Woodcok Husbond & tenant to the seid Chieff lord .. .. .. in lond | | 20s | in goods £24 | & hath a Jak & a pair splynts |
| Archer | John Bowman Husbond & tenant to the seid lord .. .. .. .. in lond | | £4 | in goods £4 | — |
| | Thomas Slye Husbond & tenant to the seid Chieff lord .. .. .. in lond | | nil | in goods £20 | — |
| | Robert Russell Husbond & tenant to the seid lord .. .. .. in lond | | 15s | in goods £20 | — |
| | | | **£22 7s** | **£138 13s 4d** | |

**f.22 (41)**

| | | | in lond | in goods | |
|---|---|---|---|---|---|
| | Water Wyburn Husbond & tenant to the seid lord .. .. .. in lond | | 20s | in goods 40s | — |
| | John Guytet Husbond & tenant to the seid lord .. .. .. in lond | | nil | in goods 40s | — |
| Bill man | William Prestley Husbond & tenant to the seid lord .. .. .. in lond | | 5s | in goods £24 | — |
| | William Johnson Husbond & tenant to the seid lord .. .. .. in lond | | nil | in goods £20 | — |
| Bill man | William Newbon Husbond & tenant to the seid lord .. .. .. in lond | | 10s | in goods £10 | — |
| | William Luff Husbond & tenant to the seid lord .. .. .. in lond | | 15s | in goods £28 | — |
| Bill man | Richard Hill Husbond & tenant to the seid lord .. .. .. in lond | | 15s | in goods £24 | & hath a Jak, a Sallet with a Bill |
| | William Walker laborer & tenant the seid lord .. .. .. in lond | | nil | in goods 20s | — |
| Bill man | William Newbon Husbond & tenant to the seid lord .. .. .. in lond | | 20s | in goods £24 | — |
| | John Hill Husbond & tenant to the seid lord .. .. .. in lond | | 5s | in goods £10 | — |
| Bill man | Richard Luff Husbond & tenant to the seid lord .. .. .. in lond | | 6s 8d | in goods £5 | — |
| Bill man | Henry Wyburn Husbond & tenant to the seid lord .. .. in lond | | nil | in goods £5 | — |
| Bill man | John Baker laborer & tenant to the lord .. .. .. .. in lond | | nil | in goods 20s | — |
| Bill man | William Flecher laborer & tenant to the seid lord .. .. .. in lond | | nil | in goods 20s | — |
| | Richard Sherde laborer & tenant to the seid lord .. .. .. in lond | | nil | in goods 20s | — |
| Bill man | Richard Morres Husbond & tenant to the seid lord .. .. .. in lond | | nil | in goods 40s | — |
| Archer | Thomas Luff Husbond & tenant to the seid lord .. .. .. in lond | | nil | in goods £4 | — |
| Bill man | Thomas Coluyll Husbond & tenant to the seid lord .. .. .. in lond | | nil | in goods £4 | — |
| | Harre Warren laborer & tenant to the seid lord .. .. .. in lond | | nil | in goods 30s | — |
| Bill man | Richard Kyrke[1] Husbond & tenant to the seid lord .. .. in lond | | nil | in goods £4 | — |

1. *Or Kyrbe.*

Bill man   John Newbon Husbond & tenant to
the seid lord   ..   ..   ..   .. in lond      10s      in goods   £13   6s   8d      —
Johan Newbon widowe & tenant to
the seid lord   ..   ..   ..   .. in lond    nil      in goods      40s      —
Bill man   John Closton laborer & tenant to
the seid lord   ..   ..   ..   .. in lond    nil      in goods      20s      —

         **£5   6s   8d**          **£189   16s   8d**

*f. 22v (42)*

Bikl man   William Lawe Smyth & tenant to
the seid lord   ..   ..   ..   .. in lond    nil      in goods nil      —
Biil man   Thomas Slee Husbond & tenant to
the seid lord   ..   ..   ..   .. in lond    nil      in goods   £6

Bill man   Thomas Woodcok laborer   ⎫
         Thomas Hill laborer   ..    ⎪
Bill man   William Luff the yonger   ⎪
         laborer   ..   ..   ..   ⎬    in lond    nil      in goods nil      yong men & pore
Bill man   William Cooper laborer   ⎪
Bill man   Jamys Foliame laborer   ⎪
         John Colborn laborer   ..   ⎪
         George Newton laborer   ⎭

         The Church Stoke    nil

## LEDYNGTON

         The Reuerent Father in good William
the Bishop of Lincoln is chieff lord of
the seid Town ..   ..   ..   .. in lond   £56   8d   4d   in goods nil q.e.      —
Robert Purday clerk is vicar of
the town      ..   ..   ..   .. vicarige   20 marks   in goods   £10      —
............ clerk is parson of
the seid town ..   ..   ..   .. parsonage   £24   in goods nil q.e.      —
William Skevyngton Knyght is
Steward their ..   ..   ..   .. in feez      13s   4d   in goods nil q.e.      —
Archer    Edward Watson Gent. hath londs their   —      £8   in goods £200      & hath a Jak a Sallet
                                                   & a paire of Splynts
     John Stanger Gent. Bailly to the                                & hath harnesse for
seid Bishop   ..   ..   ..   .. in lond   £4   in goods   £50      a man
John Irelond yoman & tenant to                                & hath a Jak & a
the seid lord   ..   ..   ..   .. in lond   £6   in goods   £40      Sallet
William Wells Husbond & tenant
to the seid lord      ..   ..   .. in lond    nil      in goods   £6      —
John Howlatt Husbond & tenant
to the seid lord      ..   ..   .. in lond      10s   in goods   £15      —
Archer    John Maritt Husbond & tenant to
the seid lord   ..   ..   ..   .. in lond    nil      in goods   £7      —
Bill man   Richard Fowler Husbond & tenant
to the seid lord      ..   ..   .. in lond    nil      in goods   £3      —
Bill man   Robert Peyke Husbond & tenant to
the seid lord   ..   ..   ..   .. in lond    nil      in goods   £10      —
Issabell Messinger widow & tenant to
she seid lord   ..   ..   ..   .. in lond      13s   4d   in goods      40s      —
Bill man   John Kytte Husbond & tenant to
the seid lord   ..   ..   ..   .. in lond    nil      in goods   £4      —

         **£112   11s   8d**          **£353   13s   4d**

*f.23 (43)*

| | | | | | | |
|---|---|---|---|---|---|---|
| Bill man | John Edmond Husbond & tenant to the seid lord .. .. .. .. in lond | nil | in goods £10 | | | — |
| Bill man | Robert Adams Husbond & tenant to the seid lord .. .. .. .. in lond | 20s | in goods £6 | | | — |
| | Thomas Rowyll Husbond & tenant to the seid lord .. .. .. .. in lond | nil | in goods £3 | | | — |
| Archer | John Brown the yonger tenant to the seid lord .. .. .. .. in lond | nil | in goods 40s | | | — |
| | William Selebarn laborer & tenant to the seid lord .. .. .. .. in lond | nil | in goods 26s 8d | | | — |
| Archer | Robert Awyngkull Husbond & tenant to the seid lord .. .. .. .. in lond | 5s | in goods £4 | | | — |
| Bill man | Simon Irelond Husbond & tenant to the seid lord .. .. .. .. in lond | nil | in goods 40s | | | — |
| Archer | John Bunnyng Husbond & tenant to the seid lord .. .. .. .. in lond | nil | in goods £3 | | | — |
| | Thomas Hawley Husbond & tenant to the seid lord .. .. .. .. in lond | nil | in goods £3 | | | — |
| | Richard Sampson Husbond & tenant to the seid lord .. .. .. .. in lond | nil | in goods £6 | | | — |
| | Richard Astyll Husbond & tenant to the seid lord .. .. .. .. in lond | nil | in goods 26s 8d | | | — |
| Archer | John Irelond Husbond & tenant to the seid lord .. .. .. .. in lond | 10s | in goods £5 | | | — |
| | John Fowler Husbond & tenant to the seid lord .. .. .. .. in lond | nil | in goods 40s | | | — |
| | Thomas Harne Husbond & tenant to the seid lord .. .. .. .. in lond | nil | in goods £4 | | | — |
| Bill man | Richard Hill Husbond & tenant to the seid lord .. .. .. .. in lond | 10s | in goods £15 | | | — |
| | John Day laborer & tenant to the seid lord .. .. .. .. in lond | nil | in goods 20s | | | — |
| | Richard Irelond Husbond & tenant to the seid lord .. .. .. .. in lond | nil | in goods 40s | | | — |
| | Nicolis Torpe Husband & tenant to the seid lord .. .. .. .. in lond | nil | in goods £13 | | | — |
| | Robert Heuse Husbond & tenant to the seid lord .. .. .. .. in lond | nil | in goods 40s | | | — |
| | Robert Tayller Husbond & tenant to the seid lord .. .. .. .. in lond | nil | in goods 40s | | | — |
| Archer | John Brown Husbond & tenant to the seid lord .. .. .. .. in lond | 5s | in goods £4 | | | — |
| | Henry Cossyn Husbond & tenant to the seid lord .. .. .. .. in lond | nil | in goods 40s | | | — |
| | John Sismay Husbond & tenant to the seid lord .. .. .. .. in lond | 5s | in goods £3 6s 8d | | | — |
| | John Barret Husbond & tenant to the seid lord .. .. .. .. in lond | nil | in goods £5 | | | — |
| | | **£2 15s** | **£102** | | | |

*f.23 v (44)*

| | | | | | | |
|---|---|---|---|---|---|---|
| | Robert Jeffery Husbond & tenant to the seid lord .. .. .. .. in lond | 10s | in goods £3 | | | — |
| | Johan Slay widow & tenant to the seid lord .. .. .. .. in lond | nil | in goods £7 | | | — |

| | | | | | | | | |
|---|---|---|---|---|---|---|---|---|
| Bill man | Adam Shelton laborer & tenant to the seid lord | .. .. .. .. in lond | nil | in goods | 26s 8d | — |
| | John Fenton Husbond & tenant to the seid lord | .. .. .. .. in lond | nil | in goods | 40s | — |
| | William Colwell Husbond & tenant to the seid lord | .. .. .. .. in lond | nil | in goods | £5 | — |
| Archer | John Panter laborer & tenant to the seid lord | .. .. .. .. in lond | nil | in goods | 20s | — |
| | Robert Shortred laborer & tenant to the seid lord | .. .. .. .. in lond | nil | in goods | 20s | — |
| | Richard Sismay Husbond & tenant to the seid lord | .. .. .. .. in lond | 5s | in goods | £4 | — |
| | John Pitts laborer & tenant to the the seid lord | .. .. .. .. in lond | nil | in goods | 20s | — |
| | Agnes Rutkyn widow & tenant to the seid lord | .. .. .. .. in lond | nil | in goods | 40s | — |
| Bill man | Richard Sysmay thelder Husbond & tenant to the seid lord | .. .. in lond | 5s | in goods | £20 | — |
| | John Britmay Husbond & tenant to the seid lord | .. .. .. .. in lond | nil | in goods | £6 | — |
| | Richard Irelond of Uppyngham hath lond their | .. .. .. .. — | £4 10s | in goods nil q.e. | | — |
| Bill man | John Galare laborer & tenant to the said lord | .. .. .. .. in lond | nil | in goods | 20s | — |
| | William Irelond Husbond & tenant to the seid lord | .. .. .. .. in lond | 10s | in goods | £13 | — |
| Archer | Thomas Stabulls Husbond & tenant to the seid Richard Irelond | .. .. in lond | nil | in goods | £6 | — |

| | | | | | |
|---|---|---|---|---|---|
| Archer | Brian Barker laborer .. | | | | |
| | John Banyster laborer | | | | |
| Archer | John Fowler laborer .. | | | | |
| | John Watson laborer .. | | | | |
| | Thomas Williamson laborer | | | | |
| Bill man | Richard Wallis seruant | | | | |
| Bill man | Hugh Padley laborer .. | | | | |
| Bill man | John Horsley laborer .. | in londs | nil | in goods nil | yong men & pore |
| Archer | William Hill seruant .. | | | | |
| Bill man | Austyn Embre seruant | | | | |
| Archer | John Clerk seruant .. | | | | |
| Archer | Robert Spaldyng seruant | | | | |
| Archer | Jamys Hert seruant .. | | | | |
| Bill man | Hugh Smyth seruant .. | | | | |

The Church Stoke          20s
£7                                    £73  6s  8d

f. 24 (45)

**BAROUGDON**

| | | | | | |
|---|---|---|---|---|---|
| | The Kyng ower Souereign lord is Chiff lord of the seid Town | | | | |
| | Edward Digby Esquier is Steward of the seid Town .. .. .. in Feez | 6s 8d | in goods nil q.e. | | — |
| | Rowlond Digby prest is parson of the seid Town .. .. .. parsonage | £6 6s 8d | in goods £20 | | — |
| | John Digby Knyght hath lond their .. — | 8s | in goods nil q.e. | | — |
| | Thomas Duraunt Gent. hath lond their — | 4 marks | in goods nil q.e. | | — |

| | | | | | | | |
|---|---|---|---|---|---|---|---|
| | Raff Sacheuerell Gent. hath lond their | — | 40s | | in goods nil q.e. | | |
| | The Prior of Fynneszed Abbey hath lond their .. .. .. .. | — | 26s | 8d | in goods nil q.e. | | — |
| | Issabell Conyers Gent. hath lond their | — | 13s | 4d | in goods nil q.e. | | — |
| | John Duraunt Gent. hath lond their & tenant to the Kyng .. .. .. | — | £6 13s | 4d | in goods £13 | 6s | 8d | — |
| | Henry Aunger Chappelyn & Chauntre prest .. .. .. | stipend | 46s | 8d | in goods nil q.e. | | — |
| | Thomas Basset Gent hath lond their | — | 10s | | in goods nil q.e. | | — |
| | Thomas Clerk is parich prest of the seid Town .. .. .. .. | in lond | 26s | 8d | in goods £3 | | — |
| | William Niccoll Husb. hath lond their | — | 16s | | in goods nil q.e. | | — |
| | William Walker Husb. hath lond their | — | 26s | 8d | in goods nil q.e. | | — |
| Bill man | Robert Clyff Husb. & tenant to the seid John Duraunt .. .. .. | — | 30s | | in goods £10 | | — |
| | John Teylbe Husb. & tenant to the seid John Duraunt .. .. .. | in lond | nil | | in goods £40 | | — |
| | William Goodlad thelder & tenant to the seid Thomas Duraunt .. | in lond | nil | | in goods £40 | | — |
| Archer | Badwyn Wymbysh Yoman & tenant to the Kyng & reteyned to the seid John Digby .. .. .. | in londs | nil | | in goods £8 | | & hath harnes a Sallet |
| | John Bradforth Husbond & tenant to the Kyng .. .. .. .. | in londs | nil | | in goods £20 | | & hath a Jestorn & a Sallet |
| Bill man | Thomas Clers Husb. & tenant to the seid Thomas Clerk prest .. .. | in londs | nil | | in goods 20s | | — |
| | | | £29 4s | | | £173 6s 8d | | ● |

*f. 24v (46)*

| | | | | | | | |
|---|---|---|---|---|---|---|---|
| | Richard Reynold Husb. & tenant to the seid Richard Sacheuerell .. .. | in lond | nil | | in goods £24 | | — |
| | Bartilmew Sharpe Husb. & tenant to the seid John Duraunt .. .. | in londs | 20s | | in goods £30 | | — |
| Archer | Robert Slye Husb. & tenant to the seid Thomas Duraunt .. .. .. | in lond | nil | | in goods 40s | | — |
| Bill man | Thomas Goodlad Husb. & tenant to the Kyng .. .. .. .. | in lond | nil | | in goods 40s | | — |
| Archer | William Mathew Husb. & tenant to the Kyng .. .. .. .. | in londs | nil | | in goods £4 | | — |
| | The Chauntre of the seid Town hath lond their .. .. .. .. | in lond | 46s | | in goods nil | | — |
| | Richard Style Husb. & tenant to the seid Chauntre .. .. | in lond | nil | | in goods £10 | | — |
| | John Brampton laborer & tenant the Kyng .. .. .. .. | in londs | nil | | in goods 20s | | — |
| | John Frayne Husb. & tenant to the Kyng .. .. .. .. | in lond | 10s | | in goods 40s | | — |
| | Thomas Smyth laborer & tenant to the seid Issabell Conyers .. | in londs | nil | | in goods 26s 8d | | — |
| | Agnes Goodlad widow & tenant to the Kyng .. .. .. .. | in lond | nil | | in goods £10 | | — |
| | Robert Keysbe Husb. & tenant to the seid William Niccoll .. .. | in lond | nil | | in goods £8 | | — |
| | William Goodlad the yonger Husb. & tenant to the seid Richard Sacheuerell | in lond | nil | | in goods £4 | | |

| | | | | | |
|---|---|---|---|---|---|
| | John Laurence laborer & tenant to the Kyng .. .. .. .. | in lond | nil | in goods | 20s | — |
| Bill man | John Niccoll Husb. & tenant to the Kyng .. .. .. .. | in lond | nil | in goods | £10 | — |
| Bill man | John Hunt laborer .. | | | | | |
| Archer | Simon Teylbe laborer .. | | | | | |
| Archer | Samuel Tygh laborer .. | | | | | |
| Bill man | Thomas Goodlad laborer | | | | | |
| Archer | William Ferebe laborer | in londs | nil | in goods nil | | yong men & pore |
| Bill man | John Chapman laborer | | | | | |
| Archer | Thomas Styll laborer .. | | | | | |
| Archer | John Jepson laborer .. | | | | | |
| Bill man | Robert Sharpe laborer | | | | | |
| Bill man | William Stylle laborer .. | | | | | |

The Church Stoke  £6

£3 16s                £115  6s  8d

End of this Hundred.

f.25 (47)
**WYNG**

## MERTYNSLEY HUNDRED IN COUNTY ROTLOND

| | | | | | |
|---|---|---|---|---|---|
| | The Kyng ower souereign lord is Chieff lord of the seid Town | | | | | |
| | Edward Digby Esquier is Steward of the seid Town .. .. .. .. | in feez | 6s  8d | in goods nil q.e. | | — |
| | The lord Zouch hath lond their .. | — | 24s | in goods nil q.e. | | — |
| | The Abbot of Thorney hath lond their | — | 40s | in goods nil q.e. | | — |
| | The Prior of Seint Edds hath lond their | — | 4 marks | in goods nil q.e. | | — |
| | Master Tenaunt Clerk is parson of the seid Town .. .. .. | parsonage | £12 | in goods | £10 | — |
| | Robert Rutkyn Chappelyn is parich prest their .. .. .. .. | stipend | £5 | in goods | 40s | — |
| Bill man | William Sharpe Husbond hath lond their .. .. .. .. .. | — | 33s  4d | in goods | £4 | & hath harness a Jestorn with a Bill |
| | William Sharpe the yonger & tenant to the Kyng .. .. .. .. | in londs | 12s | in goods | £4 | — |
| | John Allen Husbond & tenant to the Kyng .. .. .. .. | in lond | nil | in goods | £8 | & hath a Jestorn & a Sallet |
| | Robert Allen Husbond & tenant to the Kyng .. .. .. .. | in lond | nil | in goods | £20 | |
| | John Tyller Husbond & tenant to the Kyng .. .. .. .. | in lond | nil | in goods | £7 | |
| Bill man | Robert Bunnyng Husbond & tenant to the Kyng .. .. .. .. | in lond | nil | in goods | £10 | |
| Bill man | John Bunnyng Husbond & tenant to the Kyng .. .. .. .. | in lond | nil | in goods | £9 | |
| | William Rawlyn Husbond & tenant to the lord Zouch .. .. .. | in lond | nil | in goods | £5 | |
| | William Sharpe thelder Husbond & tenant to the Abbot of Thorney | in lond | nil | in goods | £4 | |
| | Thomas A Ridlington Husbond & tenant to the Kyng .. .. | in lond | nil | in goods | £5 | — |
| | Robert Irelond Husbond & tenant to the lord Zouch .. .. | in lond | nil | in goods | £5 | — |
| | Thomas Smyth laborer & tenant to | | | | | |

|  |  |  |  |  |  |  |
|---|---|---|---|---|---|---|
|  | the Prior of Seint Edds .. .. | in lond | nil | in goods | £3 | — |
|  | William Horsley Husbond & tenant to the seid Prior of Seint Edds .. | in londs | nil | in goods | £3 | — |
|  | Hugh Barnes Husbond & tenant to the seid Abbot .. .. .. | in lond | nil | in goods | 40s | — |
|  |  |  | **£25 10s 4d** |  | **£101** |  |

**f.25 v (48)**

|  |  |  |  |  |  |  |
|---|---|---|---|---|---|---|
|  | John Peper Husbond & tenant to the seid Abbot .. .. .. .. | in lond | nil | in goods | £3 | — |
|  | William Peper Husbond & tenant to the seid Prior .. .. | in londs | nil | in goods | 40s | — |
|  | Robert Sharpe Husbond & tenant to the Kyng .. .. .. | in lond | nil | in goods | 40s | — |
| Bill man | John Bigarton Husbond & tenant to the seid Abbot .. .. | in lond | nil | in goods | £3 | — |
| Bill man | William Brown Husb. & tenant to the seid Prior .. .. .. | in lond | nil | in goods | 40s | — |
|  | Jamys Affairley laborer & tenant to the seid Abbot .. .. | in lond | nil | in goods | 40s | — |
| Bill man | Thomas Kylbe Bocher & tenant to the seid lord Zouch .. .. | in lond | nil | in goods | 40s | — |
|  | Thomas Dunmowe laborer & tenant to the seid Abbot .. .. | in lond | nil | in goods | 20s | — |
| Archer | Richard Hellary laborer .. |  |  |  |  |  |
| Bill man | William Smyth laborer .. |  |  |  |  |  |
| Archer | Robert Rawlyns seruant .. | in lond | nil | in goods nil |  | yong men & pore |
|  | Thomas Sharpe seruant .. |  |  |  |  |  |
|  | Richard Tiller seruant .. |  |  |  |  |  |
|  | The Church Stoke 40s |  |  |  |  |  |

### PRESTON

|  |  |  |  |  |  |  |
|---|---|---|---|---|---|---|
|  | The Kyng ower souereing lord is Chiff lord of the seid Town |  |  |  |  |  |
|  | Edward Digby Esquier is Steward their .. .. .. | in feez | 6s 8d | in goods nil q.e. |  | — |
|  | Cristofer Goodworth is parson of the seid Town .. .. .. | parsonage | 10 marks | in goods nil q.e. |  | — |
| Bill man | John Digby gentilman & fermer to the seid parson .. .. | in lond | £5 | in goods | £4 | & hath a Sallet & a pair of Briggandines a gorgit with a Bill |
| Bill man | Thomas Irelond Husbond & tenant to the seid Chieff lord .. | in lond | nil | in goods | £25 | & hath a Jestorn with a Bill |
|  | Gilbert Thompson Husbond & tenant to the seid lord .. .. | in lond | nil | in goods | £15 | & hath a Jestorn |
| Bill man | John Sheld Husb. & tenant to the seid Chieff lord .. .. | in lond | nil | in goods | £10 | — |
| Archer | William Rudkyn Husbond & tenant to the seid lord .. .. | in lond | nil | in goods | £10 | — |
|  | Thomas Whetley Husbond & tenant to the seid Chieff lord .. | in lond | nil | in goods | £14 | — |
|  | Thomas Cooper Husbond & tenant to the seid Chieff lord .. | in lond | nil | in goods | £15 | — |
|  |  |  | **£14** |  | **£110** |  |

*f.26 (49)*

|  | | | | | | |
|---|---|---|---|---|---|---|
|  | John Faconer Husb. & tenant to the seid Chieff lord .. .. .. | in lond | nil | in goods | £15 | — |
|  | Robert Sheryngton Husbond & tenant to the seid Chieff lord .. .. | in lond | nil | in goods | £4 | — |
|  | William Langton Husb. & tenant to the seid Chieff lord .. .. .. | in lond | nil | in goods | £3 | — |
|  | Thomas Andres Husbond & tenant the seid Chieff lord .. .. | in lond | nil | in goods | £8 | — |
| Bill man | Robert Ward Husb. & tenant to the seid Chieff lord .. .. .. | in lond | nil | in goods | £5 | — |
|  | John Wynter Husb. & tenant to the seid Chieff lord .. .. | in lond | nil | in goods | 4 marks | — |
| Bill man | Robert Thompson Husb. & tenant to the seid Chieff lord .. .. | in lond | nil | in goods | £6 | — |
| Bill man | Richard Faconer Husb. & tenant to the seid Chieff lord .. .. .. | in lond | nil | in goods | £3 | — |
|  | William Allen Husb. & tenant to the seid Chieff lord .. .. .. | in lond | nil | in goods | 40s | — |
| Archer | Clement Tiller laborer & tenant to the seid Chieff lord .. .. | in lond | nil | in goods | 20s | — |
| Bill man | John Irelond laborer & tenant to the seid Chieff lord .. .. | in lond | nil | in goods | 40s | — |
|  | John Jerman laborer & tenant to the seid Chieff lord .. .. | in lond | nil | in goods | 20s | — |
| Bill man | William Wynter laborer & tenant to the seid Chieff lord .. .. | in lond | nil | in goods nil | | — |
|  | Robert Cooper laborer & tenant to the seid Chieff lord .. .. | in lond | nil | in goods | 20s | — |

| Archer | Thomas Jerman laborer .. .. |
|---|---|
| Archer | John Goole seruant .. .. |
| Archer | William Pas seruant .. .. |
| Archer | William Sheld seruant .. .. |
| Archer | William Wynter seruant .. .. |
|  | Robert Andrew seruant .. .. |
|  | John Smyth seruant .. .. |

in lond   nil     in goods nil     yong men & pore

The Church Stoke nil

## NORMANTON

|  | | | | | | |
|---|---|---|---|---|---|---|
|  | George Mackworth Esquier is Chieff lord of the seid Town .. .. | in lond | £5 | in goods nil q.e. | | — |
|  | William Ouerton is Steward their .. | in feez | [blank] | in goods nil q.e. | | — |
|  | Thomas Walker prest is parson of the seid Town .. .. .. | parsonage | 8 marks | in goods | £7 | — |
|  | Peter Stevyn is parich prest of the seid Town .. .. .. | stipend | £5 | in goods | 20s | — |
|  | Thomas Greneham the yonger gent & fermer to the seid parson .. .. | in lond | £10 | in goods | £4 | — |
|  | | | £25 6s 8d | | £65 13s 4d | |

*f.26 v (50)*

|  | | | | | | |
|---|---|---|---|---|---|---|
| Bill man | John Naillour Husb. & tenant to the seid George .. .. .. | in lond | nil | in goods | £20 | — |
|  | William Sherwood Husbond & tenant to the seid George .. .. .. | in lond | 14s | in goods | £4 | — |

|  |  |  |  |  |  |  |
|---|---|---|---|---|---|---|
|  | Richard Smyth Husb. & tenant to the seid George | in lond | nil | in goods | £3 | — |
| Bill man | George Swetbon' Husb. & tenant to the seid George | in lond | nil | in goods | £5 | — |
|  | Thomas Hoston Husb. & tenant to the seid George | in lond | nil | in goods | £4 | — |
|  | Thomas Meryll Husb. & tenant to the seid Chieff lord | in lond | nil | in goods | 40s | — |
|  | Jssabell Sherwood widow & tenant to the seid lord | in lond | nil | in goods | £4 | — |
|  | Thomas Tilton Husb. & tenant to the seid George | in lond | nil | in goods | 40s | — |
|  | Simon Swaffeld gentilman hath londs their | in londs | 40s | in goods nil q.e. |  | — |
|  | Thomas Sherrard Esquier hath londs their | in lond | 10s | in goods nil q.e. |  | — |
|  | John Smyth laborer & tenant to the seid Simon | in lond | nil | in goods | 20s | — |
|  | William Sherwood the yonger laborer | in lond | nil | in goods | 20s | — |
| Archer | Robert Walker seruant |  |  |  |  |  |
| Bill man | John Taillor laborer |  |  |  |  |  |
| Bill man | John Meryll laborer | in lond | nil | in goods nil |  | yong men & pore |
| Bill man | John Sherwood seruant |  |  |  |  |  |

The Church Stoke nil

## LYNDON

|  |  |  |  |  |  |  |
|---|---|---|---|---|---|---|
|  | Robert Peyton Esquier is Chieff lord of the seid Town | in lond | £18 | in goods nil q.e. |  | — |
|  | Ambrose Barker yoman & tenant to the seid lord | in lond | 20s | in goods | £20 | — |
|  | William Barker prest is parson of the seid Town | parsonage | 6 marks | in goods | £3 | — |
|  | John Harbar Husb. & tenant to the seid lord | in lond | nil | in goods | £20 | — |
|  | Gregory Barkar Husb. & tenant to the seid lord | in lond | nil | in goods | £20 | — |
|  |  |  | £27  4s |  | £109 |  |

*f. 27 (51)*

|  |  |  |  |  |  |  |
|---|---|---|---|---|---|---|
|  | Edmond Standelond Husb. & tenant to the seid Robert Peyton | in lond | nil | in goods | £16 | — |
| Archer | William Diccons Husb. & tenant to the seid Robert Peyton | in lond | nil | in goods | £18 | — |
| Archer | Thomas Thornham Husb. & tenant to the seid chieff lord | in lond | nil | in goods | £5 | — |
|  | John Rawlyn Husbond & tenant to the seid chieff lord | in lond | nil | in goods | £6 | — |
|  | John Miller Husb. & tenant to the seid chieff lord | in lond | nil | in goods | £3 | — |
| Bill man | Robert Grene laborer & tenant to the seid chieff lord | in lond | nil | in goods | 20s | — |
|  | Edward Sauell laborer & tenant to the seid chieff lord | in lond | nil | in goods | 20s | — |

The Church Stoke nil

**AYSTON**

|  | | land | | goods | |
|---|---|---|---|---|---|
|  | Robert Brudenell Knyght is Chieff lord of the seid Town .. .. .. in lond | [blank] | | in goods nil q.e. | — |
|  | William Ouerton Gent. is Steward their in feez | 40d | | in goods nil q.e. | — |
|  | Thomas Burley prest is Parson of the seid Town .. .. .. .. parsonage | £10 | | in goods £20 | — |
|  | Richard Cletar Husb. & tenant to the seid Chieff lord .. .. .. in lond | nil | | in goods £26 | — |
| Bill man | Thomas William Husb. & tenant to the seid lord .. .. .. .. in lond | nil | | in goods £15 | — |
|  | Thomas Colson Husb. & tenant to the seid lord .. .. .. .. in lond | nil | | in goods £16 | — |
|  | William Drayton Husb. & tenant to the seid Chieff lord .. .. .. in lond | nil | | in goods £10 | — |
|  | John Kyrke thelder tenant to the seid Chieff lord .. .. .. in lond | nil | | in goods £7 | — |
|  | John Jakson Husbond & tenant to the seid Chieff lord .. .. .. in lond | nil | | in goods £5 | — |
|  | Thomas Wellis Husb. & tenant to the seid Chieff lord .. .. .. in lond | nil | | in goods £4 | — |
|  | Thomas Kyrke Husb. & tenant to the seid Chieff lord .. .. .. in lond | nil | | in goods £3 | — |
| Bill man | William Turlyngton Husb. & tenant to the seid Chieff lord .. .. in lond | nil | | in goods £4 | — |
|  |  | £10 3s 4d | | £160 | |

*f. 27v (52)*

| Bill man | Thomas Whetley laborer & tenant to the seid Chieff lord .. .. in lond | nil | | in goods 40s | — |
|---|---|---|---|---|---|
| Archer | John Kyrke the yonger laborer & tenant to the seid lord .. .. in lond | nil | | in goods 40s | — |
| Archer | William Dare Husb. & tenant to the seid Chieff lord .. .. .. in lond | nil | | in goods £3 | — |
| Bill man | John Atkynson laborer .. } Fraunces Billyng laborer .. } in lond | nil | | in goods nil | yong men & pore |

The Town hath a Jestorn a Sallet with a Sword & a Buckler

The Church Stoke 16s

**RIDLINGTON**

| | The Kyng owr souereign lord is chieff lord of the seid Town | | | | |
|---|---|---|---|---|---|
|  | Edward Digby Esquier hath lond their in fez | 6s 8d | — | — | |
|  |  in lond | 10s | | in goods nil q.e. | — |
|  | John Calcot Esquier hath lond their — | 40s | | in goods nil q.e. | — |
|  | Margaret Symmys widow .. .. in lond | 53s 4d | | in goods £10 | — |
|  | Richard Chisselden Gent. .. .. in lond | 30s | | in goods nil q.e. | — |
| Archer | Rowlond Sheffeld Gent. .. .. in lond | £4 | | in goods £10 | & hath a jestorn & a sallet |
| Bill man | Richard Peyke Husbond & tenant to the Kyng .. .. .. .. in lond | nil | | in goods £25 | — |
| Archer | Cristofer Lacy ys Husb. & tenant to the Kyng & seruant in the Howsehold with the lord Hastyngs .. .. in lond | nil | | in goods £15 | & hath a jestorn & a sallet |

| | | | | | | |
|---|---|---|---|---|---|---|
| | John Swaynston Husb. & tenant to the seid chieff lord | in lond | nil | in goods | £10 | & hath a jestorn |
| | Henry Persson Husb. & tenant to the seid chieff lord | in lond | nil | in goods | £10 | — |
| Bill man | Richard Bonyng Husb. & tenant to the seid chieff lord | in lond | nil | in goods | £8 | — |
| Bill man | William Curtes Husb. & tenant to the seid lord | in lond | nil | in goods | £10 | — |
| | Thomas Taillor Husb. & tenant to the seid lord | in lond | nil | in goods | £10 | — |
| | Agnes Berige widow & tenant to the seid lord | in lond | nil | in goods | £6 | — |
| | | | £11 6s | | £121 | |

*f. 28 (53)*

| | | | | | | |
|---|---|---|---|---|---|---|
| Archer | Henry Goodlad Husb. & tenant to the seid Chieff lord | in lond | nil | in goods | £4 | — |
| | John Padley Husb. & tenant to the seid lord | in lond | nil | in goods | £3 | — |
| Archer | John Billyng Husb. & tenant to the seid lord | in lond | nil | in goods | 40s | — |
| Bill man | William Teyller laborer & tenant to the seid John Calcot | in lond | nil | in goods | 30s | — |
| Bill man | John Sharpe Husb. & tenant to the seid John Calcot | in lond | nil | in goods | £15 | — |
| | John Tympson Husb. & tenant to the seid Chieff lord | in lond | nil | in goods | £8 | — |
| Archer | Thomas Haryngton gent. & seruant to John Haryngton the yonger | in lond | nil | in goods | £7 | — |
| | Niccolis Clerk seruant to the seid John Haryngton | in lond | nil | in goods | £4 | — |
| | Thomas Sharpe laborer & tenant to the seid Chieff lord | in lond | nil | in goods | 20s | — |
| | John Baker Husb. & tenant to the seid Chieff lord | in lond | nil | in goods | 40s | — |
| Archer | William Sarson laborer & tenant to the seid Chieff lord | in lond | nil | in goods | 40s | — |
| | William Presgrave laborer & tenant to the seid Chieff lord | in lond | nil | in goods | 20s | — |
| Archer | Cristofer Webster tenant to the seid Chieff lord & howsehold seruant to the seid lord Hastyngs | in lond | nil | in goods | £12 | & hath a Sallet & a paire of splynts |
| | William Tympson Husb. & tenant to the seid Chieff lord | in lond | nil | in goods | £4 | — |
| Bill man | Edmond Milner laborer & tenant to the seid Chieff lord | in lond | nil | in goods | 20s | — |
| | Robert Issabell laborer & tenant to the seid Chieff lord | in lond | nil | in goods | 20s | — |
| | John Pykwell laborer & tenant to the seid John Calcot | in lond | nil | in goods | 20s | — |
| | Agnes Magdaunce widow & tenant to the seid Chieff lord | in lond | nil | in goods | 20s | — |
| | John Berige seruant | } in lond | nil | in goods nil | | yong men & pore |
| | John Sowter seruant | | | | | |

The Church Stoke nil

| | | | | | |
|---|---|---|---|---|---|
| | John Childurley prest is parich prest of the seid Town .. .. .. | stipend | 8 marks | in goods £7 | — |
| | John Haryngton the yonger Esquier hath lond .. .. .. .. | in lond | £20 | in goods £20 | — |
| | | | **£25  6s  8d** | **£97 10s** | |

*f. 28v (54)*

**MANTON**

| | | | | | |
|---|---|---|---|---|---|
| | The Warden of Tatershall is chieff lord of the seid Town .. .. .. | in lond | £7 | in goods nil q.e. | — |
| | ...... Newton is parson of the seid Town .. .. .. .. | parsonage | £20 | in goods £30 | — |
| | The same ...... Newton parson hath lond their .. .. .. | — | [blank] | in goods nil | — |
| | Antony Ardes gent. hath lond their | — | £7 | in goods nil q.e. | — |
| | William Feldyng Esquier hath lond their | — | 46s  8d | in goods nil q.e. | — |
| | Henry Wryght yoman hath lond their | — | 3s | in goods nil q.e. | — |
| Archer | John Feldyng gent. & tenant to the seid William Feldyng .. .. .. | in lond | 10 marks | in goods £8 | — |
| | Thomas Burneby Husb. & tenant to the seid Warden .. .. .. | in lond | nil | in goods £22 | & hath a jestorn a Sallet with a Bowe & a Sheff of Arrows |
| | Henry Rutkyn Husb. & tenant to the seid Warden .. .. .. | in lond | nil | in goods £16 | & hath a jake with a Bill |
| Bill man | William Laurence Husb. & tenant to the seid Warden .. .. .. | in lond | nil | in goods 20 marks | — |
| Bill man | Richard Chiselden Husb. & tenant to the seid Antony Ardes .. .. | in lond | nil | in goods £10 | — |
| Archer | William Burnby Husb. & tenant to the seid Warden .. .. .. | in lond | nil | in goods £8 | — |
| Bill man | William More Husb. & tenant to the seid Newton .. .. .. | in lond | nil | in goods £4 | — |
| Archer | John Burneby Husb. & tenant to the seid Warden .. .. .. | in lond | nil | in goods £6 | — |
| Bill man | Antony Bunnyng Husb. & tenant to the seid Warden .. .. .. | in lond | nil | in goods £4 | — |
| | John Blande Husb. & tenant to the seid Antony Ardes .. .. | in lond | nil | in goods £5 | — |
| | William Bradford Husb. & tenant to the seid Warden .. .. .. | in lond | nil | in goods 40s | — |
| Bill man | Thomas Laurence Husb. & tenant to the seid Warden .. .. .. | in lond | nil | in goods £5 | — |
| Archer | Henry Burby Husb. & tenant to the seid Newton, parson .. .. | in lond | nil | in goods 40s | — |
| | John Standerd Husb. & tenant to the seid Antony .. .. .. | in lond | nil | in goods 40s | — |
| | George Harys laborer & tenant to the seid William Feldyng .. .. | in lond | nil | in goods 20s | — |
| Bill man | Richard Lowyth Husb. & tenant to the seid Warden .. .. .. | in lond | nil | in goods 40s | — |
| | Thomas Porter laborer & tenant to the seid William Feldyng .. .. | in lond | nil | in goods 20s | — |
| Bill man | William Norris laborer & tenant to the seid Antony Ardes .. .. | in lond | nil | in goods 20s | — |
| | | | **£43  3s** | **£142 6s  8d** | |

*f. 29 (55)*

| | | | | | |
|---|---|---|---|---|---|
| Archer | Henry Thornton seruant to the seid Newton .. .. .. | in lond | nil | in goods nil | — |
| Bill man | Cristofer Fereby laborer & seruant to the seid parson .. | | | | |
| Bill man | John Corbe laborer .. .. | | | | |
| Bill man | Thomas Strynger laborer .. | in lond | nil | in goods nil | yong men & pore |
| Archer | John Rutkyn laborer .. | | | | |
| | Richard Bell laborer .. .. | | | | |
| | Robert Preston Taillor .. | | | | |

The Church Stoke 40*s*

| | | | | | |
|---|---|---|---|---|---|
| | Thomas Scott is parich prest of the seid Town .. .. .. | stipend | 7 marks | in goods 13 marks | 6*s* 8d |

**EDIWESTON**

| | | | | | |
|---|---|---|---|---|---|
| | The Prior of the Charterhouse of Coventry is Chieff lord of the seid Town | | 40 marks | in goods nil q.e. | — |
| | ...... Walthrop is Steward | in fez | 6*s* 8*d* | in goods nil q.e. | — |
| | Gere Flower gent. & farmer to the parson their .. .. .. | in lond | 20 marks | in goods £16 | — |
| | Antony Bretten prest is parson of the seid Town .. .. .. | parsonage | £5 6*s* 8*d* | in goods £10 | — |
| | John Richards is parich prest of the seid Town .. .. .. | stipend | 8 marks | in goods 26*s* 8*d* | — |
| | John Page Husb. & tenant to the seid prior .. .. .. | in lond | nil | in goods £24 | — |
| | Hugh Sey Husb. & tenant to the seid prior .. .. .. | in lond | nil | in goods £20 | — |
| Bill man | William Barker Husb. & tenant to the seid prior .. .. .. | in lond | nil | in goods £20 | — |
| | Thomas Barker Husb. & tenant to the seid Prior .. .. .. | in lond | nil | in goods £12 13*s* 4*d* | — |
| | Alis Stephen widow & tenant to the seid prior .. .. .. | in lond | nil | in goods £12 | — |
| | Robert Freman Husb. & tenant to the seid prior .. .. .. | in lond | nil | in goods £5 | & hath a Sallet with a Bill |
| Bill man | Thomas Barker the yonger tenant to the seid prior .. .. .. | in lond | nil | in goods £5 | — |
| Bill man | William Ward Husb. & tenant to the seid prior .. .. .. | in lond | nil | in goods £4 | — |
| | John Clerk Husb. & tenant to the seid prior .. .. .. | in lond | nil | in goods £4 | — |
| | | | **£56 6s 8d** | **£143** | |

*f. 29v (56)*

| | | | | | |
|---|---|---|---|---|---|
| Bill man | Robert Ward Husb. & tenant to the seid prior .. .. .. | in lond | nil | in goods £3 | — |
| | John Cook Husb. & tenant to the seid prior .. .. .. | in lond | nil | in goods 40*s* | — |
| Bill man | Robert Wright Husb. & tenant to the seid prior .. .. .. | in lond | nil | in goods £5 | — |
| Bill man | John Graunt Husb. & tenant to the seid prior .. .. .. | in lond | nil | in goods 40*s* | — |
| | Robert Cook Husb. & tenant to the seid prior .. .. .. | in lond | nil | in goods £4 | — |

|          | | | | | | |
|----------|------------------------------------------------------|-----------|-----|----------|------------|---|
|          | Thomas Turnor Husb. & tenant to the seid prior .. .. .. .. | in lond | nil | in goods | £3 | — |
| Bill man | Peter Hare Husb. & tenant to the seid prior .. .. .. .. | in lond | nil | in goods | £3 | — |
|          | Thomas Ellit Husb. & tenant to the seid prior .. .. .. .. | in lond | nil | in goods | £5 | — |
| Archer   | John A Waters Husb. & tenant to the seid prior .. .. .. | in lond | nil | in goods | £3 | — |
|          | Robert Page Husb. & tenant to the seid prior .. .. .. .. | in lond | nil | in goods | 40s | — |
| Archer   | William Beneson laborer & tenant to the seid prior .. .. .. .. | in lond | nil | in goods | 20s | — |
|          | Robert Wright thelder & tenant to the seid prior .. .. .. .. | in lond | nil | in goods | 20s | — |
| Bill man | John Taillor Husb. & tenant to the seid prior .. .. .. .. | in lond | nil | in goods | £3 | — |
|          | Henry Bretten[1] laborer & tenant to the seid prior .. .. .. | in lond | nil | in goods | £3 | — |
| Bill man | John Sey Husb. & tenant to the seid prior .. .. .. .. | in lond | nil | in goods | £4 | — |
| Bill man | Laurence Fox laborer & tenant to the seid prior .. .. .. .. | in lond | nil | in goods | 20s | — |

The Church Stoke 40s

The Town hath the fyft part of a hoole harness for a man

                             nil                      £46

*f. 30 (57)*

**HAMYLDON**

|          | | | | | | |
|----------|------------------------------------------------------|-----------|----------|----------|-----------------|---|
|          | Edward Ferris knyght is chieff lord of the seid Town .. .. .. .. | in lond | £35 | in goods nil q.e. | | — |
|          | John Haryngton thelder Esquier is Steward of the seid Town .. | Fez | 6s 8d | in goods nil q.e. | | — |
|          | Edward Derby clerk is parson of the seid Town .. .. .. | parsonage | 20 marks | in goods q.e. | | — |
|          | Edward Smyth is Vicar of the seid Town .. .. .. | vicarige | 10 marks | in goods | 40s | — |
|          | Edward Burton Gent. & fermer to the seid Edward Digby parson .. | in lond | £10 | in goods | £50 | & hath harnesse sufficient for ij men with a bow & a sheff or arrowis |
|          | William Fowler Husb. & tenant to the seid chieff lord .. .. | in lond | nil | in goods | £20 | — |
|          | John Fowler Husb. & bailly to the seid chieff lord .. .. .. | in lond | nil | in goods | £24 | & hath ij bills |
|          | John Atkynson Husb. & tenant to seid chieff lord .. .. .. | in lond | nil | in goods | £15 | & hath a Sallet with a bow & a Sheff of arrowis |
|          | Robert Freman Husb. & tenant to the seid chieff lord .. .. | in lond | nil | in goods | £20 | & hath a bill |
| Bill man | Thomas Fowler Husb. & tenant to the seid chieff lord .. .. | in lond | nil | in goods | £10 | & hath a bill |
|          | Margaret Draper widow & tenant to the seid chieff lord .. .. | annuite | £5 | in goods | £12 13s 4d | — |

1. *The initial letter is ambiguous and could be 'C'. I prefer 'Bretten' which occurs several times.*

|  | Name | in lond |  | in goods |  | Note |
|---|---|---|---|---|---|---|
|  | William Richardson Husb. & tenant to the seid chieff lord | in lond | nil | in goods | £10 | & hath a bill |
|  | Thomas Bradley Husb. & tenant to the seid chieff lord | in lond | nil | in goods | £10 | — |
|  | George Amore Husband. & tenant to the seid chieff lord | in lond | nil | in goods | £12 13s 4d | — |
|  | Robert Wyles Husb. & tenant to the sied chieff lord | in lond | nil | in goods | 40s | — |
|  | William Whitwell Husb. & tenant to the seid chieff lord | in lond | nil | in goods | £6 | — |
| Bill man | John Bell Husb. & tenant to the seid chieff lord | in lond | nil | in goods | £3 | — |
|  | Johan Ward widow & tenant to the seid chieff lord | in lond | nil | in goods | £4 | — |
| Archer | John Mathew laborer & tenant to the seid chieff lord | in lond | nil | in goods | £3 | — |
|  | John Whitwell Husb. & tenant to the seid chieff lord | in lond | nil | in goods | £7 | — |
|  | John Fynne Husb. & tenant to the seid chieff lord | in lond | nil | in goods | £6 | — |
|  | William Gunthorp Husb. & tenant to the seid chieff lord | in lond | nil | in goods | £6 | — |
|  |  | **£70 6s 8d** | | **£222 6s 8d** | | |

*f. 30v (58)*

|  | Name | in lond |  | in goods |  | Note |
|---|---|---|---|---|---|---|
| Bill man | Robert Noot Husb. & tenant to the seid chieff lord | in lond | nil | in goods | £6 | — |
|  | Thomas Broke Husb. & tenant to the seid chieff lord | in lond | nil | in goods | £3 | — |
| Bill man | John Gunthorp Husb. & tenant to the seid chieff lord | in lond | nil | in goods | £4 | — |
| Bill man | Richard Asshwell Husb. & tenant to the seid chieff lord | in lond | nil | in goods | £5 | — |
|  | William Burges Husb. & tenant to the seid chieff lord | in lond | nil | in goods | 40s | — |
|  | Thomas Walker Husb. & tenant to the seid chieff lord | in lond | nil | in goods | 40s | — |
|  | Henry Fowler laborer & tenant to the seid chieff lord | in lond | nil | in goods | 20s | — |
|  | Robert Newell Husb. & tenant to the seid chieff lord | in lond | nil | in goods | 40s | — |
| Bill man | Robert Redhed laborer & tenant to seid the chieff lord | in lond | nil | in goods | 30s | — |
|  | William Thompson laborer & tenant to the seid chieff lord | in lond | nil | in goods | 20s | — |
|  | John Coole laborer & tenant to the seid chieff lord | in lond | nil | in goods | 20s | — |
| Bill man | Robert Howis laborer & tenant to the seid chieff lord | in lond | nil | in goods nil | | a pore yong man |
| Archer | Edward Richardson son to the seid William Richardson | in lond | nil | in goods nil | | yong men & pore |
| Bill man | John Freman seruant & son to the seid Robert Freman | | | | | |
| Archer | Robert Fynne seruant to the seid Johan Warde | | | | | |

| | | | | | |
|---|---|---|---|---|---|
| Bill man | Raff Nott son to the seid Robert Nott .. .. .. | | | | |
| Archer | William Reysyng seruant to Edward Burton .. .. | in lond    nil | | in goods nil | yong men & pore |
| Archer | Robert Asshwell seruant to Margaret Draper .. .. | | | | |

The Church Stoke    20s

20s    £28 10s

*f. 31*

## UPPYNGHAM

| | | | | | |
|---|---|---|---|---|---|
| | The Kyng owr souereign lord is chieff lord of the seid Town | | | | |
| | Edward Digby Esquier is Steward of the seid Town .. .. .. .. | in Fez | 6s 8d | in lond  nil q.e. | — |
| | William Moldar Clerk is parson of the seid Town .. .. | parsonage | £17 | in goods nil q.e. | — |
| | Edward Chisselden gent. & hath lond their .. .. .. | — | £16 | in goods   20 marks | — |
| | Richard Chisselden gent, & tenant to the seid chieff lord .. .. | in lond | 40s | in goods nil q.e. | — |
| | William Ingwardby is parich prest .. | stipend | £5 | in goods    40s | — |
| Archer | Richard Irelond the yonger yoman hath lond their .. .. .. | — | £5 | in goods £20 | — |
| Bill man | John Welles Husb. & tenant to the seid chieff lord .. .. .. | in lond | 26s 8d | in goods £20 | — |
| | Bartilmewe Ouerton gent. hath londs, seruant to the lord Hastynges .. | in lond | nil | in goods £16 | — |
| | John Choueney Husband & fermer to the parson .. .. | in lond | nil | in goods £16 | — |
| Bill man | William Brige Draper & tenant to the seid chieff lord .. .. .. | in lond | nil | in goods £30 | — |
| | William Bell haberdasher & tenant to the seid chieff lord .. .. | in lond | nil | in goods £30 | & hath a Sallet |
| | Thomas Affell Husb. & tenant to the seid chieff lord .. .. .. | in lond | nil | in goods £20 | — |
| Archer | Ambrose Grene Bocher & tenant to the seid chieff lord .. .. | in lond | nil | in goods £20 | — |
| Bill man | William Salysbury Husb. & tenant to the Kyng .. .. .. | in lond | nil | in goods £30 | — |
| Archer | John Bocher Husb. & tenant to the seid chieff lord .. .. | in lond | nil | in goods £20 | — |
| Archer | Richard Horsley Husb. & tenant to the seid chieff lord .. .. | in lond | nil | in goods £20 | — |
| Bill man | Edward Sympson Husb. & tenant to the seid chieff lord .. .. | in lond | nil | in goods £10 | — |
| Archer | Roger Wilson Husb. & tenant to the seid chieff lord .. .. | in lond | nil | in goods £10 | — |
| Archer | Thomas Chitwood Husb. & tenant to the seid chieff lord .. .. | in lond | nil | in goods £15 | — |
| | Richard Lyncold Draper & tenant to the seid chieff lord .. .. | in lond | nil | in goods £15 | — |
| | Roger Laughton Husb. & tenant to John Digby gent. .. .. .. | in lond | nil | in goods £7 | & hath a jestorn with a Sallet |

£46 13s 4d    £312 6s 8d

*f. 31v*

| | | | | | |
|---|---|---|---|---|---|
| Archer | Phillip Awyncull Husb. & tenant to the seid Edward Chisselden .. .. in lond | nil | in goods £10 | — |
| Archer | Richard Chitwood mercer & tenant to the seid chieff lord .. .. in lond | nil | in goods £10 | — |
| Bill man | Richard Hogekyn Husb. & tenant to the seid chieff lord .. .. .. in lond | nil | in goods £15 | — |
| Archer | George Pakman Husb. & tenant to the seid chieff lord .. .. .. in lond | nil | in goods £10 | — |
| Bill man | Robert Drayton Husb. & tenant to the seid chieff lord .. .. .. in lond | nil | in goods £7 | — |
| Bill man | William Lokwood Husb. & tenant to the seid chieff lord .. .. in lond | nil | in goods £3 6s 8d | — |
| | John Adaway Husb. & tenant to the seid chieff lord .. .. .. in lond | nil | in goods £4 | — |
| Archer | William Bull Husb. & tenant to the seid chieff lord .. .. .. in lond | nil | in goods £5 | & hath a paire of cors[lets] |
| | Alice Chitwood widow & tenant to the seid chieff lord .. .. in lond | nil | in goods £4 | — |
| | Hugh Downe Husb. & tenant to the seid chieff lord .. .. .. in lond | nil | in goods £7 | — |
| | John Bennyt Husb. & tenant to the seid chieff lord .. .. .. in lond | nil | in goods £5 | — |
| Bill man | Richard Wilson Husb. & tenant to the seid chieff lord .. .. .. in lond | nil | in goods £3 | — |
| Archer | John Robynson Husb. & tenant to the seid chieff lord .. .. .. in lond | nil | in goods £5 | — |
| Bill man | John Horseley laborer & tenant to the seid lord .. .. .. in lond | nil | in goods £3 | — |
| Bill man | Richard Fox Waxchaundeller & tenant to the seid lord .. .. in lond | nil | in goods £4 | — |
| | Robert Lyon laborer & tenant to the seid chieff lord .. .. .. in lond | nil | in goods 40s | — |
| | John Agroue laborer & tenant to the seid chieff lord .. .. .. in lond | nil | in goods 40s | — |
| Bill man | Richard Walker laborer & tenant to the seid chieff lord .. .. in lond | nil | in goods 40s | — |
| Archer | John Richardson Husb. & tenant to the seid chieff lord .. .. in lond | nil | in goods 40s | — |
| | Richard Irelond thelder Husb. & tenant to the seid chieff lord .. .. in lond | nil | in goods nil | a pore old man |
| [Archer] | William Oxon laborer & tenant to the seid chieff lord .. .. in lond | nil | in goods 40s | — |
| | William Glouer laborer & tenant to the seid chieff lord .. .. in lond | nil | in goods 40s | — |
| Archer | Richard Murdok laborer & tenant to the seid Richard Chisselden .. .. in lond | nil | in goods 20s | — |
| | | **20s** | **£108 6s 8d** | |

*f. 32*

| | | | | | |
|---|---|---|---|---|---|
| Bill man | Richard Presgrave laborer & tenant to the seid chieff lord .. .. in lond | nil | in goods 20s | — |
| | Richard Gravell laborer & tenant to the seid lord .. .. .. in lond | nil | in goods 20s | — |

| | | | | | |
|---|---|---|---|---|---|
| | Bartilmew Kyrk seruant | in lond | nil | in goods | 20s | — |
| | Thomas Glouer laborer & tenant to the seid chieff lord | in lond | nil | in goods | 30s | — |
| | John Brigstoke laborer & tenant to the seid chieff lord | in lond | nil | in goods | 20s | — |

|  |  |  |  |  |  |
|---|---|---|---|---|---|
| | Henry Botton laborer .. .. | | | | |
| | Thomas Smyth laborer .. | | | | |
| | Humfrey Down laborer .. | | | | |
| Archer | John Down laborer .. .. | | | | |
| | William Andrew laborer .. | | | | |
| | Thomas Gravell laborer .. | | | | |
| | Thomas Harreson laborer .. | | | | |
| | Edmund Bull laborer .. .. | | | | |
| | Humfrey Hill seruant to Edward Digby Esquier .. | | | | |
| Bill man | John Bele laborer .. .. | in lond | nil | in goods nil | yong men & pore |
| Bill man | Raff Atkyn laborer .. .. | | | | |
| | Richard Atkyn laborer .. | | | | |
| Bill man | William Lacy laborer .. | | | | |
| Bill man | John Taillor laborer .. .. | | | | |
| | John Murdok laborer .. .. | | | | |
| Bill man | John Colbe laborer .. .. | | | | |
| | John None laborer .. .. | | | | |
| Bill man | John Baker laborer .. .. | | | | |
| | John Long seruant .. .. | | | | |
| | Henry Lokwood laborer .. | | | | |

The Church Stoke   nil
The Stoke of the Gyld   40s
End of this Hundred

*f. 32v*
**EGILTON**                       **OKAM SOKON IN COUNTY RUTLOND**

| | | | | | |
|---|---|---|---|---|---|
| | The Kyng Ower souereign lord is Chieff lord of the seid Town | | | | |
| | Roger Radclyff Esquier is Steward of the seid Town .. .. | Fez | 3 marks 6s 8d | in goods nil q.e. | — |
| | The Abbot of Westminster is parson of the seid Town & summed in Okham hoole .. .. .. | parsonnage goes in the sum of Okham Rectory | | in goods nil q.e. | — |
| Bill man | Robert Fowler Husbond & tenant to the seid chieff lord .. .. | in lond | nil | in goods £16 | — |
| | Thomas Barforth is parich prest of the seid town .. .. .. | stipend | £5 | in goods £4 | — |
| | Thomas Maltson Husb. & tenant to the seid chieff lord .. .. | in londs | nil | in goods £10 | — |
| | Robert Leyff Husb. & tenant to the seid chieff lord .. .. .. | in londs | nil | in goods £10 | — |
| [Bill man] | John Fowler Husb. & tenant to the seid chieff lord .. .. | in lond | nil | in goods £10 | — |
| | Richard Redmyld Husb. & tenant to the seid chieff lord .. .. | in londs | nil | in goods £6 | — |
| | Thomas Sharpe Husb. & tenant to the seid chieff lord .. .. .. | in londs | nil | in goods £6 | — |

| | | | | | | |
|---|---|---|---|---|---|---|
| Bill man | Robert A Manton Husb. & tenant to the seid chieff lord .. .. .. | in lond | nil | in goods | £8 | — |
| | John Porter Husb. & tenant to the seid chieff lord .. .. .. | in londs | nil | in goods | £5 | — |
| | Thomas Sharp laborer & tenant to the seid chieff lord .. .. .. | in lond | nil | in goods | £5 | — |
| | Richard Leyff laborer .. .. <br> William Hyeway laborer .. <br> John Hichecok laborer .. <br> John A Manton laborer .. <br> Richard Seyton laborer .. <br> John [Eytor ?] laborer .. .. | in lond | nil | in goods | nil | old men & pore |
| | Richard Lednam laborer .. | in lond | nil | in goods | nil | yong man & pore |

The Church Stoke   nil

**£7   6s   8d**        **£80**

*f. 33*

## KYLPESHAM

| | | | | | | |
|---|---|---|---|---|---|---|
| | The lord Souch is chieff lord of the seid Town .. .. .. | in lond | £10 | in goods | nil q.e. | — |
| | John Haryngton thelder is Steward of the seid Town .. .. | in Fez | 13s 4d | in goods | nil q.e. | — |
| | Sir Richard Fowler is parson of the seid Town .. .. .. | parsonage | £7 | in goods | nil q.e. | — |
| | Richard Taillor prest is chauntre prest their .. .. .. | in lond | £7 | in goods | £7 | — |
| | Hugh Coo is parich prest of the seid Town .. .. .. | stipend | £5 | in goods | 20s | — |
| | Thomas Bowre Husb. & tenant to the seid chieff lord .. .. | in lond | nil | in goods | £18 | & hath a Jestorn a Sallet with a Bill |
| | John Parker yoman & tenant to the seid lord .... .. | in lond | nil | in goods | £7 | — |
| Bill man | Thomas Garaway Husb. & tenant to the seid lord .. .. .. | in lond | nil | in goods | 50s | — |
| Bill man | Thomas Osterby Husb. & tenant to the seid lord .. .. .. | in lond | nil | in goods | £10 | — |
| Bill man | Thomas Carter Husb. & tenant to the seid lord .. .. .. | in lond | nil | in goods | £3 | — |
| | William Carter the yonger laborer & tenant to the seid lord .. | in lond | nil | in goods | 40s | — |
| | John Harryson tenant to the seid lord | in lond | nil | in goods | 40s | — |
| | Thomas Trowgton laborer & tenant to the seid lord .. .. | in lond | nil | in goods | 40s | — |
| | John Lynby laborer & tenant to the seid lord .. .. .. | in lond | nil | in goods | 40s | — |
| | John Garrard laborer & tenant to the seid lord Souch .. .. | in lond | nil | in goods | 20s | — |
| | Margarit Raff widow & tenant to the seid lord .. .. .. | in lond | 5s | in goods | £3 | — |
| Archer | Richard Croose laborer .. <br> Robert Carter laborer .. <br> William Carter laborer .. | in lond | nil | in goods | nil | yong men & pore |

The Church Stoke   6s 8d

**£29 18s   4d**       **£60 16s   8d**

*f. 33v*
**BROKE**

| | | | | | |
|---|---|---|---|---|---|
| | The prior of Broke Abbey is Chieff lord of the seid Town .. .. .. in lond | 20 marks | in goods £13 6s 8d | — |
| | The lord Hastyngs other weis called George Hastyngs knyght the lord of Hastyngs is Steward of the seid Town fez | 20s | in goods nil q.e. | — |
| | The Abbot of Westminster hath lond their .. .. .. .. — | 10s | in goods nil q.e. | — |
| Archer | Thomas Rigeley Husbondman & tenant to the seid prior .. .. in lond | nil | in goods £5 | — |
| | Thomas Knolles Husb. & tenant to the seid prior .. .. .. .. in lond | nil | in goods £7 | — |
| | Raff Peper Husb. & tenant to the seid prior .. .. .. .. in lond | nil | in goods £12 | — |
| Archer | John Barnes Husb. & tenant to the seid prior .. .. .. in lond | nil | in goods £5 | — |
| Archer | Thomas Ward Husb. & tenant to the seid prior .. .. .. in lond | nil | in goods £7 | — |
| Bill man | William Allen laborer & tenant to the seid prior .. .. .. in lond | nil | in goods 20s | — |
| | William Ward Husb. & tenant to the seid prior .. .. .. in lond | nil | in goods £8 | — |
| | William Dikons Husb. & tenant to the seid prior .. .. .. in lond | nil | in goods £8 | — |
| | Robert Smale Husb. & tenant to the seid prior .. .. .. in lond | nil | in goods £6 | — |
| Archer | Richard Bailly seruant to the seid prior & tenant .. .. in lond | nil | in goods 20s | — |
| Bill man | Edmund Leyff howsehold seruant to John Haryngton Esquier .. .. in lond | nil | in goods 40s | — |
| | William Perkyns laborer & tenant to the seid Prior .. .. .. .. in lond | nil | in goods 40s | — |
| | Ellyn Wilcokes widow & tenant to the seid Prior .. .. .. .. in lond | nil | in goods £3 | — |
| | Thomas Hawley laborer & tenant to the seid prior .. .. .. in lond | nil | in goods 20s | — |
| | Margaret Swaynston widow & tenant to the seid prior .. .. .. in lond | nil | in goods £7 | — |
| | Thomas One laborer & tenant to the seid prior .. .. .. in lond | nil | in goods 40s | — |

Richard [Rogers] seruant to
Thomas Knollis        ..      ..

Archer    John Hoby seruant to
William Warde      ..      ..                    in lond    nil        in goods nil        yong men & pore

[Bill man] Robert Swaynston seruant
to Ellyn Wilcokes      ..      ..

[Bill man] John [Harpon] seruant to
Margaret Swaynston      ..

John Perkyns laborer      ..

| | | | |
|---|---|---|---|
| | The Church Stoke | £4 | |
| | Robert Wylies is parich prest their of the seid Town .. .. .. stipend | £5 | in goods 3 marks | — |

|   |   |
|---|---|
| [faded] | £93 |

*f. 34*
**WARDLEY**

| | | | | | | |
|---|---|---|---|---|---|---|
| | Robert Brudenell Knyght is chieff lord of the seid town .. .. .. | in lond | £8 | in goods nil q.e. | | — |
| | William Ouerton Gent. is steward of the seid Town .. .. .. .. | feez | 40*d* | in goods nil q.e. | | — |
| | Robert Baxster yoman hath lond their | | 6*s* 8*d* | in goods nil q.e. | | — |
| | Edward Chisselden gent. hath lond their .. .. .. .. | | 10*s* | in goods nil q.e. | | — |
| Bill man | John Roberd Husb. .. .. .. | in lond | 10*s* | in goods | £4 | — |
| Bill man | William Brome Husb. & tenant to the seid lord .. .. .. .. | in lond | nil | in goods | £24 | — |
| [Bill man] | Thomas Roberd Husb. & tenant to the seid lord .. .. .. .. | in lond | nil | in goods | £15 | — |
| | Robert Cantyng Husb. & tenant to the seid lord .. .. .. .. | in lond | nil | in goods | £10 | — |
| | Henry Grov' Husb. & tenant to the seid Edward Chisselden .. .. | in lond | nil | in goods | 40*s* | — |
| | Richard Whitt Husb. & tenant to the seid Edward Chisselden | in lond | nil | in goods | 40*s* | — |
| [Archer] | Thomas Cleypole yoman & seruant to the lord Hastyngs .. .. | in lond | nil | in goods | £3 | & hath harness sufficient for a man |
| Archer | John Cleypole seruant to the prior of Laund Abbey .. .. .. | in lond | nil | in goods | £3 | — |
| | William Taillor Husb. & tenant to the seid lord .. .. .. .. | in lond | nil | in goods | 40*s* | — |
| | Thomas Taillor Husb. & tenant to the seid lord .. .. .. .. | in lond | nil | in goods | 40*s* | — |
| | Richard Elsham Husb. & tenant to the seid lord .. .. .. .. | in lond | nil | in goods | 40*s* | — |
| | John Canyng laborer & tenant to the seid lord .. .. .. .. | in lond | nil | in goods | 20*s* | — |
| | William Asshley laborer .. | } in lond | nil | in goods nil | | yong men & pore |
| Archer | Richard Redish laborer .. | | | | | |
| | Edmond Hustler is parson of the seid Town .. .. .. .. | parsonage | 11 marks | in goods | 12 marks | — |

The Church Stoke   nil

[faded]                         £78

*f. 34v*
**BELTON**

| | | | | | |
|---|---|---|---|---|---|
| The Kyng owr souereign lord is chieff lord of the seid Town .. .. .. | | | | | |
| The lord Mountioy hath lond their .. | in lond | £18 | in goods nil q.e. | | — |
| The Prior of Laund Abbey is parson of the seid Town .. .. .. | parsonage | 5 marks | in goods nil q.e. | | — |
| William Haukinge chappelyn is Vicar their .. .. .. .. | vicarige | 6 marks | in goods | £11 | — |
| Thomas Brokesby Gent. is steward of the seid Town .. .. .. | in feez | 6*s* 8*d* | in goods nil q.e. | | — |
| The seid Prior of Laund hath lond their .. .. .. .. .. | | 20*s* | in goods nil q.e. | | — |
| The Prior of Broke Habbey hath lond their .. .. .. .. .. | | 40*s* | in goods nil q.e. | | — |
| The Abbot of Osolueston hath lond their .. .. .. .. .. | | 2*s* | in goods nil q.e. | | — |

| | | | | | | |
|---|---|---|---|---|---|---|
| | John Ward Husb. & tenant to the seid lord Mountioy .. .. .. | in lond | 13s 4d | in goods | £3 | — |
| [Archer] | Thomas [Aleyster], Husb, & tenant to the seid lord Mountioy .. | in lond | 6s | in goods | 40s | — |
| [Archer] | Thomas Leyster Husb. & seruant to Oustyn Hasylbrige gent. .. | in lond | 8s | in goods | £6 | & hath sufficient harnes for hymself |
| | Hugh Dalkes yoman .. .. .. | in lond | 8s | in goods | £6 | — |
| | Robert Phillip Husb. & tenant to the seid lord Mountioy .. .. | in lond | 4s | in goods | 40s | — |
| | Cristofer Webster Husb. .. .. | in lond | 4s | in goods nil q.e. | | — |
| | Thomas Olyuer Husb. .. | in lond | 5s | in goods nil q.e. | | — |
| | Richard Tailler Yoman & bailly to the seid lord Mountioy .. .. | in lond | nil | in goods | £8 | & hath harness a Sallet [a paire] of Brigga[ndines] a paire of splynts, a shert of [mail], a gorgit with a Bill |
| Archer | John Parker Yoman reteyned to the lord Hastynges & tenant to the seid lord Mountioy .. .. .. .. | in lond | [faded] | in goods | £4 | — |
| Bill man | Robert Suston Husb. & tenant to the seid lord Mountioy .. .. .. | in lond | [faded] | in goods | £8 | — |
| | Robert Newman Husb. & tenant to the seid lord Mountioy .. .. | in lond | nil | in goods | £6 | — |
| | Thomas Newman Husb. & tenant to the seid lord Mountioy .. .. | in lond | nil | in goods | £6 | — |
| | Watter Angell Husb. & tenant to the seid lord Mountioy .. .. | in lond | nil | in goods | £3 | — |
| | John Royse Husb. & tenant to the seid lord Mountioy .. .. | in lond | nil | in goods | £5 | — |
| | | | [faded] | | £65 | |

*f. 35*

| | | | | | | |
|---|---|---|---|---|---|---|
| | John Clement Husb. & tenant to the seid prior of Broke .. .. | in lond | nil | in goods | £4 | — |
| Bill man | William Hayle Husb. & tenant to the seid lord Mountioy .. .. | in lond | nil | in goods | £5 | — |
| | Thomas Tillowstell Husb. & tenant to the seid lord Mountioy .. .. | in lond | nil | in goods | £3 | — |
| | Richard Barker Husb. & tenant to the seid lord Mountioy .. .. | in lond | nil | in goods | £3 | — |
| | Thomas Clement Husb. & tenant to the seid lord Mountioy .. .. | in lond | nil | in goods | £4 | — |
| | Thomas A Ridlington Husb. & tenant to the seid prior of Laund .. .. | in lond | nil | in goods | £7 | — |
| Bill man | William Colles Husb. & tenant to the seid lord Mountioy .. .. | in lond | nil | in goods | £4 | — |
| | Robert Wyggenton laborer & tenant to the seid lord Mountioy .. .. | in lond | nil | in goods | 20s | — |
| | Thomas Saunder laborer & tenant to ther seid Hugh Dalkes .. .. | in lond | nil | in goods | 20s | — |
| | Cristofer Saunder Husb. & tenant to the seid lord Mountioy .. .. | in lond | nil | in goods | £3 | — |
| | Thomas Hall Husb. & tenant to the seid lord Mountioy .. .. | in lond | nil | in goods | £4 | — |

| | | | | | |
|---|---|---|---|---|---|
| | William Hart laborer & tenant to the seid Thomas A Leyster | in lond | nil | in goods 20s | — |
| | William Clement Husb. & tenant to the seid lord Mountioy | in lond | nil | in goods £3 | — |
| | Richard Cooper laborer & tenant to the seid lord Mountioy | in lond | nil | in goods 20s | — |
| | Bartilmewe P[*MS torn*] laborer & tenant to the seid lord Mountioy | in lond | nil | in goods 20s | — |
| | John Marchaunt laborer & tenant to the seid lord Mountioy | in lond | nil | in goods 20s | — |
| | Hugh Marshall laborer | | | | |
| | Robert Palfreman laborer | | | | |
| | Thomas Connell laborer | | | | |
| Archer | Laurence Taillor laborer | in lond | nil | in goods nil | yong men & pore |
| Bill man | Richard Laurence laborer | | | | |
| Bill man | John Roose laborer | | | | |

The Church Stoke   nil

nil                                £40

*f. 35v*

## OKHAM

| | | | | | |
|---|---|---|---|---|---|
| | The Kyng owr souereign lord is Chieff lord of the seid Town | | | | |
| | Roger Ratclyff Esquier is Steward of the seid Town | in feez | 5 marks | in goods nil q.e. | — |
| | The Abbot of Westminster is parson of the seid Town with Langham, Egilton & Barleythorp | parsonage | £49 | in goods nil q.e. | — |
| | William Butler Clerk is vicar of the seid Town | vicarige | 20 marks | in goods nil q.e. | — |
| | William Pereson is parich prest of the seid Town | stipend | £5 6s 8d | in goods £5 | — |
| | Thomas Sheperd Chappelyn | stipend | £5 | in goods 40s | — |
| | John Townsend chaplyn | stipend | £5 | in goods 40s | — |
| | Hugh Mervyn chaplyn to Jamys Waren gent. | stipend | £5 | in goods 20s | — |
| | Robert Gunby Warden of the Almeshowse of Okham | stipend | 20 marks | in goods 40s | — |
| | Jamys Waren gent. | in lond | 40s | in goods £33 | & hath on horse & harness for tow men sufficient |
| Bill man | William Plavis Yoman & tenant to the Kyng | in lond | 40s | in goods £200 | & hath harness sufficient for ij men |
| | Richard Morecroft grocer & tenant to the chieff lord | in lond | nil | in goods £50 | & hath harnes for on man |
| Bill man | Henry Jervis Yoman & tenant to the seid chieff lord | in lond | nil | in goods £20 | & hath harnes sufficient for iiij men |
| Bill man | Henry Wyght Yoman & tenant to the seid chieff lord | in lond | nil | in goods £40 | & hath harnes sufficient for a man |
| Archer | Niccolis Hill Yoman & seruant to the Kynges grace & tenant | in lond | nil | in goods £8 | — |
| Bill man | Robert Armystrong Draper & tenant to the seid chieff lord | in lond | nil | in goods £25 | — |
| Bill man | Cristofer Grene Shomaker & tenant to the seid chieff lord | in lond | nil | in goods £20 | — |

| | | | | | | |
|---|---|---|---|---|---|---|
| | William Symmys Husb. & tenant to the seid chieff lord .. .. .. | in lond | nil | in goods | £20 | — |
| Archer | William Eltham mercer & tenant to the seid chieff lord .. .. .. | in lond | nil | in goods | £20 | & hath harnes for a man |
| Archer | William Wright miller & tenant to the seid chieff lord .. .. .. .. | in lond | nil | in goods | £8 | — |
| Archer | William Glouer Barbour & tenant to the seid chieff lord & reteyned to John Digby Knyght .. .. .. | in lond | nil | in goods | £8 | & hath a bill |
| Archer | William Woodcok shomaker & tenant to the seid chieff lord .. .. | in lond | nil | in goods | £8 | — |
| | | | **£117 6s 8d** | | **£561** | |

*f. 36*

| | | | | | | |
|---|---|---|---|---|---|---|
| | William Nawnby Smyth & tenant to the seid chieff lord .. .. .. | in lond | nil | in goods | £5 | — |
| [Bill man] | William [Groue] Husb. & tenant to the seid chieff lord .. .. .. | in lond | nil | in goods | £5 | — |
| | Raff Symmys laborer & tenant to the seid chieff lord .. .. .. | in lond | nil | in goods | 20s | — |
| Archer | Hugh Turnor baker & tenant to the seid Jamys Waren | in lond | nil | in goods | £8 | — |
| | [Jamys][1] Sotherland glouer & tenant to the seid chieff lord .. .. | in lond | nil | in goods | £4 | & hath a Sallet with a bill |
| | Hugh Thorp bocher & tenant to the seid chieff lord .. .. .. | in lond | nil | in goods | £15 | — |
| | John Vellam bocher & tenant to the seid chieff lord .. .. .. | in lond | nil | in goods | 40s | — |
| | [John John ..][2] Husb. & tenant to the seid chieff lord .. .. .. | in lond | nil | in goods | £5 | — |
| | Thomas Medows laborer & tenant to the seid chieff lord .. .. | in lond | nil | in goods | 40s | — |
| | Thomas Lodyngton Husb. & tenant to the seid chieff lord .. .. .. | in lond | nil | in goods | £15 | — |
| | Thomas Trayford Dier & tenant to the seid chieff lord .. .. .. | in lond | nil | in goods | £5 | — |
| | William Guadryng laborer & tenant to the seid chieff lord .. .. | in lond | nil | in goods | 20s | — |
| | Raff Sharpe Sherman & tenant to the seid chieff lord .. .. .. | in lond | nil | in goods | £6 | & hath a Jak with a Sallet |
| | John Barker Dier & tenant to the seid chieff lord .. .. .. | in lond | nil | in goods | £7 | — |
| | William Bannyng Husbondman & tenant to the seid chieff lord .. .. | in lond | nil | in goods | £7 | — |
| | Stephen Bunnyng Husbond & tenant to the seid chieff lord .. .. | in lond | nil | in goods | £5 | — |
| | Henry Hachet Husbondman & tenant to the seid chieff lord .. .. .. | in lond | nil | in goods | £5 | — |
| | | | **nil** | | **£100** | |

1. *The Ms being faded, the name is conjecturally reconstructed from the Subsidy Return.*
2. *Cf. John Johnson, Husbandman, in the Subsidy Return.*

*f. 36v*

| | | | | | | |
|---|---|---|---|---|---|---|
| | William Bate Husbondman & tenant to the seid chieff lord .. .. .. | in lond | nil | in goods | £15 | — |
| Archer | Stepvyn Ouerend Shomaker & tenant to the seid chieff lord .. .. | in lond | nil | in goods | £6 | — |
| | Ottewell Crannowe Husbond & tenant to the seid chieff lord .. .. .. | in lond | nil | in goods | £6 | — |
| | Robert Paroter Husbondman & tenant to the seid chieff lord .. .. | in lond | nil | in goods | £5 | — |
| Archer | Robert Gilbert Husb. & tenant to the seid chieff lord .. .. .. | in lond | nil | in goods | £5 | — |
| | John Jakson Husb. & tenant to the seid chieff lord .. .. .. | in lond | nil | in goods | 40s | — |
| | John Dikman Bocher & tenant to the seid chieff lord .. .. .. | in lond | nil | in goods | 40s | — |
| Bill man | John Bennet Smyth & tenant to the seid chieff lord .. .. .. | in lond | 13s | in goods | £4 | — |
| Bill man | Henry Rathby Turnor & tenant to the seid chieff lord .. .. .. | in lond | nil | in goods | £6 | & hath a sallet |
| | Richard Carter Chapman & tenant to the seid chieff lord .. .. .. | in lond | nil | in goods | 20s | — |
| | Thomas P[att] glouer & tenant to the seid chieff lord .. .. .. | in lond | nil | in goods | 20s | — |
| Bill man | Miles Kyng seruant to the seid Robert Armystrong .. .. .. | in lond | nil | in goods | 40s | — |
| | Thomas Bregges Husb. & tenant to the seid chieff lord .. .. | in lond | nil | in goods | 20s | — |
| | John Adcok Husb. & tenant to the seid chieff lord .. .. .. | in lond | nil | in goods | 20s | — |
| | John Caterns Baker & tenant to the seid chieff lord .. .. .. | in lond | nil | in goods | 20s | — |
| | Thomas Marten laborer & tenant to the seid chieff lord .. .. | in lond | nil | in goods | 20s | — |
| | Robert Gounbe laborer & tenant to the seid chieff lord .. .. | in lond | nil | in goods | 26s 8d | — |
| | | | **13s** | | **£60 6s 8d** | |

*f. 37*

| | | | | | | |
|---|---|---|---|---|---|---|
| | Thomas Stanyerd seruant to the seid William Plovis .. .. | in lond | nil | in goods | 20s | — |
| | John Sharpe laborer & tenant to the seid Henry Wryght .. .. | in lond | nil | in goods | 20s | — |
| | John [Ousten] laborer & tenant to the seid chieff lord .. .. .. | in lond | nil | in goods | 26s 8d | — |
| | Richard Sharpe Tailler & tenant to the seid chieff lord .. .. | in lond | nil | in goods | 20s | — |
| | Dauid Bunnyng seruant .. | in lond | nil | in goods | 40s | — |
| | Thomas Fyndern seruant to William Wright .. .. | in lond | nil | in goods | 20s | — |
| Archer | John Jamys laborer .. ..<br>Cristofer Page laborer .. ..<br>John Dynsell laborer .. ..<br>John Andrew laborer .. ..<br>John Jarden laborer .. ..<br>Cristofer Johnson laborer .. | in lond | nil | in goods nil | | yong men & pore |

Richard Hoogyn laborer ..
William Vellam laborer ..
William Kellit laborer ..
Richard Luter minstrell ..
Thomas Richworth laborer ..
John Grey seruant .. ..
William Barret seruant to
John Vellam .. .. ..
Richard Fyrkyll seruant to
Thomas Crayford .. ..
[Thomas] Clerk seruant [to the
seid] Cristor Grene .. ..
Cristor Benson Furbissher ..
Roger seruant to Raff Sharpe
John Ward seruant to the seid
Harry Hacher .. .. ..

in lond    nil      in goods nil      yong men & pore

nil      **£7   6s   8d**

*f. 37v*

Thomas Grenebank seruant to
William Eltham .. .. in lond   nil    in goods nil    yong man & pore
Thomas Sharpe laborer ..
William Baldok laborer ..
William Nawnbe laborer ..
John Catton laborer .. ..
Richard Gybson laborer ..
Rowlond Barbour laborer ..
John Fairechild laborer ..
John Selue laborer .. ..
William Snell laborer ..
William Edson laborer ..
William Clyff laborer ..
John Jamys laborer .. ..
Cristor Page sadler .. ..

in lond   nil    in goods nil    old men & pore

## OKAM SOKON INFRA FEODUM ABBATIS WESTMONASTERII (The Abbot's Fee)

| | | | | | |
|---|---|---|---|---|---|
| | The Abbot of Westminster is Chieff lord of the seid fee .. .. .. in lond | £21 | in goods nil q.e. | — |
| | John Digby Knyght is steward of the seid fee .. .. .. .. Feez | 6s 8d | in goods nil q.e. | — |
| Bill man | Maunder Crannow Husb. & tenant to the seid Abbot .. .. .. in lond | 20s | in goods £10 | & hath a jestorn .. a sallet .. .. |
| Bill man | Robert Hopkyn weuer & tenant to the seid Abbot .. .. .. .. in lond .. .. .. | | in goods £5 | [MS torn] |
| | William Pylkyngton Tanner & tenant to the seid Abbot .. .. .. in lond | nil | in goods £6 | — |
| | William Fyrkell Husb. & tenant to the seid Abbot .. .. .. .. in lond | nil | in goods £3 | — |
| | Richard Scherpe Sherman & tenant to the seid Abbot .. .. in lond | nil | in goods 40s | — |

[faded]      **£36**

*f. 38*

## OKAM CUM BARLYTHORP

| | | | | | | |
|---|---|---|---|---|---|---|
| Bill man | William Cantyng laborer & tenant to the seid Abbot .. .. .. .. | in lond | nil | in goods | 20s | — |
| | John Wryght the yonger Husb. & tenant to the seid Abbot .. .. | in lond | nil | in goods | 40s | — |
| | William [Hand] Husb. & tenant to the seid Abbot .. .. .. .. | in lond | nil | in goods | £8 | — |
| | Thomas Nownwyk laborer & tenant to the seid Abbot .. .. .. | in lond | nil | in goods | 20s | — |
| | Richard [Wright] Husbond & tenant seid Abbot .. .. .. .. | in lond | nil | in goods | £4 | — |
| | Thomas Cantyng Husb. & tenant to the seid Abbot .. .. .. .. | in lond | nil | in goods | £3 | — |
| | William Pylkyngton the yonger [laborer] | in lond | nil | in goods nil | | yong man & pore |
| [Archer] | Richard Pylkyngton Husb. & tenant to the seid Abbot .. .. .. | in lond | nil | in goods | £3 | — |
| | Hugh Jorden Husbond & tenant to the seid Abbot .. .. .. .. | in lond | nil | in goods | £16 | — |
| | Roger Flower gentilman hath lond their .. .. .. .. | in lond | 53s 4d | in goods nil q.e. | | — |
| | William Shepperd Husb. & tenant to the seid Abbot .. .. .. .. | in lond | nil | in goods | £4 | — |
| | John Pylkyngton Husbond & tenant to the seid Abbot .. .. .. | in lond | nil | in goods | £3 | — |
| [Bill man] | John Olyman laborer & tenant to the seid Abbot .. .. .. | in lond | nil | in goods | 20s | — |
| Archer | Thomas Thornton laborer & tenant to the seid Abbot .. .. | in lond | nil | in goods | 20s | — |
| | Peter Slye, Walker & tenant to the seid Abbot .. .. .. | in lond | nil | in goods | 20s | — |
| | John Jorden Husbond & tenant to the seid Abbot .. .. .. .. | in lond | nil | in goods | £8 | — |
| | Henry Maye Husbond & tenant to the seid Abbot .. .. .. .. | in lond | nil | in goods | £7 | — |
| | | | 53s 4d | | [£63] | |

*f. 38v*

| | | | | | | |
|---|---|---|---|---|---|---|
| Bill man | William Williams Husb. & tenant to the seid Abbot .. .. .. .. | in lond | nil | in goods | £7 | — |
| Archer | John Hall laborer & tenant to the seid Abbot .. .. .. | in lond | nil | in goods nil | | — |
| Bill man | Robert Grene laborer & seruant to Jamys Waren gent. .. .. .. | in lond | nil | in goods nil | | — |
| Archer | John Pylkyngton, the yonger, laborer | in lond | nil | in goods nil | | — |
| | William Wymfeld seruant to Maunder Crannow .. .. | | | | | |
| | John Cantyng seruant to John Olyman .. .. .. | | | | | |
| | Fraunces Hoogyn seruant to Robert Hokyn .. .. .. | in lond | nil | in goods nil | | yong men & pore |
| | William Luff seruant to William Pylkyngton .. .. | | | | | |
| Bill man | William Pylkyngton the son of John Pylkyngton .. .. | | | | | |

| | | | | | |
|---|---|---|---|---|---|
| Bill man | John Barnys laborer .. .. <br> Robert Cantyng laborer .. <br> Richard Smyth laborer .. <br> John Hareyson seruant to <br> William Hand .. .. .. <br> William Hanson seruant to <br> Hugh Jorden .. .. .. | in lond | nil | in goods nil | yong men & pore |
| | | | [nil] | £7 | |

*f. 39*

**BRAUNSTON**

| | | | | | |
|---|---|---|---|---|---|
| | The Kyng owr souereign lord is chieff <br> lord of the seid Town | | | | |
| | Roger Ratclyff Esquier is Steward of <br> the seid Town .. .. .. .. | in feez | 6s | in goods nil q.e. | — |
| Archer | Simon Swaffeld Gent. hath lond their | | £11 | in goods £20 | — |
| | Edward Chisselden gent. hath lond <br> their .. .. .. .. .. | | £9 | in goods nil q.e. | — |
| | The Prior of the Abbey of Broke <br> hath lond their .. .. .. | | £3 | in goods nil q.e. | — |
| | Richard Flower Squier hath lond their | | 11s 6d | in goods nil q.e. | — |
| | Robert Borow gent. hath lond their | | 20s | in goods nil q.e. | — |
| | John Burton Husbond & tenant to <br> the seid Simon .. .. .. .. in lond | in lond | 14s | in goods £20 | — |
| | William Kyng Yoman & tenant to <br> the seid chieff lord .. .. .. in lond | in lond | 4s | in goods nil q.e. | — |
| | William Morell Husb. & tenant to <br> the seid Edward Chisselden .. .. in lond | in lond | 7s | in goods £7 | — |
| | Richard Lacy Husbond & tenant to <br> the seid Simon .. .. .. .. in lond | in lond | 10s | in goods £4 | — |
| | Richard A Buttre Husbond .. .. in lond | in lond | 13s 4d | in goods nil q.e. | — |
| | John Framyngham Yoman hath <br> lond their .. .. .. .. | | 7s | in goods £10 | — |
| | Thomas Lacy[1] tenant to the chieff lord in lond | in lond | nil | in goods £14 | — |
| | William Lacy tenant to the seid Simon in lond | in lond | nil | in goods £16 | — |
| | William Dalby Husb. & tenant to the <br> seid Edward Chisselden .. .. in lond | in lond | nil | in goods £10 | — |
| | | | [faded] | [faded] | |

*f. 39v*

| | | | | | |
|---|---|---|---|---|---|
| Bill man | John Alee Husbond & tenant to <br> the seid prior .. .. .. .. in lond | in lond | nil | in goods £9 | — |
| Bill man | Cristor Law Husbond & tenant to the <br> seid Richard Bottre .. .. .. in lond | in lond | nil | in goods £10 | — |
| | John Clerk Husbond & tenant to the <br> seid Simon Swaffeld .. .. .. in lond | in lond | nil | in goods £7 | — |
| | Simon Mayn Husbond & tenant to <br> the seid Edward Chisselden .. .. in lond | in lond | nil | in goods 40s | — |
| | William Mayn Husbond & tenant to <br> the seid Edward Chisselden .. .. in lond | in lond | nil | in goods 40s | — |
| | John Andrew Husbond & tenant to <br> the seid John Burton .. .. .. in lond | in lond | nil | in goods £7 | — |
| | John Crooft Husb. & tenant to the <br> seid Edward Chisselden .. .. in lond | in lond | nil | in goods 20s | — |

1. *Cf. the next entry; 'Long' may be a better reading*

|  | | | | | | |
|---|---|---|---|---|---|---|
|  | John Vnderwod laborer & tenant to the seid prior of Broke | in lond | nil | in goods | 20s | — |
| Archer | John Smyth Husbond & tenant to the seid Simon Swaffeld | in lond | nil | in goods | £5 | — |
|  | Richard Ragdall Husb. & tenant to the seid Simon Swaffeld | in lond | nil | in goods | £3 | — |
|  | Thomas Bray laborer & tenant to the seid Richard Flower | in lond | nil | in goods | 20s | — |
|  | William Down' laborer & tenant to the seid Simon Swaffeld | in lond | nil | in goods | 40s | — |
|  | Henry Peper Husbond & tenant to the seid Edward Chisselden | in lond | nil | in goods | £4 | — |
|  |  |  | [faded] |  | £53 |  |

*f. 40*

|  | | | | | | |
|---|---|---|---|---|---|---|
| Bill man | Robert Miller Husb. & tenant to the seid Simon Swaffeld | in lond | nil | in goods | 40s | — |
|  | John Awyng Husb. & tenant to the seid Edward Chisselden | in lond | nil | in goods | £4 | — |
|  | Robert Acton laborer & tenant to the seid Edward Chisselden | in lond | nil | in goods | 20s | — |
|  | Henry Merytt Husbond & tenant to the seid Robert Borow | in lond | nil | in goods | 40s | — |
|  | William Amore Husb. & tenant to the seid Simon Swaffeld | in lond | nil | in goods | £4 | — |
|  | Thomas Brown Husbond & tenant to the seid Richard Flower | in lond | nil | in goods | 40s | — |
|  | John Miller Husbondman & tenant to the seid Simon Swaffeld | in lond | nil | in goods | £6 | — |
|  | Thomas Alday Husbond & tenant to the seid Simon Swaffeld | in lond | nil | in goods | £5 | — |
|  | Robert Dicman Husbond & tenant to the seid Simon Swaffeld | in lond | nil | in goods | £5 | — |
|  | Thomas Edmond sheperd & tenant to the seid prior | in lond | nil | in goods | 20s | — |
| Bill man | John Cumberlond seruant to William Lacy | in lond | nil | in goods | 20s | — |
|  | John Clakwell laborer & tenant to the seid Simon Swaffeld | in lond | nil | in goods nil |  | — |
|  | Thomas Banes seruant to William Lacy | in lond | nil | in goods nil |  | — |
|  | Mathew Nower seruant to Richard Ragdall | in lond | nil | in goods nil |  | Yong & pore |
|  | The Church Stoke | nil |  |  |  |  |
|  |  | nil |  |  | £34 |  |

*f. 40v*

**LANGHAM**

|  | | | | | | |
|---|---|---|---|---|---|---|
|  | The Kyng owr souereign lord is chieff lord of the seid Town |  |  |  |  |  |
|  | The Abbot of Westminster is parson of the seid Town | parsonage is cessed in Okham Town |  |  |  |  |
|  | William Bromewynd is parich prest of the seid Town | stipend | [£5] | in goods | 40s | — |
|  | The Prior of Broke hath lond within the seid Town |  | 8s | in goods nil q.e. |  | — |

| | | | | |
|---|---|---|---|---|
| | Roger Ratclyff Esquier is steward of the seid Town .. .. .. .. in feez | [blank] | in goods nil q.e. | — |
| | William Villers gent, hath lond their | 10s | in goods nil q.e. | — |
| | Richard Flower Esquier hath lond their | 10s | in goods nil q.e. | — |
| | John Clerk yoman & tenant to the seid chieff lord .. .. .. .. in lond | nil | in goods £26 | & hath harnes sufficient for a man |
| | Henry Hobberd Husbond & tenant to the seid chieff lord .. .. .. in lond | nil | in goods £30 | & hath harnes sufficient for a man |
| | Gregory Smyth Husb. & tenant to the seid chieff lord .. .. .. .. in lond | nil | in goods £20 | [& hath harnes sufficient for a man] |
| | Nicolis Pittes Husbond & tenant to the seid chieff lord .. .. .. in lond | nil | in goods £12 | — |
| | William Welles Husbond & tenant to the seid chieff lord .. .. .. in lond | nil | in goods £8 | — |
| | John Ball Husbond & tenant to the seid chieff lord .. .. .. .. in lond | nil | in goods £15 | — |
| | Nicolis Pittes the yonger Husbondman & tenant to the seid chieff lord .. in lond | nil | in goods £8 | — |
| | Thomas Beston tenant to the seid chieff lord .. .. .. in lond | nil | in goods £8 | — |

*f. 41*

| | | | | |
|---|---|---|---|---|
| | Thomas Crane Husbond & tenant to the seid chieff lord .. .. .. in lond | nil | in goods £5 | — |
| | William Ball thelder Husbond & tenant to the seid chieff lord .. .. in lond | nil | in goods £8 | — |
| | William [May] Husbond & tenant to the seid chieff lord .. .. .. in lond | nil | in goods £6 | — |
| | [Thomas Waters] Husbond & tenant to the seid chieff lord .. .. .. in lond | nil | in goods £6 | — |
| | John Hunt Husbond & tenant to the seid chieff lord .. .. .. in lond | nil | in goods £6 | — |
| | [Thomas Trafford] Husbond & tenant to the seid chieff lord .. .. .. in lond | nil | in goods £7 | — |
| Bill man | Thomas Willows Husbond & tenant to the seid chieff lord .. .. .. in lond | nil | in goods £10 | — |
| | John Wylhowse Husbond & tenant to the seid chieff lord .. .. .. in lond | nil | in goods £4 | — |
| [Archer] | John Watson Husbond & tenant to the seid chieff lord .. .. .. in lond | nil | in goods £6 | — |
| | Thomas Hubberd Husbond & tenant to the seid chieff lord .. .. .. in lond | nil | in goods £10 | — |
| | Thomas Eggeton Husb. & tenant to the seid chieff lord .. .. .. in lond | nil | in goods 40s | — |
| | John Hubberd Husbond & tenant to the seid chieff lord .. .. .. in lond | nil | in goods 40s | — |
| | William Dikman thelder & tenant to the seid chieff lord .. .. .. in lond | nil | in goods 40s | — |
| Bill man | John Gilburn Husb. & tenant to the seid chieff lord .. .. .. .. in lond | nil | in goods £4 | — |
| | Henry Longfote Husbond & tenant to the seid chieff lord .. .. .. in lond | nil | in goods 50s | — |
| | Thomas Ball the yonger Husbond & tenant to the seid chieff lord .. .. in lond | nil | in goods £3 | — |
| | | [blank] | £83 10s | |

*f. 41v*

|  |  |  |  |  |  |  |
|---|---|---|---|---|---|---|
|  | William Brown laborer & tenant to the seid chieff lord .. .. .. in lond | nil | in goods | 20s |  | — |
|  | Thomas Bushe thelder tenant to the seid chieff lord .. .. .. .. in lond | nil | in goods | £4 |  | — |
|  | Thomas Bushe the yonger Husb. & tenant to the seid chieff lord .. .. in lond | nil | in goods | £3 |  | — |
|  | John Gibson Husbond & tenant to the seid chieff lord .. .. .. in lond | nil | in goods | 40s |  | — |
| Archer | John Thistilton laborer & tenant to the seid prior of Broke .. .. in lond | nil | in goods | 20s |  | — |
| Bill man | John Middleton Husbondm & tenant to the seid chieff lord .. .. .. in lond | nil | in goods | £5 |  | — |
| Bill man | William Dicman thelder laborer & tenant to the seid chieff lord .. .. in lond | nil | in goods | 30s |  | — |
| [Archer] | Thomas Wylford Husb. & tenant to the seid chieff lord .. .. .. in lond | nil | in goods | 40s |  | — |
| Bill man | Nicolis Palmer laborer & tenant to the seid chieff lord .. .. .. in lond | nil | in goods | 20s |  | — |
|  | William Sharpe Husb. & tenant to the seid chieff lord .. .. .. in lond | 18s | in goods | 40s |  | — |
| [Bill man] | Richard Andrew laborer & tenant to the seid chieff lord .. .. .. in lond | nil | in goods | 20s |  | — |
|  | Robert Pyttes Husbondman & tenant to the seid chieff lord .. .. .. in lond | nil | in goods | £4 |  | — |
|  | Robert Masson laborer & tenant to the seid Richard Flower .. .. in lond | nil | in goods | 20s |  | — |
|  | William Roose laborer & tenant to the seid chieff lord .. .. .. in lond | nil | in goods | 20s |  | — |
|  |  | [MS torn] |  | [MS torn] |  |  |

*f. 42*

|  |  |  |  |  |  |  |  |
|---|---|---|---|---|---|---|---|
|  | John Writte Husbond & tenant to the the seid chieff lord .. .. .. in lond | nil | in goods | £3 |  |  |  |
|  | Thomas Herd Turner & tenant to the seid chieff lord .. .. .. .. in lond | nil | in goods | 20s |  |  | — |
|  | William Bendbowe laborer & tenant to the seid chieff lord .. .. in lond | nil | in goods | 20s |  |  | — |
|  | William Bayle Husbond & tenant to the seid chieff lord .. .. .. in lond | nil | in goods | £10 |  |  |  |
| Archer | John Laurence Husb. & tenant to the seid chieff lord .. .. .. .. in lond | nil | in goods | 30s |  |  |  |
| Bill man | Bartill Taillor Husb. & tenant to the seid William Villers .. .. .. in lond | nil | in goods | £8 |  |  | — |
|  | Robert Ives Husb. & tenant to the seid chieff lord .. .. .. .. in lond | nil | in goods | £4 |  |  | — |
| Bill man | John B[all] the yonger tenant to the seid chieff lord .. .. .. .. in lond | nil | in goods | £13 | 6s | 8d | — |
|  | William [Bery] Bocher & tenant to the seid chieff lord .. .. .. .. in lond | nil | in goods | £12 |  |  | — |
|  | Robert Bury Husbond & tenant to the seid chieff lord .. .. .. .. in lond | nil | in goods | £10 |  |  | — |
|  | Thomas Burye Husbond & tenant to the seid chieff lord .. .. .. in lond | nil | in goods | £13 | 6s | 8d | — |

John Symme Husbond & tenant to the
seid chieff lord ..    ..    ..    .. in lond    nil    in goods   £6           —
William Egeston Husbond & tenant
to the seid chieff lord ..    ..    .. in lond    nil    in goods   £5           —
Thomas Dikman Husbond & tenant
to the seid chieff lord ..    ..    .. in lond    nil    in goods   £6           —
William Ball the yonger Husb. &
tenant to the seid chieff lord ..    .. in lond    nil    in goods   £4           —

                        **nil**              **£88    3s    4d**

*f. 42v*

William Phellypot Husbond & tenant
to the seid chieff lord ..    ..    .. in lond    nil    in goods   £3           —
Thomas Gilbourn Husbondman &
tenant to the seid chieff lord ..    .. in lond    nil    in goods      40s       —
John Dikman Husbondman & tenant
to the seid chieff lord ..    ..    .. in lond    nil    in goods   £4           —
Richard Brown Husbondman &
tenant to the seid chieff lord ..    .. in lond    nil    in goods   £3           —
William Webster Husbondman &
tenant to the seid prior of Broke    .. in lond    nil    in goods   £3           —
Richard Hubberd Husbondman &
tenant to the seid chieff lord ..    .. in lond    nil    in goods   £8           —
William Pittes laborer & tenant to the
seid chieff lord ..    ..    ..    .. in lond    nil    in goods      20s       —
William Vellam Husbondman & tenant
to the seid chieff lord ..    ..    .. in lond    nil    in goods   £3           —
Henry [Hygecok] Husb. & tenant to
the seid chieff lord    ..    ..    .. in lond    nil    in goods   £7           —
Bill man [William Stephyn] Husbond & tenant
to the seid chieff lord ..    ..    .. in lond    nil    in goods   £8           —
William Wright Husbondman &
tenant to the seid chieff lord ..    .. in lond    nil    in goods      20s       —

                        [faded]              **£53**

*f. 43*

Robert Smyth laborer & tenant to the
seid chieff lord ..    ..    ..    .. in lond    nil    in goods      20s       —
William Heywod laborer & tenant to
the seid chieff lord    ..    ..    .. in lond    nil    in goods      20s       —
Ann Coldale widow & tenant to the
seid chieff lord ..    ..    ..    .. in lond    nil    in goods   £13   6s   8d    —
Issabell [Ball] widow & tenant to the
seid chieff lord ..    ..    ..    .. in lond    nil    in goods   £6           —
[Elizabeth Dawes] widow & tenant to
the seid chieff lord    ..    ..    .. in lond    nil    in goods   £8           —
[Johan Daue] widow & tenant to the
seid chieff lord ..    ..    ..    .. in lond    nil    in goods   £3           —
.. cisley Beston widow & tenant to
the seid chieff lord    ..    ..    .. in lond    nil    in goods      40s       —
.... Clerk son to John ......    .. in lond    nil    in goods   £3           —
Robert Prattes seruant to
Thomas Waters    ..    ..    .. in lond    nil    in goods      20s       —

Archer     Robert Colebam' laborer     ..
[Bill man] Robert Webster laborer       ..
           ....Egeston laborer   ..       ..
           .... Hubberd laborer           ..
           [William] Dikman son to
           John Dikman ..    ..     ..      } in lond    nil      in goods nil      yong men & pore
           [Nic] olis .... y seruant to
           ...... Bury    ..    ..     ..
           ...... bberd laborer ..       ..
           ........ laborer       ..

*f. 43v*

           John Pyttes laborer   ..    ..
           William Smyth laborer   ..    ..
           John May laborer    ..    ..
           John Mable laborer   ..    ..    } in lond    nil      in goods nil      old men & pore
           John Fairewether laborer   ..
           Gregory Hubberd laborer   ..
           Roger Hubberd laborer    ..

                              The Church Stoke   nil
              The seid Town hath a Gilde in Stoke                £4

*f. 44*
**[GU]NTHORP[1]**
           Richard Sapcot Squier is chieff lord of
           the seid village ..    ..    ..    .. in lond    £20      in goods nil q.e.        —
           The Abbot of Westminster is parson
           of the seid village    ..    ..    .. parsonage   [£22]    in goods nil q.e.        —
           The seid Abbot hath londs their   .. [in lond    10 marks]  ....................      —
           The prior of Broke hath londs their .. [in londs    20s]    ....................      —
           The Heir of Fraunces ..........    .....................   ....................      —
           *An illegible line. Possibly says;*
           ['No other inhabitants'.]

                                   land    £24 [sic]    goods    nil
                              Finis Huius Hundred

*f. 44v*
**[MARTINSTH]ORP**   Infra Martley Hundred
           Dame Gylles Feldyng widow hath
           lond their    ..    ..    ..    .. [torn]                [in goods] nil           —
           Richard Flower Esquier hath lond
           their   ..    ..    ..    .. [in lond      26s  8d ]   [in goods] nil
           Henry Sacheuerell Knyght hath
           lond their    ..    ..    ..    .. [torn]                [in goods] nil           —
           The Prior of Broke Abbey hath
           lond their    ..    ..    ..    .. [in lond       12s]    ....................      —
           Richard Sapcote Esquier hath
           lond their    ..    ..    ..    .. [torn]                ....................      —
           ....ls [Manyll] prest is parson    .. parsonage  [torn]    ....................      —
                              The Ch[urch Stoke]   nil
                   End of the book of county Rotlond

[*An illegible entry in a smaller hand*]

1.  *Most sums of money are conjectural*

# The Lay Subsidy, 1524-5

*E. 179/165/110 m2.*

This byll Trypartyte indentyd made the Thyrd day of May ye xvj*th* yere of the Ragne of oure Souerand Lorde kyng Henry theyght Betweene John Haryngton Edward Sapcottes George Makworth Fraunces Broune & John Calcot Commyssioners namyd & appoyntyd be oure Souerand lord the Kyng within hys Shyre of Rotell of & for ye fyrst parte of a Subsidy to hys Grace at hys last parlyment grauntyd to be levyed there & payable in the Vtas [octave] of ye puryficacyon of oure lady last past Wytnessyth that Ambrose Berker Robt. Fancourt John Bate Henry thyssylton & John Burton be hygh Colectors appoyntyd for ye levy & collecton of ye same & that ye seyd Commyssioners haue charged ye seyd hygh collectors & euery of them seuerally in hys hundryd to hym so alottyd as hereafter apperyth not only wyth the Subsidy & anticipacon of ye Subsidy but also w*t* suche somes of money as hath beyn auansed w*t*in ye seid Shyre by wey of ye Kinges late Commyssion of memoriall whiche particulerly doyth appere in ye sedule to one of theys Indentures annexyd in particuler & in grose as ys in this indenture conteyned that ys to sey of ambrose Berkar of Lyndon hye Collector appoyntyd for the Hundryd of Martynsley Chargyd in grose xxix*li* xvj*s* ij*d* Robt. Fancourt of Pysbroke hygh Collector appoyntyd for ye Hundryd of Wrangdek Chargyd in grose lvj*li* xj*s* vj*d* of John Bate hygh Colector of ye hundryd of Alstow Chargyd in grose xl*li* ij*s* vj*d* of Henry thyseylton hygh Colector of ye Est hundryd Chargyd in grose lvij*li* v*s* ij*d* of John Burton hygh Colector of Okam Soken Chargyd in grose xxxvj*li* xix*s* vij*d* Sum Total CCxx*li* xiiij*s* xj*d* Whereof the one parte of theys indentures of the grose sommed w*t* V Seduls of the particulers theronto annexid to be delyueryd vnto the kynges exchecure a nother parte of ye Indentres of ye grose Summes to be delyueryd to ye tresurer of the Kynges Chamber & the thyrde parte of the Indentres of ye grose sommes Remaynyth w*t* ye hygh Colectors In Witness whereof ye seyd Commyssioners to theys bylls trypartite indentyd haue Sette theyre Seals the day & yere a bove Wreton.

JOHN HARYNGTON

EDWARD SAPCOT

GEORGE MACWORTH

FRAUNCES BROWN

JOHN CALCOTE

*Endorsed*  By the hands of Richard Irelond deputy to the Commissioners within written, the last day of June in the sixteenth year of the reigh of King Henry VIII.
By the whole Commission [for] Rotel.

# RUTLOND

## WRANDIKE HUNDRETH

*m.3*

### NORTH LUFFENHAM

**1524**

| | | | |
|---|---|---|---|
| Thomas Basset, gent in londes | £17 | †Thomas Hvnte in goodes | £8 |
| Wylliam Splay in wages | 20s | John Per in wages | 20s |
| Jane Wymerke in goodes | £12 | Robard Rowlyn in wages | 20s |
| Roberd Godman in goodes | £15 | Edward Burgys in profet of wages | 20s |
| John Scheperde in wages | 20s | Roger Bombar in profet of wages | 20s |
| John Browne in wages | 20s | Thomas Harte in profet of wages | 20s |
| Wylliam Sculthorpe in goodes | £15 | Henry Whiett in profet of wages | 20s |
| Margere Wylkynson in goodes | £12 | Wylliam Islepe in goodes | £6 |
| Hewe hir seruant in wages | 20s | John Wylsone in profet of wages | 40s |
| Thomas Roys in goodes | £15 | Symon Carter in goodes | £4 |
| John Tylton in londes | 40s | Wylliam Croft in goodes | 40s |
| Richard Hopkens in profet of wages | 20s | Valentyne Nutbrowne in profet | |
| John Pare Schomaker in goodes | 40s | of wages | 40s |
| Wylliam Carter in wages | 40s | John Jonsone in goodes | 40s |
| Wylliam Glyne in wages | 40s | Robert Lamley in goodes | 40s |
| †Wylliam Scarborough in goodes | £8 | Richard Spenser in goodes | £3 |
| John Hoppar in wages | 20s | †Robert Cole in goodes | £16 |
| John Tatan in goodes | 40s | Robert Spycke in wages | 20s |
| John Multon in profet of wages | 20s | Thomas Cottes in goodes | 40s |
| †Wylliam German in goodes | 40s | Peter Gybham in goodes | £6 |
| Parsone Wymarke in londes | 4 marks | Robert Lane in profet of wages | 20s |
| Robert German in goodes | 40s | John Hart in wages | 20s |
| Thomas Buttre in profet of wages | 20s | Cristofer Cooper in profet of | |
| Wylliam Afforth in profet of wages | 20s | wages | 20s |
| Thomas Hall in goodes | £4 | The Gyldlonde in londes | £3 |

*Sum £5 4s 4d*

**1525** (*these amendments and new names can be read*)

| | | | |
|---|---|---|---|
| John Tylton in goodes | £4 | Wylliam Croft in wages | 20s |
| Wylliam Scarborough in goodes | £6 | Robert Cole in goodes | £15 |
| Wylliam German in goodes | £3 | John Jerman in wages | 20s |
| Thomas Hvnte in goodes | £4 | Thomas Forth in wages | 20s |

*Sum illegible*

## SOUTH LUFFENHAM

**1524**

| | | | | | |
|---|---|---|---|---|---|
| John Tokey in goodes | .. | .. | £14 | Johan Johson wedow in goodes .. | £3 |
| Thomas Coke in wages | .. | .. | 20s | Thomas Brydge in goodes .. | £3 |
| Wylliam Peek in goodes | .. | | 40s | Thomas Brydge jun' in wages .. | 20s |
| Wylliam Bonnet in goodes | .. | £4 | | Wylliam Bentley in goodes .. | £7 |
| Henry Bonnett in goodes | .. | | 40s | Wylliam Gudlocke in goodes .. | 40s |
| Robert Coke in goodes | .. | .. | £13 | Thomas Dowghty in wages .. | 20s |
| Bartylmewe Scharpe in goodes | .. | £16 | | John Machyne in wages .. | 20s |
| John Scarborowgh in goodes | .. | | 40s | Wylliam Multon in wages .. | 20s |
| John Wright in goodes | .. | .. | £4 | Radulphe Barkar in wages .. | 20s |
| Thomas Wyles in goodes | .. | £8 | | Wylliam Cowper in wages .. | 20s |

*Sum* **42s 4d**

**1525** (*about 14 names largely illegible*)

*Sum* **£1 16s 2d**

## SEYTON

**1524**

| | | | | | |
|---|---|---|---|---|---|
| John Scherffylde gent. in londes | | £14 | †John Yett in goodes .. | .. | £3 |
| †Thomas Beredge in goodes | .. | £20 | Henry Bowell in wages .. | .. | 20s |
| *Robert Corbye in wages | .. | 20s | Thomas Ybbys in wages .. | .. | 20s |
| Wylliam Ilstone in wages | .. | 20s | Richard Hermytage in wages .. | .. | 20s |
| †Richard Byschope in goodes | .. | £4 | Thomas Bolley in wages .. | .. | 20s |
| *Wylliam Pyckeryng in wages | .. | 20s | *John Waltrott in goodes .. | .. | 40s |
| †John Bolley in goodes | .. | £18 | *John Wylliamson in wages | .. | 20s |
| Robert Sesmey in wages | .. | 20s | Wylliam Luffe in goodes .. | .. | £3 |
| Richard Edwardes in goodes | .. | £3 | *Richard Tailour in wages | .. | 20s |
| John Waryn in wages | .. | 20s | Wylliam Bakster in goodes .. | .. | £5 |
| Henry Tokey in goodes | .. | £3 | *John Nycoll in wages .. | .. | 20s |
| *Henry Horne in goodes | .. | 40s | †Wylliam Nycoll in goodes | .. | £21 |
| †Robert Boyehowe in goodes | .. | £20 | Henry Machyn in wages .. | .. | 20s |
| †Robert Tomlynson in goodes | .. | £4 | Richard Mellys in wages .. | .. | 20s |
| Thomas Boyehowe in goodes | .. | £2 | | | |

*Sum* **£5 4s 2d**

**1525**

| | | | | | |
|---|---|---|---|---|---|
| Thomas Beredge in goodes | .. | £15 | Wylliam Hybbys in wages | .. | 20s |
| Richard Byschope in goodes | .. | £3 | John Jamys in wages .. | .. | 20s |
| John Bolley in goodes | .. | £16 | Wylliam Wylkynson in wages | .. | 20s |
| Robert Boyehowe in goodes | .. | £18 | Wylliam Nicoll in goodes | .. | £14 |

| | | | | |
|---|---|---|---|---|
| Robert Tomlynson in goodes | .. | 40s | John Kyrby in wages  ..  .. | 20s |
| John Yett in goodes  .. | .. | 40s | Richard Geffrey in wages  .. | 20s |
| Wylliam Bakster in goodes | .. | £4 | Wylliam Helson in wages  .. | 20s |

*Sum £3 1s 2d*

## MORCOTT

**1524**

| | | | | |
|---|---|---|---|---|
| Wylliam Bryghtmer in goodes | .. | £3 | *Wylliam Bewshue in wages  .. | 20s |
| †Thomas Goodman in goodes | .. | £6 | †John Grevys in goodes  ..  .. | £3 |
| *John Messenger in goodes | .. | £3 | †John Frank in goodes  ..  .. | £3 |
| *Wylliam Adyngton in wages | .. | 20s | †John Spire in goodes  ..  .. | £7 |
| Rauff Bryttoft in goodes .. | .. | £5 | †John Brone in goodes  ..  .. | £7 |
| *John Richardson in wages | .. | 20s | Thomas Pegell in profet of wages | 20s |
| *Robert Radys in goodes .. | .. | 40s | *Reynolde Kyrkby in profet of | |
| Thomas West in goodes .. | .. | £14 | wages  ..  ..  ..  .. | 20s |
| †Henry Tampon in goodes | .. | £12 | Wylliam Fawkner in profet of | |
| Wylliam Overton in goodes | .. | £10 | wages  ..  ..  ..  .. | 20s |
| *John Kettylborough in goodes | .. | 40s | *Robert Teryngton in profet of | |
| Roolonde Scherffylde in goodes | £5 | | wages  ..  ..  .. | 20s |
| †John Tampon in goodes .. | .. | £6 | *Robert Lawrence in profet of | |
| *John Smyth in goodes  .. | .. | £4 | wages  ..  ..  .. | 20s |
| Thomas Smyth in goodes | .. | 40s | *John Foster in profet of wages .. | 20s |
| John Haryngton in wages | .. | 20s | †John Bulle in profet of wages .. | 20s |
| Olyuer Taleth in wages  .. | .. | 20s | *Richard Bell in profet of wages .. | 20s |
| †Richard Cooke in goodes | .. | £7 | Wylliam Jacsone in profet of | |
| *Alys Kyrkby in goodes  .. | .. | £7 | wages  ..  ..  ..  .. | 20s |
| *Thomas Fawkener in wages | .. | 20s | Robert Schone in profet of wages | 20s |
| Thomas Presgrave in goodes | .. | £4 | John Scheparde in profet of wages | 20s |

*Sum £3 1s 8d*

**1525**

| | | | | |
|---|---|---|---|---|
| Thomas Goodman in goodes | .. | £5 | Johane Messenger widow in goodes | £3 |
| Henry Tampon in goodes | .. | £9 | Robert Bacar in goodes  ..  .. | 40s |
| John Tampon in goodes | .. | £5 | Wylliam Tyrlyngton in wages  .. | 20s |
| Richard Cooke in goodes | .. | £6 | Oliuer Billyng in wages  ..  .. | 20s |
| John Grvys in goodes  .. | .. | 40s | Margaret Kyrby in goodes  .. | £5 |
| John Frank in goodes  .. | .. | £4 | Robert Lamperte in wages  .. | 20s |
| John Spire in goodes  .. | .. | £6 | Robert Cheselden in wages  .. | 20s |
| John Brone in goodes  .. | .. | £5 | Thomas Beushire in wages  .. | 20s |
| John Bulle in goodes  .. | .. | 40s | Wylliam Pellrok in wages  .. | 20s |

*Sum 46s*

## PYLTON

**1524**

| | | | | | |
|---|---|---|---|---|---|
| †John Fawkener in goodes | .. | £5 | Thomas Smyth in goodes | .. | £3 |
| †Wylliam Carter in goodes | .. | £16 | John Wyngham in goodes | .. | 40s |
| John Bromby in goodes | .. | £6 | | | |

*Sum* **16s 0d**

**1525**

| | | | | | |
|---|---|---|---|---|---|
| John Fauconer in goodes | .. | £4 | Thomas Wyngham in wages | .. | 20s |
| Thomas Fauconer in wages | .. | 20s | Thomas Mason in wages | .. | 20s |
| Wylliam Carter in goodes | .. | £12 | Robert Tyler in wages | .. | .. | 20s |

*Sum* **13s 4d**

## CALCOTT

**1525**

| | | | | | |
|---|---|---|---|---|---|
| Thomas Wodecok in goodes | .. | £15 | John Hille in goodes | .. | .. | £10 |
| Richard Clerk in goodes .. | .. | 40s | Thomas Colvell in wages | .. | 20s |
| John Bowman in landes .. | .. | £4 | Thomas Sly thelder in goodes | .. | £4 |
| John White in wages | .. | .. | 20s | Thomas Sly the yonger in goodes | 40s |
| †Walter Newbon in goodes | .. | £6 | Wylliam Nebon in goodes | .. | £12 |
| †Wylliam Luffe in goodes | .. | £10 | Wylliam Smyth in wages .. | .. | 20s |
| Wylliam Luff [his] son in goodes | £5 | Thomas Stefynson in wages | .. | 20s |
| Richard Hyll in goodes .. | .. | £16 | Thomas Russell in goodes | .. | £4 |
| Wylliam [Dalbor?] in wages | .. | 20s | Robert Russell in goodes | .. | £14 |
| Richard Luffe in goodes .. | .. | £3 | John Nebon in goodes | .. | .. | £8 |
| Androwe Bisshope in wages | .. | 20s | John Shepherd in wages .. | .. | 20s |
| John Baker in wages | .. | .. | 20s | Roger Kyrby in goodes .. | .. | 40s |
| Richard Morys in wages .. | .. | 20s | Herry Waren in wages | .. | .. | 20s |
| Harry Wybarn in goodes | .. | 40s | | | |

*Sum* **£3 4s 10d**

**1524** (*These amendments and new names can be read*)

| | | | | | |
|---|---|---|---|---|---|
| Edwarde Casterton in wages | .. | 20s | Wylliam Luffe in goodes .. | .. | £20 |
| Thomas Wodcocke in wages | .. | 20s | Richard Hyll in goodes .. | .. | £17 |
| Walter Newbon in goodes | .. | £8 | James Gybsone in wages | .. | 22s |

*Sum illegible*

## STOKE DRY

**1525**

| | | | Nicholas Webster in wages | .. | 20s |
|---|---|---|---|---|---|
| Sir Edward Digby knyght in landes | £120 | | | | |
| John Pekke in goodes .. | .. | £10 | John Couper in wages .. | .. | 20s |
| Robert Islep' in goodes .. | .. | £10 | Laurence Weuer in wages[1] | .. | 26s 8d |
| Richard Warde in goodes | .. | 40s | John Lacy in wages | .. | 20s |
| John Fauconer in goodes | .. | £10 | Austen Emery in wages | .. | 20s |
| Richard Henning in goodes | .. | £7 | William Aunger in wages | .. | 20s |
| Wylliam Dudleye in goodes | .. | 40s | Roulande A[Were?] in wages[1] .. | | 26s 8d |
| | | | Thomas Billyng in goodes | .. | 40s |

*Sum* **£7 4s 4d**[2]

**1524** (*these additional names can be read*)

| Phillipe [Nedaur] in wages | .. | 20s | Laurence Baukham in wages | .. | 20s |
|---|---|---|---|---|---|
| [Quyntyne][3] Emery in wages | .. | 20s | John Bornys in wages .. | .. | 20s |
| Robard [Ch] apman in wages | .. | 20s | | | |

*Sum* **£7 4s ...**

## THORPE

**1524**

| †Wylliam Haryson in goodes | .. | £10 | †Wylliam Vffyngton in goodes | .. | £10 |
|---|---|---|---|---|---|
| Christofer Scherffylde in londes .. | | £5 6s 8d | †John Harysone in goodes | .. | £3 |
| †Richard Yerlonde in goodes | .. | £3 | Henry Sadylar in wages .. | .. | 20s |

*Sum* **18s 8d**

**1525** (*of 6 names these are legible*)

| Wylliam Harreson in goodes | .. | £7 | Wylliam Uffington in goodes | .. | £7 |
|---|---|---|---|---|---|
| Richard Yerlonde in goodes | .. | 40s | John Haryson in goodes .. | .. | 40s |

*Sum* **14s 8d**

## LYDYNGTON

**1525**

| Edward Watson (gent) in goodes | £200 | Thomas Hervy in wages .. | .. | 20s |
|---|---|---|---|---|
| †John Strengar (gent) in goodes .. | £30 | Wylliam [Wacreman?] in wages .. | | 20s |
| John Irelond in goodes .. | [£18] | Richard Irelond in goodes | .. | 40s |
| Wylliam Wells in goodes | [£3] | John Ireland in goodes .. | .. | 40s |

1. *These paid 6d.*
2. *Recte £7. 3s 10d.*
3. *Barely legible, should possibly read 'Austen' as in 1525.*

| | | |
|---|---|---|
| John Howlet in goodes | .. .. | £7 |
| Thomas De in wages | .. .. | 20s |
| Robert Mesendew in wages | .. | 20s |
| Robert Lame in goodes | .. | 40s |
| John Pittes in wages | .. | 20s |
| John Panter in wages | .. | 20s |
| Thomas [Stable?] in goodes | .. | . . . . |
| John Fenton in wages | .. | 20s |
| Wylliam [Colvil] in goodes | .. | . . . . |
| John [Mariet] in goodes .. | .. | . . . . |
| Adam Stelton in goodes .. | .. | [40s] |
| John Dey in wages | .. | [20s] |
| †Wylliam Irelond in goodes | .. | [£13] |
| Robert Pereson in goodes | .. | . . . . |
| †Nicolas Toppy in goodes | .. | [£3] |
| John Barwell in goodes .. | .. | . . . . |
| John Alkynson in wages .. | .. | 20s |
| John Watson in wages | .. | 20s |
| Wylliam Talle in goodes .. | .. | £3 |
| Agnes Sly in goodes | .. .. | £12 |
| John Parre in goodes | .. | [£10] |
| Wylliam Barwell in wages | .. | 20s |
| James Irelond in wages | .. | 20s |
| Richard Fauler in goodes | .. | [40s] |
| Richard Faukener in goodes | .. | 40s |
| Richard Dell in goodes | .. .. | [40s] |

| | | |
|---|---|---|
| Thomas Williamson in wages | .. | 20s |
| Richard Astell in wages .. | .. | 20s |
| Richard Samson in goodes | .. | £3 |
| Thomas Hawley in goodes | .. | 40s |
| John Bonyng in goodes .. | .. | 40s |
| Symond . . . in wages | .. | 20s |
| John Irelond in wages | .. | 20s |
| Robert S[a]vych in goodes | .. | 40s |
| Wylliam [Sa]lebarne in wages | .. | 20s |
| John Gater in wages | .. | 20s |
| Herry Cussyngham in wages | .. | 20s |
| John Brown in wages | .. | 20s |
| Thomas Rowall in wages[1] | .. | 26s |
| Robert Adam in goodes[2] | .. | £3 |
| John Stephenson in goodes | | 40s |
| John [Kyrlyt] in goodes .. | .. | £3 |
| Richard Walles in wages .. | .. | 20s |
| John Irelond at Crofft in wages | .. | 22s |
| Robert Pekke in goodes .. | .. | £7 |
| John Wryte in goodes | .. | £3 |
| Robert [Pargo] in wages .. | .. | 20s |
| Wylliam Lye in wages | .. | 20s |
| Robert [Work] in wages .. | .. | 20s |
| Wylliam . . . . in goodes .. | .. | 40s |
| [Richar]d Sis[may] in goodes | | £20 |

*Sum* **£16 13s 2d**

**1524** (*these amendments and new names can be read*)

| | | |
|---|---|---|
| John Strengar in goodes .. | .. | £40 |
| William Style in wages | .. | [20s] |
| Nycolas Toppy in goodes | .. | [£5] |
| John Banett in goodes | .. | [£3] |
| John Horsley in wages | .. | 20s |
| Wylliam Yerlonde in goodes | .. | £7 |

| | | |
|---|---|---|
| Richard Hill in goodes .. | .. | £10 |
| Thomas [Stables] in goodes | .. | 40s |
| John Edmondes in goodes | .. | £5 |
| John Stryckland in wages | .. | 30s |
| Wylliam Fowlar in wages | .. | 20s |

*Sum* **£17 2s 8d**

1. *Paid 6d.*
2. *Paid 20d.*

*m. 3v*

**PYSBROKE**

**1524**

| | | | | | |
|---|---|---|---|---|---|
| Robert Baxster in goodes | .. | £10 | Henry Cranwell in goodes | .. | £4 |
| Wylliam Byllyngs in wages | .. | 20s | Robert Cranwell in profet of wages | | 20s |
| Jane Meryman in wages .. | .. | 20s | John Sculthorpe in profet of wages | | 20s |
| Wylliam Cotes in wages .. | .. | 20s | John Crowley in goodes | .. | 40s |
| John Harrys in goodes .. | .. | £5 | Wylliam Cley in goodes .. | .. | £5 |
| James Edmounde in goodes | .. | £16 | Robert Fancourt in goodes | .. | £21 |
| John Kyrke in wages .. | .. | 30s | Richard Wright in wages | .. | 20s |
| Thomas Corby in profet of wages | | 20s | Wylliam Franke in wages | .. | 22s |
| Thomas Jackson in profet of wages | | 20s | | | |

*Sum* **47s 10d**

**1525** (*16 names: this amendment can be read*)

Robert Baxter in goodes ..     ..     £8

*Sum* **27s**

**GLASTON**

**1524**

| | | | | | |
|---|---|---|---|---|---|
| *Richard Yerlonde in goodes | .. | £9 | Thomas Murdock in wages | .. | 20s |
| †Richard Barkar in goodes | .. | £9 | *Thomas Lacy in wages .. | .. | 20s |
| John Lyghtfote in goodes | .. | £6 | John Lacy in goodes .. | .. | 40s |
| †Wylliam Fawkenar in goodes | .. | £4 | John Rookes in goodes .. | .. | 40s |
| Thomas Leycye in goodes | .. | £3 | †Wylliam Mason in goodes | .. | £4 |
| Richard Batfylde in goodes | .. | 40s | Robert Peke in wages .. | .. | 20s |
| Robert Stevenson in goodes | .. | £6 | *James Scheparde in wages | .. | 20s |
| George Jonson in wages | .. | 20s | *Robert Fowkenar in wages | .. | 20s |
| Wylliam Blake in goodes | .. | £14 | Richard Crosse in wages .. | .. | 20s |
| *Thomas Taylour in wages | .. | 20s | *Wylliam Dare in wages .. | .. | 20s |
| *Wylliam German in wages | .. | 20s | *John Cranwell in wages .. | .. | 20s |

*Sum* **34s 2d**

**1525**

| | | | | | |
|---|---|---|---|---|---|
| Edward Catesby in landes | .. | £38 | William Slanston in wages[1] | .. | 26s 8d |
| Richard Barkar in goodes | .. | £8 | Richard Wade in wages .. | .. | 20s |
| Wylliam Fawkenar in goodes | .. | 46s 8d | James Ferley in wages .. | .. | 20s |
| William Mason in goodes | .. | £3 | Edward Agas in wages .. | .. | 20s |
| John Lay in wages .. | .. | 26s 8d | | | |

*Sum* **£3 5s 6d**

1.  *Paid 6d.*

## BARADON

**1524**

| | | | | |
|---|---|---|---|---|
| John Durant in londes | .. | .. | £7 | |
| Robert Clyffe in goodes | .. | .. | £6 | |
| Wylliam Walkar in londes | .. | 20s | | |
| John Taylby in goodes | .. | .. | £20 | |
| John Taylby jun' in goodes | .. | 40s | | |
| Symon Taylbe in goodes | .. | .. | 40s | |
| Wylliam Goodlade in goodes | .. | £20 | | |
| Thomas Goodlade his sone in goodes | 40s | | | |
| Bawden Wynbusch in goodes | .. | £4 | | |
| John Atkynson in wages | .. | .. | 20s | |
| Sir Thomas Clark in londes | .. | 20s | | |
| John Barforde in goodes | .. | .. | £10 | |
| Alexander Tyth in goodes | .. | 40s | | |
| John Fawkener in wages | .. | 20s | | |
| Thomas Strawe in wages | .. | .. | 20s | |
| Thomas West in wages | .. | .. | 20s | |
| John Noble in wages | .. | .. | 20s | |
| Edmunde Strykland in goodes | .. | 40s | | |
| Christofer Tailour in profet of wages | .. | .. | .. | .. | 20s |
| Robert Slye in profet of wages | .. | 20s | | |
| John Smyth in profet of wages | .. | 20s | | |
| Wylliam Dunmoo in wages | .. | 20s | | |
| Thomas Clark in goodes | .. | .. | £10 | |

| | | | | |
|---|---|---|---|---|
| Wylliam Style in profet of wages | | 20s |
| Wylliam Foreby in profet of wages | | 20s |
| Thomas Goodelade in profet of wages | .. | .. | .. | .. | 20s |
| Rauffe Hvnte in goodes | .. | .. | 40s |
| Wylliam Mathewe in goodes | .. | 40s |
| Richard Styles in goodes | .. | .. | 40s |
| Thomas Styles in goodes | .. | .. | £4 |
| John Brampron in wages | .. | .. | 20s |
| Richard Browne in wages | .. | 20s |
| John Freny in goodes | .. | .. | 40s |
| Thomas Smyth in goodes | .. | 40s |
| John Skynner in profet of wages | | 20s |
| John Lawrence in goodes | .. | 40s |
| Alye Goodlade wedow in goodes | £5 |
| Wylliam Goodlade hir son in wages | 20s |
| Richard Reynolde in goodes | .. | £15 |
| John Symson in wages | .. | .. | 20s |
| Robert Keysby in goodes | .. | £8 |
| Wylliam Goodlade jun' in goods | 40s |
| Wylliam Goodlade hys sone in wages | .. | .. | .. | .. | 20s |
| John Nycoll in goodes | .. | .. | £4 |

*Sum £5*

## TYXOUER

**1524**

| | | | |
|---|---|---|---|
| Robert Strycar in goodes | .. | £4 | |
| Thomas Smyth in goodes | .. | £6 | |
| John Euerton in goodes | .. | .. | £6 |
| Wylliam Bretten in goodes | .. | £12 | |
| John Plattes in goodes | .. | .. | £6 |
| John Smyth in goodes | .. | .. | £14 |
| Wylliam Lyand in wages | .. | 20s | |

| | | | |
|---|---|---|---|
| Richard Johson in wages | .. | £6 |
| Richard Wytham in wages | .. | 20s |
| Richard Woode in profet of wages | 20s |
| Wylliam Suetman in profet of wages | 20s |
| Wylliam Cowper in profet of wages | 20s |
| Henry Fayrman in profet of wages | 20s |

*Sum 29s*

*Sum of the hundred, 1524 £56 11s 6d*

*m. 4*

# ESTHUNDRED

## TYKENCOTE

**1524**

| | | | | | |
|---|---|---|---|---|---|
| *John Phelip in goodes | £20 | | †Thomas Ocley in goodes .. | £3 | 6s 8d |
| †William Baxster in goodes | £15 | | †Geffrey Baxster in goodes | £4 | |
| *Robert Baxster in goodes | £3 | | William Hopkyn in wages | | 20s |
| †Thomas Baxster in goodes | | 40s | John Greneside in wages | | 20s |
| †John Tomlyn for wages | | 20s | *Richard Caruer in wages | | 20s |
| †William Pope in goodes | | 40s | *Richard Symmes in wages | | 20s |
| †John Ocley in goodes | £11 | | *Thomas Greneham in londes | £8 | |

*Sum* **49s 10d**

**1525**

| | | | | | |
|---|---|---|---|---|---|
| Wyllism Baxter in goodes | £11 | | Wylliam Pope in goodes .. | 33s | 4d |
| John Tomlyn in wages | | 26s 8d | Jone Greneham widow in landes | £8 | |
| John Okeley in goodes | £6 | | Phelippe Jonson in goodes | £14 | |
| Geffrey Baxter in goodes | £3 | 6s 8d | Thomas Baxter in wages .. | | 26s 8d |
| Thomas Oxley in goodes | £3 | | Ambros Jakeson in wages | | 26s 8d |

*Sum* **30s 10d**

## CASTERTON MAGNA

**1524**

| | | | | |
|---|---|---|---|---|
| *Dame Williams in goodes | £6 | | John Gunby in wages | 20s |
| *Thomas Vesey in wages | | 20s | *Thomas Gillam in wages | 20s |
| *Robert Horseley in wages and | | | *William Watte in wages | 20s |
|    profet for wages | | 20s | *Robert Watte in wages | 20s |
| †John Parrissh in goodes | £12 | | *Reynold Watte in wages | 20s |
| John Fayrchild in goodes | £4 | | John Strynger in goodes .. | £3 |
| Robert Bisshop in goodes | £4 | | †Thomas Fayrchild in wages | 20s |
| Thomas Bisshop in goodes | | 40s | Thomas Wilkynson in wages | 20s |
| Thomas Tomson in goodes | | 40s | *John Luffe in wages | 20s |
| *Mark A Lee in goodes | | 40s | William Rooke in wages | 20s |
| †Thomas Tauerner in goodes | | 40s | †Herry Laxton in goodes .. | £80 |
| †Herry Norys in wages & profet | | | †Herry Thistelton in goodes | £40 |
|    for wages | | 20s | | |

*Sum* **£7 2s 6d**

**1525**

| | | | | |
|---|---|---|---|---|
| John Parissh in goodes .. .. | £10 | | Thomas Smyth in wages .. .. | 20s |
| Thomas Tauerne in wages .. | | 20s | Wylliam Marke in wages .. | 20s |
| Herry Norysch in goodes .. | | 40s | John Wyllous in goodes .. .. | 40s |
| Thomas Fayrchild in goodes .. | | 40s | James Woulman in wages .. | 20s |
| Herry Laxton in goodes .. .. | £60 | | Robert Haryson in wages .. | 20s |
| Herry Thystylton in goodes | £22 | | | |

*Sum* **£5 0s 6d**

## RYALL

**1524**

| | | | | |
|---|---|---|---|---|
| †Thomas Netlam in goodes .. | £80 | | †John Colyn in goodes .. .. | 40s |
| †William Netlam in goodes .. | £80 | | †Richard Euerton in londes .. | 20s |
| †Robert Tagull in goodes .. .. | £5 | | Nicolas Bocher in wages and profet | |
| Thomas Vffyngton in goodes .. | | 40s | for wages .. .. .. | 20s |
| John Ganne in goodes .. | £8 | | *Thomas Chirch in wages and profet | |
| †Herry Waters in goodes .. .. | £10 | | for wages .. .. .. | 20s |
| †Thomas Waterfall in goodes .. | £11 | | James Peturson in wages .. | 20s |
| †John Watson in goodes .. .. | £8 | | *Thomas Dalby in wages .. .. | 20s |
| Thomas Burbage in goodes .. | | 40s | †Richard Laxton in wages .. | 20s |
| Robert Sherman in goodes .. | £14 | | *Richard Stacpole in wages .. | 20s |
| *Richard Wright in goodes .. | | 40s | Thomas Flecher in wages .. | 20s |
| †John Thistelton in goodes .. | £14 | | John Barbor in wages .. .. | 20s |
| *John Bloode in goodes .. .. | | 40s | William Blande in wages .. .. | 20s |
| Herry Scotte in goodes .. .. | £6 | | *Thomas Cote in wages .. | 20s |
| †Herry Clark in goodes .. .. | £3 | | Hugh Fuller in wages .. | 20s |
| Thomas Wadyngton in goodes .. | £5 | | *Wylliam [Wyshes][1] in wages .. | 20s |
| John Netlam in goodes .. | £12 | | Thomas Ruston in wages .. | 20s |
| Robert Walette in goodes .. | £8 | | *John Tomson in wages .. .. | 20s |
| John Reve in goodes .. .. | £3 | | | |

*Sum* **£11 4s 2d**

**1525**

| | | | | |
|---|---|---|---|---|
| Thomas Netlam in goodes .. | £60 | | Richard Euerton in goodes .. | 40s |
| Wylliam Netlam in goodes .. | £60 | | Richard Laxton Carpenter in goodes | 40s |
| Robert Tagyll in goodes .. | £3 | | Richard Vffyngton in goodes .. | 40s |
| Herry Waters in goodes .. .. | £6 | | Richarde Clarke, Wright in goodes | 40s |
| Thomas Waterfall in goodes .. | £9 | | John Wright in goodes .. .. | 40s |
| John Watson in goodes .. | £7 | | Thomas Kyrke laborer in wages | 20s |
| John Thystylton in goodes .. | £12 | | Thomas Scote in wages .. .. | 20s |
| Herry Clerk in goodes .. .. | | 40s | John Perpoynt in wages .. .. | 20s |
| Thomas Wadyngton in goodes .. | £3 | | Robert Dalbye in wages .. .. | 20s |
| John Collyn in wages .. .. | | 20s | | |

*Sum* **£8 16s 6d**

1.  *The surname is interlined.*

## INGTHORP

### 1524

| | | | | |
|---|---|---|---|---|
| John Spenlouffe in goodes | £3 | †Artour Watson in goodes | | 40s |
| †Roger Fayrchild in goodes | £6 | †John Page in goodes | £3 | |
| †Richard Thistelton in goodes | £6 | Henry Fayrchild in goodes | | 40s |

*Sum* **11s 0d**

### 1525

| | | | |
|---|---|---|---|
| Roger Fayerchylde in goodes | £5 | Artour Watson in wages | 20s |
| Richard Thystylton in goodes | £5 | John Page in goodes | 40s |

*Sum* **8s 10d**

## EMPYNGHAM

### 1524

| | | | | |
|---|---|---|---|---|
| George Makworth Esquier[1] in londes | £40 | William Golle in wages | | 20s |
| *Elizabeth Edmonds in goodes | £40 | *Thomas Preudfote in wages | | 20s |
| *William Tower in wages & profet for wages | 20s | *Richard Shepherd in goodes | £4 | |
| *William Horneby in wages | 20s | †Thomas Turnor in goodes | £4 | |
| †John Colyn in goodes | £17 | William Dicons in wages | | 20s |
| *John Lambe in wages | 20s | *Richard Johnson in wages | | 20s |
| †William Barons in goodes | £19 | Thomas Colyn in goodes | | 40s |
| John Laxton in goodes | £12 | John Faux in wages | | 20s |
| John Spenythorne in goodes | £6 | *John Weselhed in wages | | 20s |
| †Richard Colyn in goodes | £6 | *John Hill in wages | | 20s |
| †Robert Wright in goodes | £7 | †Raff Keteryns in goodes | | 40s |
| Thomas Wright in goodes | £6 | Robert Williamson in goodes | £4 | |
| †Nicolas Fouler in goodes | £7 6s 8d | *Dauid Comyn Irisshman in wages | | 20s |
| *William Peper in goodes | £9 | *Thomas Taillor in wages | | 20s |
| John Brown Schepard[1] in wages | 20s | Margret Wederley in goodes | | 40s |
| *Stephyn Miller in goodes | 40s | John Dale in wages | | 20s |
| *William Swayn in wages | 20s | William Fox Weuer in wages[1] | | 20s |
| *John Luffe in goodes | £3 | *Robert Peert in wages | | 20s |
| Richard Brown in goodes | £3 | †Thomas Symmes in wages | | 20s |
| Thomas Exton in goodes | £3 | *Richard Turnor in wages | | 20s |
| †William Sisson in goodes | £4 | †Thomas Tilton in wages | | 20s |
| †Guy Spenythorn in goodes | £5 | Richard Barette in wages | | 20s |
| *Robert Wright in wages | 20s | *William Wadyng in wages | | 20s |
| †Robert Careby in wages | 20s | †Robert Whathed in wages | | 20s |
| *Herry Creton in wages | 20s | †John Brown in wages | | 20s |
| | | †Robert Burnes in wages | | 20s |

1. *Occupations are inserted from the 1525 return.*

| | | | | |
|---|---|---|---|---|
| *John Careby in goodes .. | .. | £6 | *Herry Sherman in wages .. | 20s |
| *Robert Brown in wages .. | .. | 20s | *Thomas Mogry in wages .. | 20s |
| *William Graunte in wages | .. | 20s | *Gilbert Dale in wages .. | 20s |
| †Richard Pittes in wages .. | .. | 20s | The Church Stok in goodes .. | 40s |
| †Thomas Langton in goodes | .. | £5 | | |

Sum £8 0s 12d

**1525**

| | | | | |
|---|---|---|---|---|
| John Collyn in goodes .. | .. | £16 | Wylliam Syston in goodes .. | £6 |
| Wylliam Barnys in goodes | .. | £18 | Richard Robynson in goodes .. | £4 |
| Richard Collyn in goodes | .. | £4 | John Freman in goodes .. .. | 40s |
| Robert Wryght in goodes | .. | £5 | Steven Mylner in goodes .. .. | 40s |
| Nicholas Fouler in goodes | .. | £8 | John Plummar in wages .. .. | 20s |
| Gye Spenythorn in goodes | .. | £4 | Christopher Burnys in wages .. | 20s |
| Robert Careby in goods .. | .. | 40s | Thomas Fawkener in wages .. | 26s 8d |
| Richard Pittes Carpenter in wages | | 40s | Robert Whyethed in wages .. | 22s |
| Thomas Langton in goodes | .. | £3 | John Wadyngton in wages .. | 20s |
| Thomas Turnor in wages | .. | 22s | Thomas Telton in goodes .. | 40s |
| Raff Ketheryns in wages | .. | 26s 8d | John Waters in wages .. .. | 20s |
| Thomas Symmes in goodes | .. | 40s | Richard Holmes in goodes .. | 40s |
| John Brown in wages .. | .. | 40s | Thomas Fox in wages .. .. | 20s |
| Robert Burnes in wages .. | .. | 40s | Mysthell Manton in wages .. | 20s |
| Thomas Haryngton gent. in landes | | £5 | Thomas Edmonde in goodes .. | £3 |
| John [S . . . ande in goodes | .. | £10] | Agnes Edmonde in goodes .. | £6 |

Sum £6 10s

## CASTERTON PARUA CUM TORELTHORP

**1524**

| | | | |
|---|---|---|---|
| Frances Brown Esquier in goodes | £60 | †Sir Richard Berege preest in | |
| †Edmund Brown in his kepyng in | | goodes .. .. .. .. | £4 |
| goodes .. .. .. .. | £50 | †Richard Cosyn in goodes .. | £3 |
| †Anne Brown in his custody in .. | | William Walker in wages .. | 20s |
| goodes .. .. .. .. | £50 | *William Shepherd in wages .. | 20s |
| *Kathyn Brown in his custody in | | Gerrard Dode in wages .. | 20s |
| goodes .. .. .. .. | £40 | *William Carter in wages .. .. | 20s |
| †Herry Bukyngham in goodes .. | £60 | John Thorney in wages .. .. | 20s |

Sum £13 5s 4d

**1525**

| | | | |
|---|---|---|---|
| Herry Buckyngham in goodes .. | £40 | Wylliam Plummar in wages .. | 20s |
| Edmonde Browne gent. in goodes | £40 | Wylliam Tawiskote in wages | 20s |
| Anne Browne in goodes .. .. | £40 | Herry Clark in wages .. .. | 20s |
| Sir Richard Berege in goodes .. | 40s | Wylliam Vale in wages .. .. | 20s |
| Richard Cosyn in goodes .. | 40s | Nycholas Cooke in wages .. | 20s |
| John Robynson in wages .. | 20s | | |

*Sum* **£9 5s 6d**

## ESSENDEN

**1524**

| | | | |
|---|---|---|---|
| Roger Fissher in goodes .. .. | £5 | *John Freman in goodes .. .. | £3 |
| †John Bayard in goodes .. .. | £4 | John Revell in goodes .. .. | £5 |
| Thomas Smyth in goodes .. | £5 | Robert Dey in goodes .. .. | £4 |
| William Wadford in goodes .. | 40s | William Laxton in wages .. | 20s |
| †Thomas Dalby in goodes .. | £6 | †Herry Bullok in wages .. .. | 20s |
| †Richard Roo in goodes .. .. | £12 | *Roger Gilbert in wages .. .. | 20s |
| †Richard Cobsey in goodes .. | 40s | | |

*Sum* **25s**

**1525**

| | | | |
|---|---|---|---|
| John Byarde in goodes .. .. | £3 | Henry Bullok in goodes .. .. | 40s |
| Thomas Dalby in goodes .. | £7 | Richard Roo in goodes .. .. | £10 |
| Richard Cobsye in wages .. | 20s | | |

*Sum* **22s 2d**

*m.4v*
## TINWELL
**1524**

| | | | |
|---|---|---|---|
| *Sir Richard Hawe preest in goodes | £14 | †Richard Knotte in wages .. | 20s |
| *William Fayrchild in wages .. | 20s | *Richard Geyman in wages .. | 20s |
| *Herry Sange in wages .. .. | 20s | *Richard Fayrday in wages .. | 20s |
| *Thomas Smyth in goodes .. | £12 | John Freyman in goodes .. .. | £3 |
| †Thomas Thistelton in goodes .. | £12 | John Armestrong in wages .. | 20s |
| William Careby in goodes .. | £5 | †John Fayrchild in goodes .. | 40s |
| Roger Knotte in goodes .. .. | £5 | John Wynce in wages .. .. | 20s |
| *Richard Andrew in wages .. | 20s | *Richard Stanherd in wages .. | 20s |
| *John Johnson in goodes .. .. | 40s | | |

*Sum* **[30s 6d]**

**1525**

| | | | | |
|---|---|---|---|---|
| Thomas Thystylton in goodes | .. | £10 | Thomas Manley in goodes | .. £11 |
| Richard Knotte in goodes | .. | £2 | John Wetherley in wages | .. 20s |
| John Fayerchyld in wages | .. | 20s | Wylliam Bradeley in wages | .. 20s |
| Bonyface Martyn in goodes | .. | £13 6s 8d | | |

*Sum* **27s 4d**

## KETTON

**1524**

| | | | | |
|---|---|---|---|---|
| †John Caldecote in londes | .. £30 | *Herry Burgh in wages | .. .. | 20s |
| †Richard Willughby in goodes | .. £30 | Thomas Sisson in goodes | .. | £9 6s 8d |
| †William Kyng in goodes .. | .. £40 | †Herry Adam in goodes | .. | £8 |
| *Richard Wyllon in wages | .. 20s | *Nicolas Hogeson in goodes | .. | £3 |
| Alexander Gibson in wages | .. 20s | Thomas Mathew in goodes | .. | 40s |
| *Richard Cruker in wages | .. 20s | †William [Hatton]¹ in goodes | .. | 40s |
| William Flecher in wages | .. 20s | †William Kechyn in goodes | .. | £4 |
| John Smyth in wages | .. 20s | †Robert Vtterby in goodes | .. | £4 |
| †John Flecher in goodes .. | .. 40s | *Richard Willemer in goodes | .. | 40s |
| Herry Bretten in goodes .. | .. £12 | William Brawell in goodes | .. | 40s |
| †John Exton in goodes | .. £30 | *William Lewen in goodes | .. | 40s |
| †Thomas Luffe in goodes .. | .. £3 | *Robert Walker in goodes | .. | 40s |
| *John Tomson in wages .. | .. 20s | *Richard Brayle in goodes | .. | 40s |
| Richard Nicoll in goodes | .. £30 | †Thomas Grey in goodes .. | .. | £5 6s 8d |
| †John Benyng in wages .. | .. 20s | William Johnson in goodes | .. | 40s |
| †Thomas Hogeson in goodes | .. £12 | Richard Clark in goodes .. | .. | 40s |
| *Thomas Wode in goodes | .. 40s | *Raff White in goodes .. | .. | £3 |
| †Richard Aburn in goodes | .. £10 | †William Knyght in goodes | .. | 40s |
| †John Wode in goodes .. | .. £4 | *Thomas Johnson Irisshman in wages | | 20s |
| *William Normanton in goodes .. | £8 | *Thomas Porter in wages .. | .. | 20s |
| †Thomas Normanton in goodes .. | £10 | William Herkyn in goodes | .. | 40s |
| John Colyn in goodes .. | .. £4 | *William Wright in goodes | .. | 40s |
| *William Wyly in goodes .. | .. £14 | *William Shepherd in goodes | .. | 40s |

*Sum* **£11 16s**

**1525**

| | | | | |
|---|---|---|---|---|
| John Caldecote Esquier in landes | 40 marks | Wylliam Kyng in goodes | .. £30 |
| Richard Willowby in goodes | .. £34 | Robert Wylmer in wages | .. 20s |
| John Flecher in goodes .. | .. £5 | Bartylmew Mylner in wages | .. 20s |
| John Exton in goodes .. | .. £20 | John Walker in wages .. | .. 20s |
| Thomas Love in goodes .. | .. £4 | Robert Sutton in wages .. | .. 20s |
| John Bonyng in goodes .. | .. 40s | Wylliam Astell in goodes | .. £12 |
| Richard Abron in goodes | .. £8 | John Plattes in goodes .. | .. £5 |
| John Wode in goodes .. | .. 40s | Wylliam Lovett in goodes | .. £3 |
| Thomas Normanton in goodes .. | £8 | Radulphe Nutte in goodes | .. £4 |

| | | |
|---|---|---|
| Herry Adam in goodes .. .. | £6 | Robert Nycols in goodes .. 40s |
| Wylliam Schatton[1] in goodes .. | £4 | Wylliam Johnson in goodes .. 40s |
| Wylliam Kechyn in goodes .. | £5 | John Boyeall in goodes .. .. £5 |
| Robert Vtterby in goodes .. | £5 | Thomas Hodgeson in goodes .. £10 |
| Thomas Grey in goodes .. .. | £5 | Richard Nycholas in goodes .. £20 |
| Wylliam Knyght in goodes .. | £3 | Wylliam Mason in wages .. 20s |

*Sum* **£10 2s 10d**

*Sum of the hundred,* 1524   **£57 5s 2d**
                         1525   **£44 4s 6d**

*m.5*

# THE HUNDRED OF MARTYNSLEY

## PRESTON

**1524**

| | | |
|---|---|---|
| John Dygby Gent. in londes .. | £5 | John Wyntar laber. in goodes .. 40s |
| Thomas Ierlond husb. in Goodes | £20 | William Turlyngton thacker in goodes .. .. .. .. 40s |
| Gylberd Tompson husb. in goodes | £12 | William Wyntar laber. in goodes 40s |
| John Fawkner husb. in Goodes .. | £12 | William Shyld laber. in goodes .. 20s |
| Thomas Coper husb. in goodes .. | £8 | William Wyntar, laber. in goodes 20s |
| Thomas Wheteley husb. in goodes | £9 | Richerd Jarman laber. in goodes 20s |
| Thomas Andrew husb. in goodes | £6 | William Jarman laber. in goodes 20s |
| Robert Tompson husb. in goodes | £3 | John Coper laber in goodes .. 20s |
| John Shyld husb. in goodes .. | £5 | John Ierlond laber. in profyt of wages .. .. .. .. 20s |
| William Rutkyn husb. in goodes | £3 | Robert Andrew laber. in lyk profyt 20s |
| Robert Ward husb. in goodes .. | £3 | William Fawkner laber. in lyke profyt .. .. .. .. 20s |
| Robett Sheryngton husb. in goodes | £3 | William Jerman laber. in goodes 20s |
| Clement Tyler laber. in goodes .. | 40s | |
| William Langton laber. in goodes | 40s | |
| Richerd Fawkner laber. in goodes | 40s | |

*Sum* **£3 11s**

## WING

**1524**

| | | |
|---|---|---|
| Robert Alyn, Smyth in goodes .. | £14 | Hew Banys laber. in goodes .. 40s |
| John Alyn husb. in goodes .. | £12 | Thomas Smyth laber. in profyt of wages .. .. .. .. 20s |
| Richerd Bunnyng husb. in goodes | £9 | Thomas Robynson laber. in lyke profyte .. .. .. .. 20s |
| John Tyler husb. in goodes .. | £4 | |
| William Sharp husb. in goodes .. | £4 | |

1.  *'Hatton' in 1524, which is a difficult reading, is probably the same as 'Schatton' in 1525.*

| | | | |
|---|---|---|---|
| William Sharp jun' husb. in goodes .. .. .. .. | £4 | Christofor Coplond laber. in wages | 20s |
| John Bunnyng husb. in goodes .. | £3 | Richerd Ierlond laber. in profyte of wages .. .. .. | 20s |
| John Peper Carpenter in goodes | £3 | Edmond Stubley Shepherd in lyke profyte .. .. .. .. | 20s |
| William Haull husb. in goodes .. | 40s | | |
| Robert Ierlond husb. in goodes .. | 40s | William Rawkyns laber in goodes | 40s |

Sum 32s 8d

**1525**, *14 names, illegible; sum about* **£1 10s 8d**

## REDLYNGTON

**1524**

| | | | |
|---|---|---|---|
| John Haryngton Esquire in londes | £60 | William Worthyngton husb. in goodes .. .. .. .. | 40s |
| Richerd Pek husb. in goodes .. | £18 | John Douve laber. in goodes .. | 20s |
| Richerd Horsley husb. in goodes | £10 | Thomas Sharp laber. in wages .. | 20s |
| Christofor Lacy husb. in goodes | £8 | Richerd Rose wefer in goodes .. | 20s |
| John Webster keper in goodes .. | £10 | Richerd Roger laber. .. .. | 20s |
| John Sharp husb. in goodes .. | £6 | John Fylyon laber. .. .. | 20s |
| William Haryngton Gent. in goodes .. .. .. .. | £3 | William Blomer Tayler in goodes | 20s |
| Richerd Bonyng husb. in goodes | £3 | John Hely yoman in wages .. | 20s |
| Thomas Tayler husb. in goodes .. | £6 | William Perkyn laber. in wages .. | 20s |
| William Curtseye husb. in goodes | £4 | Henry Sysmey laber. in profyte of wages .. .. .. .. | 20s |
| John Swaynson husb. in goodes .. | £6 | Thomas Dikman laber. in lyke profyte .. .. .. .. | 20s |
| John Tymson husb. in goodes .. | 40s | | |
| Johan Beryge wedow in goodes .. | 40s | John Coke in lyke profyte .. | 20s |
| William Timson husb. in goodes | 40s | John Lanbashy laber in wages .. | 20s |
| Margyt Symmys wedow in goodes | £5 | | |

Sum £5 7s 10d

**1525**, *about 28 names, illegible*

## NORMANTON

**1524**

| | | | |
|---|---|---|---|
| Thomas Greneham husb. in londes | £10 | John Hart laber. in profyte of wages .. .. .. .. | 20s |
| John Nayler husb. in goodes .. | £12 | John Shyrwod laber. in lyke profyte .. .. .. .. | 20s |
| Ysabell Shyrwode wedow in goodes | £3 | | |
| Richerd Smyth husb. in goodes .. | 40s | John Merell laber. in lyke profyte .. .. .. .. | 20s |
| Thomas Awston in goodes .. | 40s | | |
| Thomas Merell husb. in goodes | 40s | Ambrose Awsten laber. in lyke profyte .. .. .. .. | 20s |
| William Sherewode husb. in goodes | £3 | | |
| George Welbone husb. in goodes | 40s | | |

Sum 24s 4d

**1525**, *12 names, illegible; sum about* **23s.**

## HAMYLDON

**1524**

| | | | |
|---|---|---|---|
| Edward Burton Gent. in goodes | £30 | Rafe Nutt laber. in lyke profyte .. | 20s |
| John Atkyns husb. in goodes .. | £15 | †Robert Newell laber. in lyke profyte .. .. .. .. | 20s |
| William Fowley husb. in goodes | £16 | Robert Scott laber. in lyke profyte .. .. .. .. | 20s |
| †Robert Freman husb.[1] in goodes | £13 | †Robert Fynne laber. in lyke profyte .. .. .. .. | 20s |
| †Thomas Fowler husb. in goodes | £10 | †Thomas Redhed laber. in lyke profyte .. .. .. .. | 20s |
| Thomas Bradley husb. in goodes | £8 | Robert Jacson laber in lyke profyte .. .. .. .. | 20s |
| George More husb. in goodes .. | £6 | †Edward Richerdson laber. in lyke profyte .. .. .. .. | 20s |
| William Richerdson husb. in goodes .. .. .. .. | £5 | Thomas Broke laber. in goodes .. | 40s |
| Symond Fowler husb. in goodes | £8 | John Mathew laber. in goodes .. | 40s |
| Richerd Aswell husb. in goodes | £5 | Johne Fowler wedow in goodes .. £5 | |
| John Whytwell husb. in goodes .. | £3 | †Henry Fowler laber. in profyte of wages .. .. .. .. | 20s |
| John Baldoke husb. in goodes .. | £3 | William Whytwell laber. in goodes £3 | |
| John Fynne husb. in goodes .. | 40s | †William Burges laber. in goodes | 40s |
| Robert Aswell husb. in goodes .. | 40s | Robert Wyles laber. in profyte of wages .. .. .. .. | 20s |
| Robert Freman husb. in goodes | £3 | | |
| John Bell husb. in goodes .. | 40s | | |
| †William Gunthorp husb. in goodes | £3 | | |
| John Gunthorp husb. in goodes | 40s | | |
| †John Cole laber in profyte of wages .. .. .. .. | 20s | | |
| †Thomas Walker laber. in lyke profyte .. .. .. .. | 20s | | |

*Sum £4 12s 10d*

**1525**

| | | | |
|---|---|---|---|
| Robert Jerman in goodes .. | £11 | Thomas Redhed in goodes .. | 20s |
| Thomas Fowler in goodes .. | £5 | Robert Neyvell in goodes .. | 20s |
| Thomas Fowler in goodes .. | £3 | Edward Richardson in goodes .. | 20s |
| John Broke in goodes .. .. | 40s | John Coole in goodes .. .. | 20s |
| William Gunthorp in goodes .. | 40s | Harry Fowler in goodes .. .. | 20s |
| Robert Miller in goodes .. .. | 40s | Robert Harris in goodes .. .. | 20s |
| William Fyn in goodes .. .. | 20s | Robert Fyn in goodes .. .. | 20s |
| Thomas Walker in goodes .. | 20s | Richard [Red]hed in goodes .. | 20s |
| William Burgeys in goodes .. | 20s | [MS torn] in wages .. .. | 20s |
| William Royse in goodes .. | 20s | in goodes .. .. .. | 20s |

*Sum missing*

---

1. *Paid 6s 8d, the rate for £13. 6s 8d; probably becomes 'Jerman' in 1525.*

## EDYWESTON

**1524**

| | | | | | |
|---|---|---|---|---|---|
| John Page husb. in goodes | £12 | | Robert Coks laber in profytt | | |
| Thomas Tu[rnor] husb. in goodes | | 40s | for wages .. .. .. | | 20s |
| Robert Ward husb. in goodes .. | £4 | | Peter Hare laber in profyt of | | |
| John Graunt husb. in goodes .. | £3 | | wages .. .. .. | | 20s |
| John Graunt jun' husb. in | | | John Watars laber in lyke | | |
| goodes .. .. .. .. | | 40s | profyttes .. .. .. | | 20s |
| William Pykwell husb. in goodes | £6 | | William Androw yoman in lyke | | |
| William Barker husb. in goodes | £8 | | profyttes .. .. .. | | 20s |
| Hew Say husb. in goodes .. | £11 | | Christofor Coke laber. in lyke | | |
| John Tayler husb. in goodes .. | £3 | | profyttes .. .. .. | | 20s |
| Thomas Barker husb. in goodes | £8 13s 4d | | William Wryde laber. in lyke | | |
| Robert Freman husb. in goodes | | 40s | profyttes .. .. .. | | 20s |
| Thomas Berkar husb. in goodes | £5 | | Hew Say husb. in goodes .. | £4 | |
| John Aburn husb. in goodes .. | £12 | | William Ward husb. in goodes .. | | 40s |

*Sum* **44s 4d**

## MANTON

**1524**

| | | | | | |
|---|---|---|---|---|---|
| Thomas Burnby husb. in goodes | £20 | | Thomas Porter labe. in lyke | | |
| Henry Rutkyn husb. in goodes .. | £12 | | profyttes .. .. .. | | 20s |
| William Larons husb. in goodes | £10 | | Thomas Banys laber. in lyke | | |
| William Burnby husb. in goodes | £8 | | profyttes .. .. .. | | 20s |
| Richerd Chysylden husb. in | | | William Neyll laber. in lyke | | |
| goodes .. .. .. .. | £10 | | profyttes .. .. .. | | 20s |
| Thomas Laurence husb. in goodes | £5 | | John Godle laber. in lyke | | |
| John Bland husb. in goodes .. | £3 | | profyttes .. .. .. | | 20s |
| William Mores husb. in goodes .. | | 40s | Henry Thornton laber. in lyke | | |
| John Stande husb. in goodes .. | | 40s | profyttes .. .. .. | | 20s |
| Antony Bunnyng husb. in goodes | | 40s | Christofor Fereby laber. in lyke | | |
| William Bradford husb. in goodes | | 40s | profyttes .. .. .. | | 20s |
| William Brown husb. in goodes | | 40s | Henry Burnby husb. in goodes .. | | 40s |
| Richard Louth laber. in profytte | | | | | |
| for wages .. .. .. | | 20s | | | |

*Sum* **52s 4d**

*Sum of the hundred* **£29 16s 2d**

## VPPYNGHAM

**1525**

| | | | | | |
|---|---|---|---|---|---|
| Widow Brige in goodes .. .. | £18 | | William Lokwood in goodes .. | | 40s |
| Bartilmew Ouerton in goodes .. | £12 | | John Baker in goodes .. .. | | 20s |
| Richard Chitwood in goodes .. | £7 | | Roger Wilson in goodes .. .. | £5 | |
| William Salisbury in goodes .. | £14 | | William Oxon in goodes .. .. | | 40s |

| | | | | |
|---|---|---|---|---|
| William Andrew in goodes | .. | £4 | Hughe Duffe in goodes .. .. | £5 |
| John Vnderwood in goodes | .. | £12 | John Bennet in goodes .. .. | £3 |
| Thomas Affell in goodes .. | .. | £8 | George Pakman in goodes .. | £3 |
| Richard Hogekyn in goodes | .. | £8 | Thomas Nicolles in goodes .. | 40s |
| John Atwell in goodes .. | .. | £8 | John Brigstoke in goodes .. | 20s |
| Ambros Grene in goodes | .. | £10 | Robert Affell in goodes .. | 40s |
| Edward Sampson in goodes | .. | £4 | Richard Gravell in goodes .. | 20s |
| Nicolles Lacye in goodes | .. | £10 | William Bull in goodes .. | £3 |
| Harry Preston in goodes .. | .. | £3 | John Horseley in goodes .. .. | 40s |
| Thomas Pakman in goodes | .. | 20s | John Richardson in goodes .. | 20s |
| William Vnderwood in goodes | .. | £10 | Robert Burrell in goodes .. | 20s |
| John Robynson in goodes | .. | 20s | Richard Fox in goodes .. | 20s |
| William Lacye in goodes | .. | 40s | Thomas Hill in goodes .. | 40s |
| William Rudhull in goodes | .. | £12 | Harry Hyll in goodes .. | 40s |
| Robert Drayton in goodes | .. | £10 | Clement Tiller in goodes .. | 40s |
| William Atwell in goodes | .. | £14 | Thomas Glover in goodes .. | 40s |
| Roger Lawghton in goodes | .. | £3 | Thomas Lokit keper in goodes .. | £3 |
| Richard Walker in goodes | .. | 20s | Thomas Keysbe in goodes .. | 20s |
| Bartilmew Nayll in goodes | .. | 20s | Mathew of the parsonage in | |
| Richard Lincoln in goodes | .. | £6 | goodes .. .. .. .. | £4 |

*Sum* **£5 12s 2d**

## LYNDON

**1525**

| | | | | |
|---|---|---|---|---|
| Ambrose Barker in goodes | .. | £10 | William Baxster in goodes .. | 20s |
| Gregory Barker in goodes | .. | £12 | John Miller in goodes .. .. | 20s |
| Edmond Stanelond in goodes | .. | £8 | William Horseley in goodes .. | 40s |
| William Stanelond in goodes | .. | 40s | John Warnoke in goodes .. | 40s |
| Thomas Fay[rman] in goodes | .. | 40s | John Chapman in goodes .. | £3 |
| William Th . . . . in goodes | .. | 20s | William Chamber in goodes .. | 20s |

*Sum* **[21s 10d]**

## AYSTON

**1525**

| | | | | |
|---|---|---|---|---|
| Richard Olever in goodes | .. | £15 | Robert Kyrke in goodes .. .. | 40s |
| Thomas Williams in goodes | .. | £8 | John Atkynson in goodes .. | 20s |
| Thomas Colson in goodes | .. | £8 | Thomas Whetley in goodes .. | 20s |
| John Peyke in goodes .. | .. | £6 | Thomas Kyrke in goodes .. | 20s |
| William Drayton in goodes | .. | £6 | Thomas Welles in goodes .. | £3 |
| John Kyrke in goodes .. | .. | £11 | [Harry Watson] in goodes .. | 20s |
| John Jakson in goodes .. | .. | £3 | John . . . . . seruant in wages .. | 20s |
| Richard Allyn in goodes .. | .. | £3 | . . . . . . . . seruant in wages .. | 20s |
| Thomas [Dooster] in goodes | .. | 40s | | |

*Sum* **32s 6d**

*m. 6*

# THE HUNDRED OF ALSTOW

## WYSSENDEN

**1524**

| | | | |
|---|---|---|---|
| Laurens Bartley Gent. in londes | £14 | Rycherd Bentley husb. in goodes | 40s |
| James Obyns husb. in goodes | £30 | Christofor Batson laber. in goodes | 40s |
| Thomas Wetley husb. in goodes | £20 | William Lovyt laber. in goodes | 40s |
| Thomas Watkyns husb. in goodes | £17 | William Man laber. in goodes | 40s |
| Richerd Wortley husb. in goodes | £7 | Richerd Snow laber. in goodes | 40s |
| Hew Sharp husb. in goodes | £20 | Henry Makedaunce laber. in goodes | 40s |
| John Cecell husb. in goodes | £6 | Robert Hopkyns laber. in wages | 20s |
| John Greneham husb. in goodes | £10 | John Perkyn laber. in profyte of wages | 20s |
| Richerd Lovyt husb. in goodes | £3 | William Standell laber. in lyk profyte | 20s |
| Richerd Laurens husb. in goodes | £5 | John Grouue laber. in lyk profyte | 20s |
| William Beryge husb. in goodes | £4 | Thomas Smyth laber. in lyk profyte | 20s |
| Robert Melton husb. in goodes | £4 | William Hereford laber. in lyk profyte | 20s |
| John Wortley husb. in goodes | £4 | John Kyrkdale laber. in lyk profyte | 20s |
| James Reve husb. in goodes | £3 | John Hochyn laber in lyk profyte | 20s |
| John Wayte husb. in goodes | £3 | Thomas Shovell laber. in goodes | 20s |
| Robert Robyns husb. in goodes | £3 | Robert Man laber. in goodes | 20s |
| William Wortley husb. in goodes | 40s | Richerd Wayte laber. in profyte of wages | 20s |
| William Mason husb. in goodes | 40s | Thomas Browne laber. in lyk profyte | 20s |
| Richerd Coke husb. in goodes | 40s | John Morton laber. in lyk profyte | 20s |
| Robert Machyn husb. in goodes | 40s | | |
| Roger Ryley laber. in goodes | 40s | | |
| William Pay laber. in goodes | 40s | | |
| John Man husb. in goodes | 40s | | |

*Sum* **£6 15s 10d**

## MARKYT OUERTON

**1524**

| | | | |
|---|---|---|---|
| Robert Ryse yoman in goodes | £3 | John Pleyer laber. in wages | 20s |
| William Stalok husb. in goodes | £3 | Andrew Hoggynson laber. in lyk profyte | 20s |
| William Porter husb. in goodes | 40s | | |

| | | | | |
|---|---|---|---|---|
| Richerd Whyghted husb. in goodes | £11 | Richerd Smart Wryght in lyk profyttes | .. .. .. | 20s |
| Richerd Nyk husb. in goodes .. | £3 | Thomas Rosyll laber. in lyk | | |
| James Holt husb. in goodes .. | £3 | profyttes .. .. .. | | 20s |
| Henry Porter husb. in goodes .. | £4 | William Ward laber. in lyk | | |
| †Henry Baxster husb. in goodes .. | £4 | profyttes .. .. .. .. | | 20s |
| William Grey husb. in goodes .. | 40s | John Porter laber. in lyk profyttes | | 20s |
| Richerd Hull laber. in goodes .. | 40s | William Whythed laber. in lyk | | |
| John Bartfeld husb. in goodes .. | 40s | profyttes .. .. .. | | 20s |
| Thomas Blowfeld husb. in goodes | 40s | Richerd Samson laber. in lyk | | |
| Thomas Snokystobe husb. in goodes | 20s | profyttes .. .. .. | | 20s |
| John Spenyng husb. in goodes .. | 20s | John Nyk in goodes .. .. | | £4 |
| †John Snokystobe husb. in goodes | £3 | | | |

*Sum* **27s 4d**

**1525** (*incomplete; 11 names only*)

| | | | |
|---|---|---|---|
| John Snokstob in goodes .. | 40s | Henry Baxster in goodes .. .. | 20s |
| Thomas Wilson in goodes .. | 20s | Robert Faconer in goodes .. | 20s |
| Thomas Dasse in goodes .. | 20s | | |

*Sum* **26s 4d**

## BARROW

**1524**

| | | | |
|---|---|---|---|
| William Nicols husb. in goodes .. | £16 | *John Allom mylner in goodes .. | 20s |
| William Christian[1] husb. in goodes .. .. .. .. | £14 | Robert Grene laber. in wages .. | 20s |
| Nycolas Castlyn husb. in goodes | £5 | Peter Hawkyns laber. in lyk profyte .. .. .. .. | 20s |
| Roger Steven husb. in goodes .. | £7 | *Henry Frekyngham laber. in lyk | |
| Thomas Clark husb. in goodes .. | £6 | profyte .. .. .. .. | 20s |
| Robert Dunnow husb. in goodes | 40s | John Christian[1] laber. in wages .. | 40s |
| *Robert Rosse husb. in goodes .. | 40s | Robert Christian[1] laber. in | |
| John Nicoll husb. in goodes .. | 40s | goodes .. .. .. .. | 40s |
| Thomas Roberd laber. in profyttes of wages .. .. .. | 20s | *Robert Clark laber. in wages .. | 20s |
| | | Henry Palmer laber. in lyk profyte | 20s |

*Sum* **31s 4d**

**1525**

| | | | |
|---|---|---|---|
| Robert Christian in goodes .. | £3 | Harry Pykwell in goodes .. | 20s |
| Thomas Wade in goodes .. | 20s | | |

*Sum* **29s 10d**

1.  '*Xpian*' *in MS.*

## THYSSILTON

**1524**

| | | | |
|---|---|---|---|
| *John Jacson husb. in Goodes .. | £9 | John Raffe husb. in goodes .. | 40s |
| Thomas Cooper husb. in goodes | £10 | William Rey laber. in wages .. | 20s |
| *John Lame husb. in goodes .. | £4 | John Rey laber. in profyttes of | |
| John Broughton husb. in goodes | £3 | wages .. .. .. .. | 20s |
| William Medybroke[1] husb. in goodes | £3 | Robert Fyslak yoman in goodes | 20s |
| Robert Peter husb. in goodes .. | 40s | Richerd Schort laber. in goodes | 40s |

*Sum* **18s 6d**

**1525**

| | | | |
|---|---|---|---|
| . . . . . Whithed in goodes .. | £11 | William [Grene] in goodes .. | 20s |
| William Whithed in goodes .. | 40s | | |

*Sum* **20s 10d**

## TYGH

**1524**

| | | | |
|---|---|---|---|
| Richerd Grene husb. in goodes .. | £20 | William Chapman husb. in goodes | 40s |
| William Money husb. in goodes | 40s | John Chapman husb. in goodes | 20s |
| Richerd Waltham husb. in goodes | £3 | Thomas Plunger husb. in goodes | 40s |
| Robert Chapman husb. in goodes | £8 | John Waltham husb. in goodes .. | 40s |
| John Pulleyn husb. in goodes .. | 20s | John Dyng husb. in goodes .. | £4 |
| Thomas Mony husb. in goodes .. | £10 | William Wayde husb. in goodes | £4 |
| Richerd Beyt husb. in goodes .. | 20s | William Quenyborough husb. in | |
| William Wylcok husb. in goodes | £3 | goodes .. .. .. .. | £3 |
| John Standerlond laber. in | | Richerd Grene husb. in goodes .. | £4 |
| goodes .. .. .. .. | 20s | Laurens Waltham laber. in wages | 20s |

*Sum* **45s 2d**

## EXTON

**1524**

| | | | |
|---|---|---|---|
| Alys Haryngton wedow in londes | £40 | Phylyp Colls laber. in goodes .. | 20s |
| Robert Clarke husb. in goodes .. | £10 | Edward Grene husb. in goodes .. | 40s |
| William Moyse husb. in goodes | £12 | John Freyne husb. in goodes .. | 40s |
| John Royse husb. in goodes .. | £13 | William Park husb. in goodes .. | 40s |
| John Freman husb. in goodes .. | £15 | William Souter husb. in goodes .. | 40s |
| Robert Loke husb. in goodes .. | £10 | John Tauerer husb. in goodes .. | 40s |
| Richerd Wryght husb. in goodes | £9 | William Muse husb. in goodes .. | 40s |
| Thomas Sowter husb. in goodes | £8 | Thomas Ouerton Tailer in goodes | 20s |
| Thomas Sysson husb. in goodes | £4 | John Apark laber. in goodes .. | 20s |
| John Smyth husb. in goodes .. | £4 | William Stevyn laber. in goodes | 20s |

1. *'Middelbroke' in 1525.*

| | | | | |
|---|---|---|---|---|
| Thomas Smyth husb. in goodes .. | £10 | | Robert Gunthorp Tayler in goodes | 40s |
| Thomas Walcheman husb. in goodes | £5 | | Robert Stevynson husb. in goodes | £3 |
| John Nyk husb. in goodes    .. | £4 | | Thomas Nuttson Smyth in goodes | 20s |
| Hew Clarke husb. in goodes    .. | £6 | | Robert Clarke laber. in wages    .. | 20s |
| George Souter husb. in goodes .. | £4 | | Robert Loke laber. in profytes | |
| Thomas Tyler husb. in goodes | £3 | | of wages ..    ..    ..    .. | 20s |
| Thomas Watson husb. in goodes | £3 | | William Souter laber. in lyk | |
| Robert Colls husb. in goodes    .. | £3 | | profyttes    ..    ..    .. | 20s |
| John Clarke husb. in goodes    .. | | 40s | Robert Smyth laber. in lyk | |
| Richerd Darby husb. in goodes .. | £3 | | profyttes    ..    ..    .. | 20s |
| John Wryght husb. in goodes    .. | £3 | | William Velam Sheperd in lyk | |
| James Amore husb. in goodes    .. | | 40s | profytes ..    ..    ..    .. | 40s |
| Raffe Abryg husb. in goodes    .. | | 40s | Robert Haryngton in londes    .. | £10 |
| Robert Sharp husb. in goodes .. | | 40s | Thomas Haryngton laber. in wages | 20s |
| John Perysvale husb. in goodes .. | | 40s | John Rygston in wages    ..    .. | 20s |
| John Colls husb. in goodes    .. | | 40s | Thomas Smyth in wages ..    .. | 20s |

*Sum* **£6 13s 4d**

## STRETTON

**1524**

| | | | | |
|---|---|---|---|---|
| Robert Wells husb. in goodes    .. | £12 | | Thomas Lamme laber. in goodes | 20s |
| Robert Skelyngton husb. in goodes | £12 | | Thomas Kensall husb. in goodes | 40s |
| William Wethed husb. in goodes | £11 | | William Wassyngborogh laber. | |
| John Skelyngton husb. in goodes | £8 | | in goodes    ..    ..    .. | 40s |
| John Quenyborogh jun. husb. | | | John Skellet netherd in goodes .. | 40s |
| in goodes    ..    ..    .. | £6 | | Richard Fyslak laber. in goodes | 20s |
| John Dollymer husb. in goodes .. | £3 | | Thomas Kensall jun. in profytte | |
| Thomas Wesythed laber. in goodes | £3 | | of wages ..    ..    ..    .. | 20s |
| Robert Dalymer husb. in goodes | £3 | | Thomas Watson laber. in wages | 20s |
| George Rogerson husb. in goodes | £3 | | [John] Backby laber. in wages    .. | 20s |
| John Quenyborogh sen. husb. | | | John Skelyngton laber. in wages | 20s |
| in goodes    ..    ..    .. | £3 | | Richerd Skelyngton sheperd in | |
| Thomas Goole laber. in goodes | | 20s | wages    ..    ..    ..    .. | 20s |
| William Coke laber. in goodes    .. | | 20s | | |

*Sum* **38s**

## GRETHAM

**1524**

| | | | | |
|---|---|---|---|---|
| †John Bronne yoman in goodes    .. | £10 | | †Thomas Hopkyn husb. in goodes | £3 |
| *Robert Laxston husb. in goodes | £16 | | Robert Rych husb. in goodes    .. | 40s |
| †John Wooston husb. in goodes    .. | £5 | | †John Stark husb. in goodes    .. | 40s |
| †John Somerby husb. in goodes    .. | £4 | | †John Bronne laber. in goodes    .. | 40s |
| †Thomas Wells husb. in goodes    .. | £6 | | †Stevyn Beell smyth in goodes    .. | 40s |
| *William Lee husb. in goodes    .. | £4 | | *John Howley laber. in goodes    .. | 20s |

| | | | |
|---|---|---|---|
| †Robert Nyk husb. in goodes .. | £4 | Richerd Parker laber. in goodes | 40s |
| *Thomas Terry husb. in goodes .. | £4 | *Henry Freman laber. in goodes .. | 20s |
| Robert Coper husb. in goodes .. | £4 | *Robert Sawer laber. in goodes .. | 20s |
| †Robert Parker husb. in goodes .. | £4 | *John Herdy netherd in goodes .. | 20s |
| †Rowlond Blak husb. in goodes .. | £3 | Richerd Crosse laber. in goodes | 20s |
| *Thomas Swyft husb. in goodes .. | £3 | William Hauley laber. in goodes | 20s |
| *Thomas Netyls husb. in goodes .. | £3 | Rycherd Royse laber. in goodes | 20s |
| John Chamberlen husb. in | | *Thomas Johnson laber. in goodes | 20s |
| goodes   ..        ..        ..        .. | £3 | John Haryson laber. in goodes .. | 20s |

*Sum* **46s**

**1525**

| | | | |
|---|---|---|---|
| [John Bronne][1] in goodes .. | £9 | Thomas Wells in goodes ..        .. | £5 |
| John Somerby in goodes .. | £5 | Thomas Silkylste in goodes      .. | 40s |
| John Woyssen in goodes .. | £3 | John Doble in goodes    ..       .. | 40s |
| William Lednam in goodes .. | £6 | Robert Winch in goodes ..        .. | 40s |
| Rowlond Blake in goodes .. | £3 | William Peper in goodes ..       .. | 40s |
| Richard Netham in goodes .. | £3 | John Stark in goodes    ..       .. | 30s[2] |
| Thomas Hopkyn in goodes .. | 40s | Steven Bell in goodes   ..       .. | 20s |
| Robert Nyke in goodes  ..    .. | 40s | John Brown in goodes    ..       .. | 20s |
| Robert Parker in goodes ..    .. | 40s | Henry Frekyngham in goodes      .. | 20s |

*Sum* **30s 4d**

### BURLEY

**1524**

| | | | |
|---|---|---|---|
| Edward Sapcotes Esquier in londes | £55 | William Curl laber. in goodes  .. | 40s |
| †William Wilkinson husb. in goodes | £16 | Robert Baker laber. in wages  .. | 20s |
| John Tyler husb. in goodes     .. | £18 | Richerd Antony laber. in wages | 20s |
| Robert Velam husb. in goodes  .. | £4 | Robert Croft laber. in wages  .. | 20s |
| John Hunton husb. in goodes  .. | £6 | Robert Hogeson laber. in wages .. | 20s |
| †John Wymark husb. in goodes  .. | £5 | John Armstrong laber. in wages .. | 20s |
| John Bakhous husb. in goodes  .. | £3 | Richerd Johnson laber. in wages | 20s |
| John Astorby husb. in goodes  .. | £4 | Thomas Day laber. in wages    .. | 20s |
| William Hoggeson husb. in goodes | £4 | Richerd Dalby laber. in wages .. | 20s |
| William Thyrmeston husb. in | | Robert Bronne laber. in wages .. | 20s |
| goodes   ..        ..        ..        .. | £3 | Richerd Brygges laber. in wages | 20s |
| John Hand laber. in goodes     .. | 40s | Thomas Dekynson laber. in wages | 20s |
| William Kyrkman laber. in goodes | 40s | John Cotton laber. in wages   .. | 20s |
| John Webster laber. in goodes .. | 40s | Thomas Velam laber. in wages .. | 20s |

*Sum* **£4 14s 10d**

1. *Conjectural, the entry being almost illegible.*
2. *Paid 6d.*

**1525** (*a fragment containing 6 names*)

| | | | |
|---|---|---|---|
| William Wylkynson in goodes .. | £18 | John Wymerk in goodes .. .. | £6 |

## COTTYSMORE

*The 1524 return must have contained about 45 entries originally, but 11 or 12 are now illegible where the MS is torn; the 1525 one is complete but much shorter. Both are therefore printed in full.*

### 1524

| | | | |
|---|---|---|---|
| Thomas Dorant gent. in goodes | £20 | Richerd Stubbes laber. in goodes | 20s |
| John Bate yoman in goodes .. | £18 | Richerd Cyttysdery in wages .. | 20s |
| Robert Chamberlen husb. in goodes | £16 | John Depyng laber. in wages .. | 20s |
| John Dorant husb. in goodes .. | £4 | Nicholas Assely Tayler in goodes | 20s |
| Thomas Hunton husb. in goodes | £3 | William Parre laber. in wages .. | 20s |
| John Alyn husb. in goodes .. | £6 | Stevyn Gylon laber. in wages .. | 20s |
| William Man husb. in goodes .. | £6 | Hew Morlond Tayler in goodes .. | 20s |
| John Hygecok husb. in goodes .. | £5 | John Breton laber. in wages .. | 20s |
| Edmond [Rob] son husb. in goodes | £8 | Thomas Leylond laber. in wages | 20s |
| John . . . . . . .. .. .. | 40s | James Rankynson laber. in wages | 20s |
| John Bett yoman in goodes .. | 40s | Rafe Turpyn laber. in wages .. | 20s |
| Robert Stubbe laber. in goodes .. | 40s | William Wells laber. in wages .. | 20s |
| Edmond Coper in goodes .. | £10 | John Walker laber. in wages .. | 20s |
| John Coper husb. in goodes .. | £4 | Thomas Eygeley laber. in wages | 20s |
| Agnes Colyn wedow in goodes .. | £3 | Thomas Greneham laber. in wages | 20s |
| *MS torn* | | John Doure husb. in goodes .. | £3 |
| Thomas Kyrk Scot in goodes .. | £3 | | |

**Sum £4 11s 4d**

### 1525

| | | | |
|---|---|---|---|
| Thomas Dorant in goodes .. | £15 | John Walker in goodes .. .. | 20s |
| Jamys Vrmestone in goodes .. | £5 | Thomas Hunnton in goodes .. | £3 |
| Robert Britmer in goodes .. | £3 | John Bretten in goodes .. .. | 20s |
| Nicolles Asslyn in goodes .. | 20s | John Allyn in goodes .. .. | £6 |
| William Turpyn in goodes .. | £6 | William Man in goodes .. .. | £7 |
| Robert Chamberlyn in goodes .. | £18 | John Hichecok in goodes .. | £5 |
| John Rushell in goodes .. .. | £6 | Emmote Collyn widow in goodes | 40s |
| John Cooper in goodes .. .. | £6 | Thomas Stark in goodes .. .. | 40s |
| John Plommer in goodes .. | 40s | William Woode in goodes .. | 40s |
| John Bate in goodes .. .. | £16 | William Clere in goodes .. .. | £4 |
| Robert Stubbes jun' in goodes .. | 20s | Edmond Cooper in goodes .. | £10 |
| John Bett in goodes .. .. | 20s | Robert Hunt in goodes .. .. | 20s |
| Johan Scharpe widow in goodes | 40s | William Burchebek in goodes .. | 40s |

| | | | | |
|---|---|---|---|---|
| Edmond Robson in goodes | .. | £7 | Robert Sneth in goodes .. .. | £4 |
| Nicolles Oldham in goodes | .. | 20*s* | Hugh Morlond in goodes .. | 40*s* |
| Richard Turpyn in goodes | .. | 20*s* | Robert Baker seruant in goodes | 20*s* |
| William Dalycok in goodes | .. | 20*s* | Raffe Turpyn in goodes .. .. | 20*s* |

*Sum* **£3 12s**

## ASWELL

**1524**

| | | | |
|---|---|---|---|
| John Smyth yoman in goodes .. | 40*s* | Geferey Spynyng husb. in goodes | 40*s* |
| Thomas Rydmyed[1] husb. in goodes | £10 | *William Castlyn husb. in goodes | £3 |
| Thomas Stancion[2] husb. in goodes | £3 | Robert Wylkok husb. in goodes | £10 |
| William Chapman husb. in goodes | £4 | *John Chaveney yoman in goodes | £10 |
| *Emot Thorp wedow in goodes | 40*s* | William Spynyng laber. in goodes | 20*s* |
| *John Castlyn husb. in goodes .. | 40*s* | †John Dey laber. in goodes[3] .. | 30*s* |
| Robert Heryng husb. in goodes .. | 40*s* | *William Harmyn laber. in goodes | 20*s* |
| Thomas Carttych husb. in goodes | £3 | *William .... laber. in goodes .. | 20*s* |
| Thomas Jarmon husb. in goodes | 40*s* | John Pulloke laber. in goodes .. | 20*s* |
| Rafe Bothamen husb. in goodes | 40*s* | Thomas Spynyng laber. in goodes | 20*s* |
| John Wenoll husb. in goodes .. | 40*s* | John Hamer laber. in goodes .. | 20*s* |
| John Castlyn husb. in goodes .. | £5 | †Richerd Heryng laber. in goodes | 20*s* |
| Thomas Androw husb. in goodes | £10 | *John Rutlond laber. in londes .. | 20*s* |
| John Wells husb. in goodes .. | £5 | †Annys Castlyn wedow in londes[4] | 26*s* 8*d* |
| *Thomas Breysell husb. in goodes | £3 | *John Dylworth laber. in goodes | 20*s* |
| John Mason husb. in goodes .. | 40*s* | *Thomas Groue in goodes .. | 20*s* |
| *Henry Breydsall husb. in goodes | 40*s* | | |

*Sum* **46s 8d**

**1525**

| | | | |
|---|---|---|---|
| Richerd Heryng in goodes | .. | 40*s* | Lawrence Waltham in goodes .. | 20*s* |
| Agnes Castelyn in landes[5] | .. | 30*s* | Robert Yeman in goodes .. | 20*s* |
| William Irenes in goodes | .. | 20*s* | | |

*Sum* **36s 4d**

1. *Redingle in 1525.*
2. *Stanmoyn in 1525.*
3. *John Dow, paid 6d. in 1525.*
4. *'goodes' struck out.*
5. *Paid 6d; should be 1s 6d.*

## WHYTWELL

**1524**

| | | | | |
|---|---|---|---|---|
| †Roger [Floure] Esquyer in londes | £80 | | William Fynyngley laber. in | |
| Wylliam Belamy husb. in goodes | £10 | | wages[1] .. .. .. .. | 20s |
| †Thomas Sherfeld husb. in goodes | | 40s | Robert Belamy laber. in wages[1] | 20s |
| †Richerd Fynyngley in londes .. | | 26s 8d | William Kyng laber. in wages[1] .. | 20s |
| Richerd Wright [husb] in goodes | £5 | | Thomas Bregges laber. in wages[1] | 20s |

*Sum* **£4 12s 2d**

**1525**

| | | | | |
|---|---|---|---|---|
| Jeyr Flower Esquyer in landes .. | £60 | | Richard Fynnyngley in landes .. | £3 |
| Thomas Sheffild in goodes .. | £3 | | Robert Smyth in goodes .. .. | 20s |

*Sum* **£3 12s 6d**

*Sum of the hundred* **£40. 2s 6d**

# THE HUNDRYD OF OKAM SOKEN

## OKAM

**1524**

| | | | | |
|---|---|---|---|---|
| Jamys Waren gent. in goodes .. | 100 marks | | Thomas Ortone laber. in profyt | |
| William Plavys pewterer in | | | of wages .. .. .. .. | 20s |
| goodes .. .. .. .. | £100 | | John Sharp laber. in lyk | |
| Henry Whygh yoinor in goodes | 20 marks | | profyttes .. .. .. | 20s |
| Richerd Morecroft Mercer in | | | William Clefe laber. in lyk | |
| goodes .. .. .. .. | £40 | | profittes .. .. .. .. | 20s |
| Henry Jarves yoman in goodes .. | £14 | | Richerd Gebon laber. in lyk | |
| Robert Armestronge draper in | | | profittes .. .. .. .. | 20s |
| goodes .. .. .. .. | £17 | | John Catares laber. in lyk | |
| William Woodcok yoman in goodes | £10 | | profittes .. .. .. .. | 20s |
| Hew Thorp yoman in goodes .. | £16 | | William Quateryng laber. in lyk | |
| William Wryght yoman in goodes | £7 | | profittes .. .. .. .. | 20s |
| William Batte yoman in goodes | £10 | | Richerd Turner laber. in lyk .. | |
| Henry Raseby husb. in goodes | £10 | | profittes .. .. .... .. | 20s |
| Christopher Greene husb. in | | | John Mesell laber. in lyk | |
| goodes .. .. .. .. | £14 | | profittes .. .. .. .. | 20s |
| William Ymys husb. in goodes .. | £13 | 6s 8d | John Dunsyll laber. in lyk | |
| Thomas Haryngton husb. in goodes | £10 | | profittes .. .. .. .. | 20s |
| Nicholas Hill yoman in goodes .. | £6 | | William Hancok laber. in lyk | |
| Hew Turner husb. in goodes .. | £8 | | profittes .. .. .. .. | 20s |

1. *Taxed on goodes in 1525.*

| | | | | |
|---|---|---|---|---|
| William Glener Berber in goodes | £6 | Thomas Patt laber. in lyk | | |
| William Nauby husb. in goodes | £6 | profittes .. .. .. .. | | 20s |
| Otwell Tranow husb. in goodes .. | £5 | John Jacson laber. in lyk | | |
| James Sotherlond Glouer in goodes | £4 | profittes .. .. .. .. | | 20s |
| John Velam husb. in goodes .. | £7 | John James laber. in lyk | | |
| John Dikman husb. in goodes .. | 40s | profittes .. .. .. .. | | 20s |
| William Fewell husb. in goodes .. | £7 | John Andrew laber. in lyk | | |
| Rafe Sharp husb. in goodes .. | £5 | profittes .. .. .. .. | | 20s |
| Henry Hayt husb. in goodes .. | £6 | Robert Gunby laber. in lyk | | |
| Thomas Traforth husb. in goodes | £4 | profittes .. .. .. .. | | 20s |
| Stevyn Bunnyng husb. in goodes | 40s | Edmonde Langton laber. in lyk | | |
| John Wryngton husb. in goodes | 40s | profittes .. .. .. .. | | 20s |
| Stevyn Ouerend husb. in goodes | £6 | John Hausell laber. in lyk | | |
| John Johnson husb. in goodes .. | £3 | profittes .. .. .. .. | | 20s |
| John Benytt husb. in goodes .. | £3 | John Fouler laber. in lyk | | |
| Robert Gelburne husb. in goodes | £6 | profittes .. .. .. .. | | 20s |
| William Bunnyng husb. in goodes | £3 | William Balldok laber. in lyk | | |
| John Beker husb. in goodes .. | £6 | profittes .. .. .. .. | | 20s |
| William Eltham husb. in goodes | £3 | John Ward laber in lyk profittes | | 20s |
| Richerd Norman husb. in goodes | 40s | John Jurden laber. in lyk | | |
| John Jacson husb. in goodes .. | £3 | profittes .. .. .. .. | | 20s |
| Thomas Medons husb. in goodes | £4 | John Mey laber. in lyk profittes | | 20s |
| Christofer Pare husb. in goodes | 40s | Rafe Somer laber. in lyk profittes | | 20s |
| John Adcok laber. in goodes .. | 40s | Jamys Stanyard pewterer in goodes | | 20s |
| Thomas Stanyard laber. in | | John Haryson pewterer in wages | | 20s |
| goodes .. .. .. .. | 40s | Rafe Benet laber. in wages .. | | 20s |
| William Dovy husb. in goodes .. | £4 | John Haston laber. in wages .. | | 20s |
| Richerd Procter husb. in | | Jamys Fedyner laber. in wages | | 20s |
| goodes .. .. .. .. | £4 | William Baryt laber. in wages .. | | 20s |
| John Pereson husb. in goodes .. | £3 | Thomas Heyat laber. in wages .. | | 20s |

*Sum* **£17 7s 8d**

## THABOTTES FEE

**1524**

| | | | | |
|---|---|---|---|---|
| Robert Hopkyns husb. in goodes | £5 | John Egeston laber. in lyk | | |
| Richerd Sharp husb. in goodes .. | 40s | profittes .. .. .. .. | | 20s |
| William Sheperd husb. in goodes | £4 | William Brygges laber. in lyk | | |
| Thomas Thornton laber. in goodes | 40s | profittes .. .. .. .. | | 20s |
| John Wyllyman husb. in goodes | 40s | John Pylkyngton laber. in lyk | | |
| [William] Pylkyngton husb. in | | profittes .. .. .. .. | | 20s |
| goodes .. .. .. .. | £3 | Thomas Hewytson laber. in lyk .. | | |
| Peter Sly fuller in goodes .. | 20s | profittes .. .. .. .. | | 20s |

| | | | |
|---|---|---|---|
| John P[ylkyngton] Berbar in goodes | 20s | John She . . . . laber. in lyk | |
| John Haull laber. in Profyt for | |  profittes ..   ..   ..   .. | 20s |
|  wages   ..   ..   .. | 20s | John Barret laber. in lyk | |
| Robert Grene . . . . . .   ..   .. | 20s |  profittes   ..   ..   .. | 20s |
| Richerd Smyth laber. in lyk | | John Thorp husb. in goodes   .. | £12 |
|  profittes ..   ..   ..   .. | 20s | | |

*Sum* **18s 8d**

## LANGHAM

**1524**

| | | | | | | |
|---|---|---|---|---|---|---|
| John Clark husb. in goodes   .. | £20 | | | John Laurens husb. in goodes   .. | 40s | |
| William Clark husb. in goodes | £3 | | | Thomas Watars husb. in goodes | £4 | |
| Henry Hubbert husb. in goodes | £16 | 6s | 8d | Thomas Busche husb. in goodes | 40s | |
| Gregory Smyth Bocher in goodes | £13 | 6s | 8d | John Hunt husb. in goodes   .. | 40s | |
| John Ball sen. husb. in goodes   .. | £10 | | | John Gybson husb. in goodes   .. | 40s | |
| Nicholas Pyttes husb. in goodes | £6 | | | William Crane husb. in goodes   .. | 40s | |
| Robert Bery husb. in goodes   .. | £6 | | | John Dykman husb. in goodes   .. | 40s | |
| Thomas Walous husb. in goodes | £6 | | | John Welous husb. in goodes   .. | £3 | |
| William Dykman 1. [sic] in goodes | 20s | | | Thomas Ardyn Berkar in goodes | 40s | |
| Thomas Beyson husb. in goodes | £4 | | | John Michell laber. in goodes   .. | 40s | |
| Thomas Boylesmere husb. in goodes | 40s | | | Richerd Browne laber. in goodes | 40s | |
| Robert Ybys husb. in goodes   .. | £4 | | | Willism Wells Berkar in goodes | £5 | |
| William Stevyns husb. in goodes | £10 | | | Thomas Trayford husb. in goodes | £5 | |
| Bartylmew Tayler husb. in goodes | £4 | | | John Myddylton husb. in goodes | 40s | |
| John Ball jun. husb. in goodes   .. | £8 | | | William Webster laber. in goodes | 40s | |
| William Beyll husb. in goodes   .. | £7 | | | John Watson laber. in goodes   .. | 40s | |
| William Bery husb. in goodes   .. | £3 | | | Richerd Hubbard husb. in goodes | £4 | |
| John Gylburne husb. in goodes .. | 40s | | | Richard Andrew Taylor in goodes | 20s | |
| Henry Eggystoke husb. in goodes | 40s | | | William Bendbow Wryght in goodes | 20s | |
| William Ball sen. husb. in goodes | £4 | | | John Freman Shomaker in goodes | 20s | |
| Thomas Bery husb. in goodes   .. | £5 | | | Robert Egyston Mason in goodes | 20s | |
| William Mey husb. in goodes   .. | £3 | | | Thomas Busche sen. laber. in | | |
| John Symys husb. in goodes   .. | £3 | | |  goodes   ..   ..   ..   .. | 20s | |
| William Ball jun. husb. in | | | | Thomas Slonet laber. in goodes | 20s | |
|  goodes   ..   ..   ..   .. | 40s | | | John Thysselton laber. in goodes | 20s | |

*Sum* **£5 11s 6d**

## BELTON

**1524**

| | | | |
|---|---|---|---|
| John Warde yoman in goodes   .. | £4 | Richerd Smyth husb. in goodes .. | 40s |
| Robert Phylyp husb. in goodes | £3 | Hew Marshall husb. in goodes   .. | 40s |
| Thomas Leystar yoman in goodes | 40s | Thomas Tylewastell husb. in goodes | £3 |
| Thomas Drake husb. in goodes   .. | £5 | Richerd Barker husb. in goodes | £4 |

| | | | |
|---|---|---|---|
| Thomas Sander husb. in goodes | 40s | Thomas Clement husb. in goodes | £4 |
| Richerd Tayler yoman in goodes | £8 | Thomas Redlyngton husb. in goodes | £6 |
| John Parkar yoman in goodes .. | £12 | William Collys Dryuer in goodes | £5 |
| Waltar Awngey husb. in goodes | £4 | John Hornynghold husb. in goodes | 40s |
| John Rayse husb. in goodes .. | £5 | Christofor Sandar husb. in goodes | 40s |
| John Clement husb. in goodes .. | 40s | Thomas Hall husb. in goodes .. | £3 |
| William Clement husb. in goodes | 40s | James Nodder Laber. .. .. | 20s |
| Robert Newman husb. in goodes | £3 | Robert Pauffeman laber. in goodes | 20s |
| Robert Geferey husb. in goodes | £8 | William Andrew Smyth in goodes | 20s |
| Thomas Hetham husb. in goodes | £6 | John Marshall Wryght in goodes | 20s |
| William Hely yoman in goodes .. | 40s | William Clark laber. in goodes .. | 20s |
| John Collys Wefer in goodes .. | 20s | William Annes Tayler in goodes | 20s |
| Richerd Coper laber. .. .. | 20s | Henry Hely laber. in goodes .. | 20s |

*Sum* **54s 6d**

## BARLETHORP

**1524**

| | | | |
|---|---|---|---|
| Hew Jorden husb. in goodes .. | £14 | Richard Wryght husb. in goodes | £3 |
| William Williams husb. in goodes | £8 | Thomas Cantyng husb. in goodes | £4 |
| Henry Mey husb. in goodes .. | £7 | Robert Pekyngton husb. in goodes | 40s |
| John Jorden husb. in goodes .. | £8 | William Pekyngton laber. in wages | 20s |
| William Hande husb. in goodes .. | £8 | William Cantyng laber. . in lyke | |
| John Wryght husb. in goodes .. | £4 | profyttes .. .. .. .. | 20s |
| Thomas Nunweke husb. in goodes | £3 | | |

*Sum* **30s 8d**

## CLYPSHAM

**1524**

| | | | |
|---|---|---|---|
| Margaret Bertley wedow in goodes | £15 | Edward Bowen laber. in lyke | |
| Thomas Bowar husb. in goodes .. | £15 | profyttes .. .. .. | 20s |
| Thomas Hasterby husb, in goodes | £7 | Richerd Cussen laber. in lyke | |
| John Parker husb. in goodes .. | £5 | profyttes .. .. .. | 20s |
| Thomas Galowey husb. in goodes | 50s | John Haryson laber. in lyke | |
| John Notyngham in goodes .. | £5 | profyttes .. .. .. | 20s |
| Thomas Carter in goodes .. | 40s | Robert Carter laber. in lyke | |
| John Garryt laber. in goodes .. | 40s | profyttes .. .. .. | 20s |
| Thomas Hanton laber. in Profittes | | Thomas Wyghted laber. in lyke | |
| of wages .. .. .. | 20s | profyttes .. .. .. | 20s |
| Anthony Carter laber. in lyke | | John Wesylhed laber. in lyke | |
| profyttes .. .. .. | 20s | profyttes .. .. .. | 20s |
| Robert Darell laber, in lyke | | Vynsent Thomason laber. in lyke | |
| profyttes .. .. .. | 20s | profyttes .. .. .. | 20s |
| Henry Whyghted laber. in lyke | | Henry Wyntar laber. in lyke | |
| profyttes .. .. .. | 20s | profyttes .. .. .. | 20s |

| | | | |
|---|---|---|---|
| Clement Carter laber. in lyke profyttes .. .. .. | 20s | Richard Crosse laber. in lyke profyttes .. .. .. | 20s |
| William Blyth laber. in lyke profyttes .. .. .. | 20s | John Bawntre laber. in lyke profyttes .. .. .. | 20s |
| John Lynby laber. in profittes of wages .. .. .. .. | 20s | William Carter laber. in lyke profyttes .. .. .. | 20s |
| Henry Crofton laber. in lyke profyttes .. .. .. | 20s | | |

*Sum* **33s 1d**

## EG'L'ON

**1524**

| | | | |
|---|---|---|---|
| Robert Fowler husb. in goodes .. | £16 | John Hechecok laber. in lyke profyttes .. .. .. | 20s |
| Thomas Matson husb. in goodes | £4 | Richerd Raysse laber. in lyke profyttes .. .. .. | 20s |
| Robert Lefem husb. in goodes .. | £10 | Richerd Seyton laber. in lyke profyttes .. .. .. | 20s |
| John Fouler husb. in goodes .. | £4 | | |
| Robert Manton husb. in goodes | 40s | John Heycoper laber. in lyke profyttes .. .. .. | 20s |
| Thomas Sharp husb. in goodes .. | 40s | | |
| William Rasyn laber. in Profytte of wages .. .. .. .. | 20s | Richerd Lednam laber. in lyke profyttes .. .. .. | 20s |
| Thomas Mortsun laber. in lyke profyttes .. .. .. | 20s | Thomas Slye laber. in lyke profyttes .. .. .. | 20s |
| Thomas Maltson jun. laber. in lyke profyttes .. .. .. | 20s | Robert Howys laber. in lyke profyttes .. .. .. | 20s |
| John Porter thelder laber. in lyke profyttes .. .. .. | 20s | William Hyeway jun. laber. in lyke profyttes .. .. .. | 20s |
| Thomas Sharp jun. laber. in lyke profyttes .. .. .. | 20s | | |

*Sum* **23s 4d**

## BRAUNSTON

**1524**

| | | | |
|---|---|---|---|
| Symond Swafeld gent. in londes | £17 | William More husb. in goodes .. | £4 |
| John Burton husb. in goodes .. | £12 | John Myllond husb. in goodes .. | £3 |
| Thomas Lacy husb. in goodes .. | £10 | Thomas Awley laber. in goodes .. | 40s |
| William Lacy husb. in goodes .. | £8 | Robert Dykman husb. in goodes | £3 |
| John Clark husb. in goodes .. | £6 | Henry Peper laber. in goodes .. | 40s |
| John Awley husb. in goodes .. | £6 | John Crosse laber. in wages .. | 20s |
| William Meryell husb. in goodes | £6 | William Isak laber. in Profytte for wages .. .. .. | 20s |
| Christopher Law husb. in goodes | £5 | | |
| Robert Lacy husb. in goodes .. | £5 | Thomas Draper laber. in lyke profyttes .. .. .. | 20s |
| William Dalby husb. in goodes .. | £5 | | |

| | | | |
|---|---|---|---|
| Thomas Fremyngham husb. in goodes .. .. .. .. | £4 | John Vnderwode laber. in lyke profyttes .. .. .. | 20s |
| John Andrew husb. in goodes .. | £3 | John Gomerlonde laber. in lyke profyttes .. .. .. | 20s |
| John Fox husb. in goodes .. | £3 | | |
| John Wyng husb. in goodes .. | £4 | | |

*Sum* **£3 4s 2d**

## WARDLEY

**1524**

| | | | |
|---|---|---|---|
| William Brome husb. in goodes | £18 | Richerd Elsam laber. in lyke profyttes .. .. .. | 20s |
| Thomas Robertes husb. in goodes | £9 | John Cantyng laber. in lyke profyttes .. .. .. | 20s |
| Robert Cantyng husb. in goodes | £7 | William Nicoll laber. in lyke profyttes .. .. .. | 20s |
| William Cantyng husb. in goodes | £4 | Richard Redysch laber. in lyke profyttes .. .. .. | 20s |
| John Robertes sen' husb. in goodes | £3 | John Hone laber. in lyke profyttes .. .. .. | 20s |
| John Robertes jun' husb. in goodes | £5 | Thomas Cleypole laber. in lyke profyttes .. .. .. | 20s |
| Hary Grvby husb. in goodes .. | 40s | | |
| Richerd Whyght husb. in goodes | 40s | | |
| William Assheley laber. in Profyttes for wages .. .. | 20s | | |
| William Flecher husb. in lyke profyttes .. .. .. | 20s | | |

*Sum* **28s 4d**

## BROKE

**1524**

| | | | |
|---|---|---|---|
| Thomas Rygley husb. in goodes | £3 | John Parkyn laber. in Profytte for wages .. .. | 20s |
| Henry Coper husb. in goodes .. | £3 | John Hoby laber. in lyke profyttes | 20s |
| Rafe Peper husb. in goodes .. | £8 | William Henson laber. in lyke profyttes .. .. .. | 20s |
| John Barons husb. in goodes .. | £4 | Christopher Hold laber. in lyke profyttes .. .. .. | 20s |
| Thomas Ward husb. in goodes .. | £7 | Hamlet Gooddyear laber. in lyke profyttes .. .. .. | 20s |
| William Decons husb. in goodes | £6 | Edmond Lefe laber. in lyke profyttes .. .. .. | 20s |
| William Ward husb. in goodes .. | £6 | Richerd Bayle laber. in lyke profyttes .. .. .. | 20s |
| Thomas Knowles husb. in goodes | £7 | | |
| John Williams laber. in goodes .. | 40s | | |
| Robert Smale husb. in goodes .. | £3 | | |
| Thomas [Cu] laber. in goodes .. | 40s | | |
| Thomas Awley laber. in goodes | 20s | | |
| Hew Lefe laber. in wages .. | 20s | | |

*Sum* **37s 8d**

*Sum of the hundred* **£36 19s 7d**

*Sum total of the county* **£220 14s 7d**

# Index of Places

# Index of Persons

The two documents frequently give widely differing versions of the same name, and not all are shown here. In most cases a name is indexed under the commonest, sometimes the simplest, form. In all cases of doubt variants are indexed separately. Cross references are supplied where necessary.

Vowels are very variable. Certain letters appear to be used indiscriminately, notably 'i', 'y' and terminal 's'. Some double letters are ambiguous, especially 'll' and 'tt'.

Sharpe, Bartholomew, 58; Hugh, 17, 107; Johan, 112; John, 20, 78, 103, 112, 114; Ralph, 77, 115; Richard, 78-9, 115; Robert, 31, 59, 60, 110; Thomas, 39, 60, 64, 71-2, 97, 103, 118 (2); William, 59 (3), 84, 102-3

She...., John, 116

Sheffield (Sherfyld), Christopher, 49, 92; John, 44, 89; Richard, 51; Roland, 44, 50, 63, 90; Thomas, 114 (2)

Sheld (Shyld), John, 60, 102; William, 61, 102

Shelton, Adam, 57

Shene, Robert, 50

Shepherd, James, 94; John, 46, 88, 90-1; Richard, 44, 98; Thomas, 76; William, 80, 99, 101, 115

Sherde, Richard, 54

Sherman, Brice, 34; Henry, 99; Robert, 42, 97; William, 43

Sherrard, Thomas, 17, 22-3, 25, 32, 62

Sherwood, Isabell, 62, 103; John, 62, 103; William, 61-2, 103

Sheryngton, Robert, 61, 102

Short, Richard, 24, 109

Shorthose, Henry, 40

Shortred, Robert, 57

Shovell, Thomas, 107

Silkylste, Thomas, 111

Sismay, Henry, 103; John, 56; Richard, 57 (2), 93; Robert, 89

Sisson, Thomas, 31, 34, 101; William, 35, 98, 109

Siston, John, 25; William, 99

Skellit, John, 26, 110

Skevington, William, 53-5

Skillington, John, 26, 110 (2); Richard, 110; Robert, 26, 110

Skynner, John, 95

Slanston, William, 94

Slay (Slee). Agnes, 93; Johan, 56; Peter, 80, 115; Robert, 58, 95, Thomas, 54-5, 91 (2), 118

Slonet, Thomas, 116

Smale, Robert, 73, 119

Smarte, Richard, 22, 108

Smith, Edward, 31, 57; Gregory, 83, 116; Hugh, 57; John, 31, 41, 49, 51, 61-2, 82, 90, 95 (2); 101, 109, 110, 113; Richard, 43, 62, 81, 103, 116; Robert, 25, 85, 110, 114; Thomas, 31-2, 39, 45, 49, 51, 58-9, 71, 90-1, 95 (2), 97, 100 (2), 102, 107, 110 (2); William, 60, 86, 91

Snell, William, 79

Sneth, Robert, 20, 113

Snokystob, see Suckstob

Snow, Richard, 107

Somer, Ralph 115

Somerby John 28 110-1

Sotherland, James, 77, 115

Sowter, George, 31, 110; John, 64; Thomas, 30, 109; William, 30, 109, 110

Sparke, William, 20

Spaldyng, Robert, 57

Spencer, Richard, 18, 52, 88

Spenethorn, Guy, 36, 98-9; John, 35, 98

Spenlong, John, 38

Spenlouffe, John, 98

Spenyng, Emmot, 27; Geoffrey, 113; Iosie, 27; John, 22, 108; William, 27, 113

Spicer, John, 51; Thomas, 56

Spire, John, 56, 90 (2)

Splay, William, 88

Spyoke, Robert, 88

Stable, Thomas, 57, 93 (2)

Stacpole, Richard, 97

Stallock, William, 22, 107

Stamford almshouse, warden of, 25, 52

Stancion (Stanmoyn), Thomas, 113

Standyll, Bartholomew, 19; William, 107

Stanelond (Standerlond), Edmund, 62, 106; John, 32, 109; William, 18, 106

Stande(rd), John, 65, 105

Stanyerd, James, 115; Richard, 41, 100; Thomas, 78, 115

Starke, Henry, 20; John, 28, 110-1; Thomas, 112

Stelton, Adam, 93

Stencall, Thomas, 26

Stephen, Alice, 66; Peter, 61; Roger, 26, 108; William, 22, 85, 109, 116

Stephenson, John, 93, Robert, 31, 48, 94, 110; Thomas, 91

Stokesley, Richard, 51

Stokerston, chantry of, 47

Stombill, Margaret, 45

Stowe, John, 27

Strawe, Thomas, 95

Strawker (Stryger), Robert, 49, 95

Strengar (Stangar, Stringer), John, 40, 55, 93 (2), 96; Thomas, 66

Stryklond, Edmund, 95; John, 93

Stubbs, John, 29; Richard, 112; Robert, 20, 29, 112 (2)

Stubley, Edward, 103

Style (Styll), Richard, 58, 95; Thomas, 59, 95; William, 59, 93, 95

Suckstob (Snokystobe), John, 22-3, 108 (2); Thomas, 22, 108

Soetman, William, 95

Suston, Robert, 75

Sutton, Robert, 101

Swaffield, Simon, 62, 81, 118

Swanson, John, 23; Robert, 23

Swayns(t)on, John, 64, 103; Margaret, 73; Robert, 73

Swetbon, George, 62

Swyfte, Thomas, 28, 111

Symond, 93

Syms, John, 85, 116; Margaret, 63, 103; Ralph, 77; Richard, 42, 96; Thomas, 37, 98-9; William, 77, 114

Sym(p)son, Edward, 69; John, 95

Tagell, Robert, 42, 97 (2)

Tailor, Bartholomew, 84, 116; Christopher, 95; Edward, 53; James, 52; John, 62, 67, 71, 105; Laurence, 76; Richard, 49, 72, 75, 89, 117; Robert, 56; Thomas, 64, 74, 94, 98, 103; William, 64, 74